Interpreting Anniversaries and Milestones at Museums and Historic Sites

D0862435

INTERPRETING HISTORY

About the Series

The American Association for State and Local History publishes the *Interpreting History* series in order to provide expert, in-depth guidance in interpretation for history professionals at museums and historic sites. The books are intended to help practitioners expand their interpretation to be more inclusive of the range of American history.

Books in this series help readers:

- quickly learn about the questions surrounding a specific topic,
- introduce them to the challenges of interpreting this part of history, and
- highlight best practice examples of how interpretation has been done by different organizations.

They enable institutions to place their interpretative efforts into a larger context, despite each having a specific and often localized mission. These books serve as quick references to practical considerations, further research, and historical information.

Titles in the Series

Interpreting Anniversaries and Milestones at Museums and Historic Sites

Kimberly A. Kenney

ROWMAN & LITTLEFIELD
Lanham • Boulder • New York • London

Published by Rowman & Littlefield
A wholly owned subsidary of The Rowman & Littlefield Publishing Group, Inc.
4501 Forbes Boulevard, Suite 200, Lanham, Maryland 20706
www.rowman.com

Unit A, Whitacre Mews, 26-34 Stannary Street, London SE11 4AB

Copyright © 2017 by Rowman & Littlefield

British Library Cataloguing in Publication Information Available

Library of Congress Cataloging-in-Publication Data

978-1-4422-6446-5 (cloth)
978-1-4422-6447-2 (paper)
978-1-4422-6448-9 (electronic)

♾™ The paper used in this publication meets the minimum requirements of American National Standard for Information Sciences—Permanence of Paper for Printed Library Materials, ANSI/NISO Z39.48-1992.

Printed in the United States of America

Contents

Preface

In 2007 I was fortunate enough to be at the McKinley Presidential Library and Museum when we celebrated the 100th anniversary of the completion of the McKinley National Memorial, the final resting place of President McKinley, his wife Ida, and their two young daughters. We celebrated all year long with an exhibition, a book, a fundraising campaign, and special behind-the-scenes tours, but our signature event was the 100 Hours Celebration. Our museum stayed open for 100 consecutive hours, all day and all night, with more than 130 activities, programs, workshops, meals, and events. It took years of planning and was a huge undertaking for a relatively small staff, yet I felt nothing but pride at being a part of it. Anniversaries—especially the big ones—are once-in-a-lifetime events. I was so proud of the way our staff came together and how the community supported us. It was deeply fulfilling and remains a highlight of my museum career to this day.

The following year I was asked to speak about the event at the Ohio Association of Historical Societies and Museums' annual meeting in Columbus, Ohio. Most of the members are very small museums and historical societies, some run by just a handful of volunteers who did not have the resources to pull off an event like ours. However, they *could* borrow a few ideas, maybe stay open a little bit later, and make a very nice celebration of their own.

As the concept simmered, I soon realized that cultural institutions everywhere are celebrating and commemorating anniversaries and milestones, and yet, in most cases, we are reinventing the wheel. No one has ever written about museum anniversary events, even though almost all of us have either planned one or will plan one in the future. What if I were to gather all of these wonderful ideas, assemble them in one place, and give them to the museum field as inspiration for planning? It might not be possible for your organization to replicate a really big idea, but there are likely parts of it that translate. Or maybe you have the resources to put on a splash for your anniversary but you need somewhere to get started.

I set out to find as many museums as I could that had recently celebrated an anniversary. This book is the result of interviews with more than forty institutions from across the country and around the world that planned some truly amazing events. In most of my interviews, a common theme emerged. You need to start planning *early*. Anniversaries don't sneak up on you. Most of the people I spoke to had planned for at least two years, and some wished they had started earlier. And most of your "friends" should be in place before planning even begins. "When you are ready to celebrate a centennial, [it] is not the time to start developing relationships," said Christie Weininger, executive director of the Rutherford B. Hayes Presidential Library and Museums. "Those should already be there."[1]

All of the people I spoke with were very enthusiastic about their celebrations. Although some wished a few things had gone differently, overall institutions who have embraced an anniversary celebration could clearly articulate the benefits enjoyed in the years that followed.

Don't let this special time in your organization's history pass you by! Use it to create marketing opportunities, develop a new audience, and even meet your fundraising goals. There are endless ways to celebrate or commemorate an anniversary. This book explores what other institutions have done thematically, so you can hone in on the type of event you want to create. Or you can read them all and find inspiration in unexpected places! Chapters include Signature Events; Programs and Tours; Fundraising Campaigns; Exhibitions, Books, and Documentaries; Audience Outreach and Community Involvement; Preservation; Partnerships; and Commemorative Products and Souvenirs.

This book is for all museums—large and small—to borrow from each other what worked well and to reevaluate ideas that did not meet expectations. It is also for colleges, churches, businesses, cities, and towns. It is for anyone, anywhere, who wants to plan an event for an anniversary.

Note

1. Personal interview with author, February 19, 2016.

Acknowledgments

This is not the kind of book you can write in a vacuum. In order to share the best anniversary events, programs, exhibitions, and fundraising campaigns, I needed to talk to my colleagues in the field. It wasn't enough to research on my own; I wanted to talk to people who were directly involved in planning anniversary celebrations and commemorations to provide an "insider's" point of view. Everyone I spoke to was very generous with their time and resources, for which I am deeply grateful.

This book would not have been possible without the contributions of the following people and institutions: Maureen Ater (The Repository), Amy Bartow-Melia (National Museum of American History), Steven Brisson (Mackinac State Historic Parks), Starlyn D'Angelo (Shaker Heritage Society), Emma Dixon (The Geffrye Museum of the Home), Robert Enholm (The President Woodrow Wilson House), Melanie Fales (Boise Art Museum), Darlene Fedun (Bethel Woods Center for the Arts), Julie Frey (Stan Hywet Hall and Gardens), George Garner (Indiana University South Bend Civil Rights Heritage Center), Owen Glendening (The National WWII Museum), Lauren Gould (Gardiner Museum), Lucy Harper (Memorial Art Gallery of the University of Rochester), Heidi Hill (Crailo State Historic Site and Schuyler Mansion State Historic Site), Katie Hill (Minneapolis Institute of Art), Emily Holmes (Paul Revere House), Brad Horn (National Baseball Hall of Fame and Museum), Tracey Johns (Chesapeake Bay Maritime Museum), Christopher Kolakowski (The Macarthur Memorial Museum), Gina Koutsika (Imperial War Museums), Wade Lawrence (Bethel Woods Center for the Arts), Russell Lord (New Orleans Museum of Art), Carol Majahad (North Andover Historical Society), Beth Manwaring (Rockwell Museum), Gail Martino (Canton Symphony Orchestra), Ashley Misko (The Mob Museum), Michele Mullaly (Canton Symphony Orchestra), Paul Muller (Cincinnati Preservation Society), Su Nimon (Journey Studios and Snarky Art), James Nottage (The Eiteljorg Museum of American Indians and Western Art), Cheryl Piropato (Fort Wayne Children's Zoo), Karen Renfrow (National Corvette Museum), Amy Rohmiller (Ohio History Connection), Cindy Sober (McKinley Presidential Library and Museum), Mary Thompson (Mount Vernon), Daniel Truckey (Beaumier U.P. Heritage Center), Diane Viera (Historic New England), Jessica Warchall (The Andy Warhol Museum), Carol Ward (The Morris–Jumel Mansion), Christie Weininger (Rutherford B. Hayes Presidential Library and Museums), Jessica Williams (Intrepid Sea, Air and Space Museum), Joyce Yut (McKinley Presidential Library and Museum).

On a personal note, I want to thank the amazing team of friends and family who are always behind me, cheering me on, including Kristen Merrill, Cheryl Beach, Marjorie Vanderhoof,

Jess German, Su Nimon, Nick Heap, Michele Anderson, Cheryl Kraus, Bird Cramer, and so many others (you know who you are!). And last, but not least, I want to thank my husband Christopher Kenney for all of his support, not just through this project but with all of the opportunities I regularly tackle that keep me busy at home when I should be cross stitching, gardening, reading, or relaxing!

Introduction

Just about everyone loves to celebrate anniversaries and milestones. We do it in our own lives, marking the passage of time through birthdays, work anniversaries, college reunions, and annual holiday gatherings. Although many celebrations are personal, community anniversaries bring people together in much the same way. Getting your community excited about an anniversary is an easy sell. Who doesn't want an excuse to celebrate? An anniversary is a great reason to install a magnificent exhibition, plan a spectacular series of programs, or host one grand signature event. You can use an anniversary to launch a fundraising campaign, preserve a historic building, or reach a new audience. Anniversaries can do all these things and more, as long as you seize the opportunity.

What is it about anniversaries that we find so appealing? Psychologists have been examining the need to mark significant moments in our lives, as well as anniversaries of tragic events. In her article "Marking Time: The Significance of Anniversaries," Counselor Libby Webber writes,

> So why do we celebrate, commemorate or otherwise mark anniversaries? Human societies have always marked important stages in the life cycle—births, marriages or formal unions, deaths. And we've celebrated the natural cycles of the world around us too—the changing seasons, harvest time, the turn of the year when the days become longer again. I wonder if marking these regular events gives us a sense that life has a structure and a rhythm rather than being random, chaotic and unpredictable? Within the familiar structure given to us by anniversaries, perhaps we can tolerate a certain amount of chaos and unpredictability, knowing that we have a number of fixed points ahead in the life of the family or the community.[1]

Anniversaries are also a time to pause and evaluate our lives. "People really look to birthdays and New Year's Day as moments of reflection and celebration," said Amy Bartow-Melia, associate director for programs and strategic initiatives at the Smithsonian's National Museum of American History. "It is ingrained in our culture."[2] Cultural heritage institutions are unique places where people can explore where we came from and contemplate where we're going. Anniversaries sit at the crossroads between celebrating your history as an organization and planning for your future. If you invest even a little time, money, and energy in your institution during this special time, it is possible to reap the benefits for years to come.

It is usually best to celebrate a "round number" anniversary, such as 25, 50, 75, or 100 years. But you could go with something quirky, if a number is specific to your site. Maybe someone planted 46 apple trees on your property 46 years ago. Or maybe the major interstate through your area was built 52 years ago and it happens to be Route 52. Look for unique connections in your own area. They've been there all along; you just haven't been looking for them.

Technically speaking, anniversaries are annual events. "Anniversaries arrive every year," says Gina Koutsika, head of national and international learning and engagement at the Imperial War Museums in England in the May 1, 2014, edition of *Museums Journal*. "When the year is a rounded number, their perceived significance increases." Deciding what and when to celebrate is key. For anniversaries that span several years, such as the sesquicentennial of the Civil War or the centennial of World War I, institutions should keep "anniversary fatigue" in mind. "Isn't it up to us whether we create 'anniversary overload'?" asks Koutsika. "We have time and therefore the opportunity to coordinate efforts; avoid duplication; experiment with new programming; form partnerships; learn from mistakes; and keep our audiences stimulated and engaged. We can work together to create moments of shared experience and connect current and future generations with history."[3]

There are many ways to celebrate an anniversary. This book is full of wonderful examples from a cross section of our field. Some organizations chose to refocus their celebrations on the community instead of themselves. For example, when the Fort Wayne Children's Zoo in Fort Wayne, Indiana, celebrated its 50th anniversary in 2015, Education and Communications Director Cheryl Piropato saw it as an opportunity to get people talking about the zoo. But she also wanted it to be a celebration of community pride. "Instead of saying, 'We're great. We're turning 50,' everything we created said our community is great because they've supported us for 50 years," she said.[4] By spinning its anniversary in this way, the zoo created a feeling of personal investment in its success.

Anniversaries are also an opportunity for us to share our institution's history with others. We preserve and present many subjects, but we rarely talk about ourselves. During its 75th anniversary year, the Boise Art Museum (BAM) used a significant portion of two newsletters to provide an illustrated timeline of the museum's history, including renovations and expansions, education initiatives, acquisition of some of the most prominent pieces in the collection, and significant traveling exhibitions over the years. A special "year in review" edition of BAM's newsletter reported on the anniversary initiatives, including 1,532 individual contributions, 210 donations of artwork, and 34 corporate sponsors.

Some organizations have used an anniversary to "pump up" annual events that are already part of its programming. For example, when Stan Hywet Hall and Gardens celebrated the centennial of the completion of the historic Manor House, the Father's Day Car Show featured 100-year-old cars, guests enjoyed live music at the annual Founder's Day celebration, and the Spring Tea included a historic house tour of a neighboring home built by the same family. "Look for ways to highlight all that you offer all year long," said Julie Frey, director of museum services at Stan Hywet. "Membership numbers increased as people saw firsthand the benefits Stan Hywet had to offer."[5]

The most common anniversaries celebrate how long an institution has been open. But there are many unique opportunities within an organization's mission to celebrate as well. Bob Enholm, executive director of the Woodrow Wilson House in Washington, DC, is in the midst of celebrating the centennial of Woodrow Wilson's presidency from 2013 to 2021. With eight years of history to sift through, Enholm is fond of saying, "Every day is a centennial of something in the Woodrow Wilson administration. It's just that some days are more important than others!"[6] When asked how his organization decides what is "important" enough to celebrate, he said it boils down to three factors: it has to be historically important, personally important, or simply amazing.

"A centennial isn't in and of itself all that important," Enholm said. "It needs to have something more. We want to pick things that capture people's imaginations and draw them here. Like many museums, we rely on donors, and others, who find what we're doing worth doing and want to support it." Enholm, with input from his staff and advisory council, chooses three or four events per year that advance the museum's mission to "promote a greater awareness of Wilson's public life and ideals for future generations." Centennial events have included Wilson's second marriage to Edith, the United States joining World War I, and Armistice Day.

Some events are to be celebrated, but it is more appropriate to commemorate others. The anniversary of Wilson's second marriage, for example, was celebrated with a festive open house. However, the passing of his first wife had to be handled much differently. "You have to be careful using it, because it's poignant and personal," says Enholm. "Our president was dealing with the outbreak of war in Europe at the same time he was tending to his dying wife in the White House. How overwhelmed he must have been."

The Woodrow Wilson House decided to commemorate the First Lady's passing on August 6, 1914, with an artistic tribute. "We have in our collection a pastel portrait of Ellen Wilson that was once described by one of her daughters as the best likeness of her," Enholm said. "We hung that portrait in a place of prominence in our front hallway for a few months leading up to the centennial of her passing. In addition, we mounted an exhibition of Ellen Wilson's oil paintings, *First Lady Ellen Axson Wilson: An American Impressionist*, that traveled to several locations around the country before being displayed in Rome, Georgia, Mrs. Wilson's hometown." The exhibition was a fitting tribute for a somber anniversary of this kind.

When marking a solemn anniversary such as a death, disaster, or war, it is important for everyone in your organization to be on the same page regarding semantics. While planning for the centennial of World War I, the Imperial War Museums issued a document for members of the First World War Centenary Partnership called "Guidance for Members: Speaking of the Centenary." The introduction provides an overview of the importance of using appropriate terminology: "The language and tone we use in our centenary plans will influence the way in which the centenary is understood. We hope that this document will help us all to define our terms and develop our tone of voice and content in a way that is appropriate to our organisation." The document goes on to explain the difference between commemoration and remembrance:

> "To commemorate" or "commemoration"—the definitions of these words indicate an activity that is a shared, perhaps civic, event that may have particular formal and/or ritual aspects to it. This can be contrasted with an act of "remembrance" which is a much more personal, internal, act of thinking, remembering or paying respects. So for example, a village might choose to organise a commemorative event to mark the rededication of a war memorial, in which members of the community take part in a variety of formal activities,

such as unveiling the memorial itself, laying wreaths, etc. This is "commemoration." If the ceremony also includes a two-minute silence, then each individual has the opportunity to choose to engage in their own personal act of remembrance during that silence.[7]

It goes without saying that a commemoration should never be referred to as a celebration.

The Imperial War Museums' document further examines how the nature of remembrance changed after 1919: "The First World War and its immediate aftermath established the language and practice of Remembrance that we use today. The historian Michael Burleigh has described Remembrance as akin to a civic religion. We see a shift from memorialising the victories (and Britain was, after all, on the victorious side) with triumphant arches, etc., to one of memorialising the dead. The decision not to repatriate the bodies from the battlefields but to bury them where they had fallen caused controversy at the time, and has shaped Remembrance ever since." This spirit and tone governed the activities the museum planned surrounding the centennial.

For some museums, anniversaries are built right into the organization's purpose. "The celebration of key historical events is considered part of our mission," said Steven Brisson, deputy director of Mackinac State Historic Parks. "It is also a marketing tool as the anniversaries tend to generate interest among the media and the public."[8] During the past 20 years, Brisson's organization has commemorated many anniversaries, including the transfer of Fort Mackinac to the United States (1996), the centennial of Michilimackinac State Park (2009), the bicentennial of the attack of Fort Michilimackinac during Pontiac's Uprising (2013), the 300th anniversary of the founding of Fort Michilimackinac (2015), and the bicentennial of the War of 1812 (2012–2015). There are numerous occasions to celebrate or commemorate in any community.

Early on in your planning process, decide if you want your event to raise money or make friends. Remember, increasing your visibility in the community can lead to good things down the line—increased admissions, public awareness for collection building, and fundraising for future events. Even if you've decided the focus of your anniversary is not specifically to launch a fundraising campaign, you will still need to create a budget to pull off your event(s).

Once you've defined what it is you are celebrating, think about how much funding you will need to make it happen. Consider all angles. What seed money do you need for marketing—printing flyers or invitations, purchasing ad space or air time, creating a special logo for the event? What costs will you have up front? Will you have to pay speakers, entertainers, or caterers? Will you need to hire security or pay extra staff? Think of every possible expense and set your goals accordingly. Ideally, admission money will be all profit. Or perhaps you want to offer a "free" day that will be paid for by your sponsorships.

After you have made your specific plans, go out and find some sponsors. In this economy, it can be tough. Since many businesses are struggling, don't overlook individuals. If your membership program has higher levels, that is a great place to start. You also might want to ask people who have donated money in the past, but be sure not to go to the same well too often.

Offer sponsorship packages with various levels and specific benefits. For example, for our 100th anniversary celebration of the McKinley National Memorial, we used the levels

Presidential, Gubernatorial, and Congressional, because President McKinley was all of those things. Will sponsors get tickets to your major events? If so, how many? Will they receive a special listing in your publications, promotional materials, or signage? A membership? A free gift from the Museum Shoppe? Make the package attractive, but keep costs down too. Remember, extravagant complimentary gifts eat into sponsorship profits.

A special logo is an essential marketing tool to excite the community about your anniversary. Most museums already have a logo, but creating something specific for your anniversary can help you advertise your celebration or even anchor a fundraising campaign. According to *Entrepreneur* magazine, there are three types of logos:

- Font-based logos, such as IBM, FedEx, or Sony
- Illustrations of what a company does, like a housepainter using a paintbrush
- Abstract symbols, such as the Nike swish[9]

Most museums, unless they have already cultivated a market based on an extensive branding campaign, should avoid the abstract symbol. Americus Reed II, a marketing professor at the University of Pennsylvania's Wharton School, told *Entrepreneur* magazine, "Such a symbol is meaningless until your company can communicate to consumers what its underlying associations are." Gather ideas by taking a look at what other museums have done to celebrate their anniversaries. What do you like about a logo? What don't you like? What elements will translate to your own institution's celebration?

Logos for an anniversary can be a completely new and "fun" design, or they can build upon an existing logo that already has recognition within the community. "The picture becomes shorthand for the event," said graphic designer Su Nimon. "Multiple impressions help improve recognition for your celebration."[10] If the budget allows, Nimon suggests hiring a local professional to create your logo, but there are inexpensive options online too. College students in graphic design at a local college or university might be willing to create a logo for you as a class project.

There are some basic guidelines for what makes a good logo. "It should work in black and white or in color," Nimon said. "It should not have more than two fonts. You should imagine it on a business card and on a billboard. When it's small, can you still see it clearly?" Color choices are subjective, depending on your museum's regular color palette for signage or letterhead, but there should be enough contrast so the image is clear. Also keep in mind where your logo will be used, and what the color limitations will be in each medium.

"Your logo should appeal to the audience you're trying to reach," Nimon said. "The style of it depends on what you're trying to do. If you usually have a more traditional logo, something more playful might be appropriate." While she encourages museums to include a year or anniversary number in a logo, it should not contain too much information. "A logo is like an icon," she said, so it should be clear and concise. Additionally, *Entrepreneur* magazine suggests that you avoid clipart: "However tempting it may be, clip art can be copied too easily. Not only will original art make a more impressive statement about your company, but it will your business apart from others."

Once your logo has been designed, you should begin to use it approximately three to six months before your first anniversary event. For fundraising purposes, you should start much earlier. Include the logo on your letterhead, envelopes, email signature, social media profiles, and on all anniversary-related printed materials—such as flyers, postcards, and advertisements. When the National Baseball Hall of Fame celebrated its 75th anniversary in 2014, the 75th logo was incorporated into every aspect of the museum, including tickets and commemorative merchandise. "The logo signifies the time relevance to the individual's visit," said Brad Horn, vice president for communications and education. "All material had that mark. It provided a time and date stamp for their visit. There is a certain emotional connection. They will be able to say they were here during an anniversary."[11] If you are planning to allow partner organizations to use your logo, you may want to consider drafting a set of guidelines for proper use of the logo. (See Appendix E: SB150 Logo Guidelines.)

No matter where you work or volunteer, there is an anniversary on the horizon. These pages examine celebrations at cultural institutions across the country and around the world. There are many ideas to draw from, and plenty of sage advice from your colleagues in the field. Your anniversary can be the leverage you need to make new friends, energize your fan base, launch a fundraising campaign—or just an excuse to throw a lavish party!

Notes

1. Libby Webber, "Marking Time: The Significance of Anniversaries," Counseling Resource, last modified September 7, 2011, http://counsellingresource.com/features/2011/09/07/marking-time-anniversaries/.
2. Personal interview with author, August 20, 2015.
3. Gina Koutsika, "The Conversation," *Museum Journal*, May 1, 2014, 17.
4. Personal interview with author, June 16, 2015.
5. Personal interview with author, November 1, 2015.
6. Personal interview with author, July 6, 2015.
7. Imperial War Museums, "Guidance for Members: Speaking of the Centenary," October 17, 2013.
8. Personal interview with author, August 30, 2015.
9. "How to Create a Logo," *Entrepreneur*, accessed October 6, 2015, https://www.entrepreneur.com/article/71902.
10. Personal interview with author, October 6, 2015.
11. Personal interview with author, December 21, 2015.

CHAPTER 1

Signature Events

YOUR ANNIVERSARY celebration could be a once in a lifetime event. Why not make it magnificent by planning an over-the-top signature event? Some organizations stretch an anniversary celebration throughout the calendar year, using smaller programs to build interest for one major event. Others pour all available resources—staff, time, and money—into one spectacular celebration. Whichever you choose, the examples in this chapter provide a wealth of ideas for planning your own signature event.

McKinley Presidential Library and Museum, Canton, Ohio

The McKinley National Memorial—the final resting place of twenty-fifth U.S. President William McKinley, his wife Ida, and their two young daughters Katie and Ida—was built between 1905 and 1907. With its 100th anniversary approaching in 2007, the McKinley Presidential Library and Museum wanted to plan something spectacular to commemorate this milestone. While casually flipping through a museum conference brochure, a staff member saw a session presented by staff at the Dallas Art Museum, which had stayed open for one hundred consecutive hours to celebrate its 100th anniversary. After presenting the idea to director Joyce Yut, the staff began planning its own event—the "100 Hours Celebration."

This was no small undertaking. It required hundreds of hours of planning and a very organized committee to pull it off. The first brainstorming meeting took place two years before the event. The entire staff met to throw out ideas—nothing was out of bounds. The key to a positive brainstorming experience is not to criticize any idea that is presented "in the moment." Troubleshooting down the line will separate what is possible from "pie-in-the-sky" ideas. The initial brainstorming session is not the place to work out minute details. One outlandish idea might lead the group to a more doable idea, so you have to let the process play out without judgment. Not every staff member was on board at first, so it was important for everyone to feel included so they would "buy in" to the idea.

The staff decided early on that not every idea had to relate directly to the museum's mission. The goal was to come up with at least one hundred programs or events to fill as much of the one hundred hours as possible. The overarching theme was a celebration of the memorial's anniversary, so the individual ideas could be anything from New Age workshops to bricklaying demonstrations—and everything in between. Ideas from the first brainstorm session included the following:

Programs

Lectures (by staff and outside guest speakers), midnight cemetery walk, outdoor movie, dance with a live orchestra, piano program, Monument tours, gallery talk, storytelling, ghost stories at the outdoor hearth, speaker from NASA, special shows in Discover World (the museum's hands-on science center), behind-the-scenes tours, textile preservation workshop, Meet the President with a McKinley impersonator, roundtable history talks, book signings, speaker from the Canton Preservation Society, history talks, poetry reading, bird walk, ghost tour of Street of Shops (the museum's life-sized indoor town), silent movie night, bake-off or cook-off, senior citizen art or photo show, tribute to Stark County veterans, have some-one read the original Memorial dedication speech

Presentations/Demonstrations

Civil War cavalry and reenactors, a sunrise church service, telescopes outside, tastings from local restaurants, fire department demonstration, K9-unit demo, belly dancing demo, line dancing performance, bricklaying demonstration, circus calliope, songs from McKinley's era, local high school choir concert, rock concert, "Antiques Roadshow" event with local appraisers

Classes/Workshops

Sunrise yoga, tai chi, spa programs, crafts for kids, cooking class, finger painting, face painting, balloon animals, magic class, knitting lesson, cross-stitch class, feng shui, calligraphy class, stained glass class, meditation, drumming, model train workshop, scrapbooking or beading class

Food

Midnight open hearth pancake breakfast, spaghetti dinner, chicken barbeque, midnight snacks, Breakfast with the Animals of Discover World, make your own s'mores, wine and cheese picnic and stargazing, outside food vendors, coffee tasting

Other

Hayride, outdoor concert, remote control car race, jewelry date appraisal, raffle prizes, on-site local radio broadcast, volunteer information session, historic headlines from local newspaper *The Repository*, penny collection events, bagpipers, petting zoo, flag raising ceremony with the Masons, carriage rides, play centered on love letters, time capsule, movies about museums, old fashioned baseball game, BINGO night, parachuting, camp-out on the grounds, walk-a-thon, send up balloons or release doves, 5K race, dance-a-thon

Staff Related

Special t-shirts for staff and volunteers, sales and/promotions at certain times in the Museum Shoppe, hand out a small gift to the first one hundred visitors, half-price admission overnight, port-a-potties on the grounds, free admission to anyone who is one hundred years old or more

Participants in the first brainstorming meeting also debated when the event should take place. The Memorial (often called the Monument locally) was officially dedicated on September 30, 1907, but that did not seem like a good time to hold an event of this kind. Since the museum already had a long-standing and successful Cruisin' Thru History Car Show on the grounds at the end of June, it was decided that the celebration should be built around that event. Plus it would be the beginning of summer, so families would be able to attend. After doing some math to figure out how long one hundred hours would actually be, the staff decided the event would begin on Wednesday June 27 at noon and end on July 1 at 4:00 p.m.

One of the first issues the planning committee encountered was which departments of the Museum would need to be staffed twenty-four hours a day. Admissions, the Museum Shoppe, and maintenance/security would be essential. An outside security officer would be hired for the overnight hours. It was also decided that at least one person from the planning committee should be on-site at all times. The morning and night people self-selected and took on the appropriate shifts. Special considerations included making sure the outdoor lights remained on all night, keeping the HVAC and phone systems on for the entire event, and using the staff "in and out" board so front office personnel knew who was and was not in the building.

The planning committee also decided this would *not* be a fundraising event, but rather a "friendraising" event. Admission was reduced to the student price of $5 per person. Visitors would have in-and-out privileges for one day only, controlled by a different colored-ink hand stamp each day. Visitors would also have the option to buy a four-day pass for $10 per person, which would be available through midnight on the first day of the event. The pass would be a tear- and water-resistant Tyvek wristband in a bright color. The pass would not be honored if it was removed from the wrist. All sponsors received a gift certificate that could be redeemed any time for a four-day pass bracelet. The committee decided no coupons or discounts would apply during the event. Members and Association of Science—Technology Centers (ASTC) reciprocals were admitted free, as always. There would be little or no cost for workshops and classes, and food prices would be kept to a minimum. All outdoor events needed an alternative plan in place in case of bad weather. Some events could be moved inside, but others would need to be canceled.

The planning committee did not meet for several weeks to allow the ideas to "simmer." At the follow-up meetings, ideas that were too difficult to pull off with everything else that was going on, or would make better ideas as stand-alone events, were eliminated from the plan and/or saved for another time.

As planning continued, the committee refined the list of programs and events and divided the responsibility of contacting presenters. Everyone was charged with keeping an eye out for potential programs that could be added to the list. "Ideas came from the strangest places," said Christopher Kenney, director of education. "One day someone from our maintenance staff was working late on the grounds when a hot air balloon team from RE/MAX Realtors drove up and asked if they could launch their balloon from our site. The staffer had told the Realtors about our 100 Hours event and asked if they would be willing to provide tethered balloon rides. They enthusiastically agreed. They charged $5 per person for a ride, and then surprised us by donating all of the money they collected to the museum."[1] Some presenters asked for a fee, but most gave the museum a reduced rate or accepted a complimentary family membership as payment.

As plans were finalized, it became clear that one person needed to be in charge of scheduling the building. The curator created a chart to keep track of everything and to avoid double-booking. Across the top were times, by the hour, and down the side were venues inside the museum. As programs were confirmed, she marked off the time slot on the master schedule. Due to space or catering requirements, some workshops and meals were limited. The committee planned an information desk, staffed by volunteers, to keep track of sign-ups for free events. All paid programs would be handled by staff through the front office. Everything was included in the price of admission except meals (midnight snacks were free), horse-drawn carriage rides, tethered balloon rides, and monument tours.

Staff used the event to recruit new volunteers and energize those who had been on the volunteer team for several years. About a month ahead of time, volunteers were invited to a meeting to discuss details of the celebration. Staff asked what they would like to do and when they were available. This information was used to create a work schedule that was mailed to the volunteer team in advance.

To promote the event, the museum purchased a countdown clock and set it up in the main lobby. It was incorporated into a sponsor sign, which was changed as new partners were added. A board member arranged for the planning committee to meet with a local public relations firm, who set up two guest appearances on a Cleveland television morning show. Since there was a fee associated with the show, the public relations (PR) representative also secured corporate funding to sponsor the TV spots. Staff cross-promoted 100 Hours at all other museum events up to one year before the celebration, volunteers delivered posters and flyers to local businesses and public library branches, and an exterior banner advertised the event to visitors on the grounds who did not come into the museum itself. During field trip season, the student welcome speech included a short promotion for 100 Hours, and each teacher received a flyer with their schedule and evaluation paperwork.

The final newsletter sent to the membership before 100 Hours was a commemorative issue, featuring the entire schedule of events for all four days:

Wednesday

- Opening Ceremony, featuring the mayor and a flag-raising ceremony by the local Masonic lodge
- Bee Talk, by the Stark County Beekeepers Association

- Just What Is in the Library?, tour of the research library
- Rubber Stamping Workshop
- Bricklaying Demonstration, over 2 million local bricks were used in the Memorial foundation
- "Shaking the Family Tree," exploration of local genealogy resources
- Counted Cross-Stitch Workshop
- Facelift Massage
- Rigatoni Dinner
- Book Signing with Local Authors
- Magic Class
- NASA Speaker
- Storytime for Kids
- Telescopes on the Memorial Plaza
- Aromatherapy Workshop
- Ghost Tour of the Street of Shops

Thursday

- Bird Walk
- Exercise Class
- "The McKinley and Saxton Letters," featuring the archival collection
- "Music, Music, Music," featuring the research library's sheet music collection
- Pizza Lunch
- Model Train Workshop
- Science Experiments
- Buttermaking Demonstration
- Scrapbooking Workshop
- Introduction to Massage
- BBQ Dinner
- Line Dancing Demonstration
- Canton Preservation Society Speaker
- Behind-the-Scenes Tour

Friday

- Sunrise Yoga
- Tree Walk
- Recycling Crafts for Kids
- Bat Program, with live bats from the Gorman Nature Center
- Sub Sandwich Lunch
- "So You Think You're Related to President McKinley"
- The House on North Market, a program about McKinley's Front Porch Campaign house
- Spinning and Weaving Demonstration

- CSI: Canton Dinner, featuring a speaker from the Stark County Crime Lab
- Tethered Balloon Rides
- Lighting Bugs and Glow-in-the-Dark Experiments
- Poetry Reading and Coffee Tasting

Saturday

- Stained Glass Demonstration
- Annual Cruisin' Thru History Car Show
- Finger Printing, program through the Stark County Sheriff's Office
- Picnic Lunch
- Akron Zoomobile
- Self-Hypnosis Workshop
- Heirloom Jewelry Dating, with a local jeweler
- S'mores and Ghost Stories
- Horse and Carriage Rides
- Wine and Cheese Stargazing
- Healing with Sound
- Midnight Open Hearth Pancake Breakfast

Sunday

- Reiki Workshop
- Ice Cream Social
- Petting Zoo
- Old Fashioned Baseball Game
- Closing Ceremony

Regular museum programming, such as History Tours, Monument Tours, Planetarium Shows, and Discover World presentations and shows were offered several times throughout the event. Brand new library and archive programming listed above were also repeated several times. A DVD player and board games were provided for visitors to use overnight. The World's Largest Puzzle, consisting of 18,000 pieces, was available to work on twenty-four hours a day. The Museum Shoppe gave a product away every hour. Each visitor received a free raffle ticket with admission that was turned in at the Museum Shoppe. The raffle encouraged visitors to step into the Shoppe to make an additional purchase or to come back at a later date to find unique gift items.

Nearly 2,200 people attended the four-day event, which did not include people who came to the outdoor events on the grounds and did not pass by the admissions window to be counted. More than one hundred volunteers gave over 1,000 hours of service. The museum raised over $1,700 in food sales, RE/MAX donated $845 back to the museum, and Saturday was the largest admissions day with $1,975 in sales. The event included 130 activities over 100 hours, surpassing the committee's goal.

At the McKinley Presidential Library & Museum, staff and volunteers wore "100 Hours 100 Years" t-shirts during the 100 Hours Celebration to mark the 100th anniversay of the McKinley National Memorial. McKinley Presidential Library & Museum, Canton, Ohio.

While the 100 Hours celebration was a resounding success, there were some things that did not work well. Due to liability issues, the adjacent cemetery refused to grant permission for a cemetery walk after dark. The planning committee discovered that early morning events and late afternoon events were not well attended. Breakfast was the least popular meal offered for sale. Obtaining a liquor license for the Wine and Cheese Stargazing event was quite difficult, although local laws will vary. Also, after the initial brainstorming session the community was invited to submit their own ideas for programs or events. Not one form was returned, which surprised the staff. Even though community members were not

The McKinley Presidential Library & Museum had a special logo designed for the anniversary year. McKinley Presidential Library & Museum, Canton, Ohio.

As part of the 100 Hours Celebration, the McKinley Presidential Library & Museum offered horse-drawn carriage rides up to the McKinley National Memorial, where a wine and cheese party was taking place. McKinley Presidential Library & Museum, Canton, Ohio.

interested in helping to plan the event, they certainly attended and enjoyed themselves. The museum received no complaints and had no security issues, even during the overnight hours.

The event was a smashing success that not only elevated the museum's profile in the community, but also boosted staff morale. "The 100 Hours celebration for the McKinley National Memorial Anniversary was one of the most ambitious events we have ever done," said director Joyce Yut. "Even though the staff was exhausted on the last day, the sense of accomplishment gave each and every one of us a very confident feeling of success."[2] Several years after the event, people still approach the museum to share how much they enjoyed themselves.

Fort Wayne Children's Zoo, Fort Wayne, Indiana

Sometimes it is possible to adopt someone else's successful signature event as your own. When the Fort Wayne Children's Zoo celebrated its 50th anniversary in 2015, the staff used a board connection to propose Here's to Zoo! as the theme of the annual Three Rivers Festival parade. Each year, all of the 160 floats in the parade have to relate to the theme. Each float entry is responsible for building its own float, so the zoo was able to get a lot of exposure about their celebration at no cost. Additionally, the American Association of Zookeepers built the zoo's float which will upgrade its parade appearances for years to come.

Billed as "Fort Wayne's biggest Summer party since 1969," the festival already has a significant following in the region. By capitalizing on another organization's success, the zoo was able to raise its profile in the community, while providing a fun theme for a parade that is always looking for a good idea. More than 50,000 people attend the kick-off parade every year, which made it an excellent vehicle to celebrate the zoo's 50th anniversary.

Cincinnati Preservation Society, Cincinnati, Ohio

"Location, location, location" isn't just a mantra in real estate. Finding the right space for your anniversary celebration can make all the difference.

Part of the Cincinnati Preservation Society's 50th anniversary celebration in 2014 included a gala at the Cincinnati Renaissance Hotel, a recently restored historic building. "We helped get the project millions of dollars of historic tax credits as a fee for service," said Paul Muller, director of the Cincinnati Preservation Society. "This shows we don't just complain about losing historic buildings, we help with the economics of saving them."[3] The state of Ohio has a 25 percent historic tax credit that is granted on a competitive basis. The building received one of the highest scores recorded since the program began in 2007.

The building provided the perfect backdrop for a black-tie anniversary gala with a preservation theme. "It was the home of Fifth Third Bank and our founders were associated with it," Muller said. "As an eighteen-story 1909 high rise by Chicago architect Daniel Burnham, at the heart of our financial district, it was important for its architecture and for its role downtown. Bringing it back after being vacant for many years was a major civic success. Plus it was a great place for our band, the Hot Magnolias, which plays New Orleans jazz."

Tickets were $150 per person, which is a much higher price point than most events the organization has hosted in the past. The invitation list included members, the public, donors, and all subcontractors who worked on the building's restoration. The program for the evening included three short welcome speeches and a brief review of the organization's history to highlight early members, many of whom were in attendance. The Preservation Society also used it as an opportunity to underscore the new, actively engaged mode they are creating as they move into the future.

"The main value of the evening was the joy and sense of purpose people came away with," Muller said. "We brought our community together in an astonishing space, one that made the case for preservation better than any speech ever could. We celebrated 50 years that began with a few visionary women and noted that their work laid the groundwork for Cincinnati's current renaissance. We celebrated that the city is being rapidly transformed by reuse of our historic structures."

The Mob Museum: The National Museum of Organized Crime and Law Enforcement, Las Vegas, Nevada

The Mob Museum opened to the public in 2012, appropriately on the 83rd anniversary of the St. Valentine's Day Massacre in Chicago in 1929. Every year since, the museum has celebrated its "birthday" with special unveilings, programs, and events. Locals can get in for free that day, and out-of-town guests receive buy-one-get-one-free admission. The museum chooses to celebrate its anniversary regularly to "showcase its commitment to the community," said Ashley Misko, director of marketing and public relations. "The museum gave out 4,488 free passes in celebration of both its anniversary and Kefauver Day (November 15)."[4]

So what, exactly, is Kefauver Day? A general Mob Museum press release explains:

The Museum is located in what many consider the ultimate artifact, the former federal courthouse and United States Post Office. Completed in 1933 and listed on the Nevada and National Registers of Historic Places, it houses the courtroom where in 1950 one of 14 national Kefauver hearings was held to expose organized crime in America. Meticulously rehabilitated for The Mob Museum, the building is significant not only for its neo-classical architecture reminiscent of the period in which it was built, but also for the historic events that unfolded inside of it.

The Mob Museum also celebrates November 15 each year with free admission for locals. "Nearly 9,000 Nevadans, representing all ages, income levels and cultures, have enjoyed the Mob Museum for free as part of the museum's anniversary celebrations," Misko said. "For many of these guests, this was the first time any had ever visited a museum."

According to the museum's fact sheet, the Mob Museum "presents an exciting and authentic view of the mob's impact on Las Vegas history and its unique imprint on America and the world. With tales so intriguing they need no embellishment, The Mob Museum reveals an insider's look at the events and people on both sides of this continuing battle between organized crime and law enforcement. True stories of mob history are brought to life in a bold and contemporary style via engaging exhibits and multi-sensory experiences. The Mob Museum puts the visitor in the middle of the action through high-tech theater presentations, iconic one-of-a-kind artifacts and interactive, themed environments."

The Mob Museum interprets a unique aspect of history that allows for a great deal of innovative and fun ideas for programming and events. "Our museum has a culture that encourages ongoing brainstorming," said Misko. "We have an active and creative board that works with staff that approaches everything we do through dual lenses of 'how can we give back to the community' and 'how can we create excitement for our content.' One of our most iconic artifacts is the bullet-ridden wall from that infamous crime. That date therefore provides ample avenues to pursue in how we mark our anniversary each year."

Playing on the fact that the St. Valentine's Day Massacre was literally a blood bath, The Mob Museum hosts a signature blood drive each year for its anniversary. In 2013 anyone who took the "Blood Oath," that is to say registered to give blood in the museum's multi-purpose room during the blood drive, received two free admission tickets. In subsequent years, blood drive participants have received one admission ticket in exchange for their blood donation. The museum partners with United Blood Services for this initiative.

The first one thousand guests who visited the museum on its first anniversary received a collectible commemorative pin and a special line-up photo opportunity with Valentine's Day messages such as "Just Married" and "It's Complicated." "There was also an over-sized postcard on display for guests to write well wishes in the lobby," Misko said.

For its second and third anniversaries in 2014 and 2015, the museum displayed, for a limited time only, two Thompson machine guns that were used in the St. Valentine's Day Massacre. The guns were exhibited in front of the actual brick wall where the massacre took place, which is part of the museum's permanent exhibitions. "The wall is always available for viewing at the museum," Misko said, "but the two Thompson machine guns, #7580 and #2347, were the only weapons scientifically proven to have been used in the massacre. The guns aren't available at the museum year-round, but they go hand-in-hand with the wall on the anniversary date and bring a whole lot more 'reality' to the exhibit."

For a fledgling museum, the media attention The Mob Museum receives as a result of its annual festivities is invaluable. "Our anniversary celebrations have generated a lot of excitement in media from around the world, generating more than $2.5 million in advertising value. In the three years we have been celebrating our anniversary, we have received coverage from countries ranging from France to Australia, from Detroit to Dallas, and from news outlets all across the West," Misko said.

The Mob Museum plans to continue its annual anniversary celebration, adding new ideas drawn from brainstorming sessions with the staff and board. "The museum has an internal culture of thinking outside the box," Misko said. "Its content provides ample resources for doing so on a regular basis."

National World War II Museum, New Orleans, Louisiana

When your museum's mission is to explore the history of war, most of your anniversary events are commemorative, rather than celebratory. But since the National World War II Museum opened to the public on June 6, 2000, its annual commemoration of D-Day is a unique combination of somber and festive.

"We celebrate the anniversary of the museum every year," said Owen Glendening, associate vice president of education and access at the National World War II Museum. "We want to remember this is the museum's birthday, and we want to thank everyone who made this possible. But we also commemorate sacrifice on the same day. We make sure we're focused on those who served. It is a marriage of public memory and personal memory that is extremely powerful."[5] In addition to the D-Day remembrance, the museum also hosts commemoration ceremonies on Armed Forces Day, Memorial Day, Veterans Day, and certain milestones of World War II, such as VE Day and VJ Day. The museum has become known as a place where veterans and civilians can come together for an appropriate and patriotic ceremony honoring these dates. Commemorations almost always include personal narratives from veterans or their families, who give their own testimony as part of the program. "They share what it means to them today, and how it affected their family," Glendening said. "At Memorial Day one woman read family letters and telegrams, and the room was in rapt attention." The ceremonies also include formal remarks, a military honor guard, and a quintet or band of some sort. "People look to us and come out for this regular series of annual commemorations," Glendening said. "It's almost like it's our civic obligation to do it." The space in which these ceremonies take place at the museum has become "the new town square."

When an anniversary is a "significant" number, the museum ramps up the event and adds more components to it. "In our business, even numbered anniversary dates tend to get the highest level of government recognition," Glendening said. For example, the 70th anniversary of D-Day on June 6, 2014, was a much larger commemoration than usual. The museum ran two major events at the same time. "We rented a cruise ship and took 300 customers on a very immersive learning cruise in Europe," Glendening said. For ten days, the museum pulled out all the stops, providing excellent access to key historic sites related to World War II. In Normandy, for example, participants were able to hear firsthand accounts from French citizens who experienced the war, as well as from veterans who were there. In addition, the museum deployed all of its collections for the cruise, such as oral histories and archival materials, to provide a rich historical experience for the participants. On board the ship there were lectures every night given by a range of well-known historians, including Tom Brokaw, Rick Atkinson, and Dr. Donald L. Miller. Phil Reed, founder of the Churchill Museum in London, and Dr. Gordon H. "Nick" Mueller, president and CEO of the National World War II Museum, also presented to the group. Dr. Mueller described the cruise as a "once-in-a-lifetime opportunity for scholars of WWII, history buffs and those who experienced World War II firsthand to visit these famous sites during this momentous anniversary."

Back in New Orleans, the public ceremony began at 6:30 a.m. with a live message from Dr. Mueller, who was standing on the beach at Normandy as part of the cruise at the exact hour the invasion began. The public ceremony included the annual ringing of a full-scale replica of the Liberty Bell, which had been a gift to the museum from the people of Normandy, and the presentation of the French Legion of Honor to several World War II veterans who helped liberate France. Throughout the day, the museum hosted lectures by authors and academics, covering all aspects of the D-Day invasion, including the role of the chaplains, the weather that day, and how the perspectives of the French, Germans, and Americans are different. Museum staff gave frequent "D-Day Briefings" so visitors could follow the Allies' progress. Musical programming included the U.S. Marine Corps Brass Quintet, the Baton Rouge Concert Band, and the museum's own Liberty Belles, who sing classic 1940s-era popular songs in the style of the Andrews Sisters. Visitors also had the rare opportunity to board an authentic Higgins Boat, while a museum curator explained the boat's role in the invasion. The museum constructed a set of stairs to provide access to the boat, which had never been done before. Every hour on the hour, the museum showed *Beyond All Boundaries*, an exclusive 4D film narrated and produced by Tom Hanks that featured "dazzling effects, CGI animation, multi-layered environments and first-person accounts from the trenches to the Home Front read by Brad Pitt, Tobey Maguire, Gary Sinise, Patricia Clarkson, Wendell Pierce, and more," according to the museum's special D-Day 70 website. That evening the museum hosted a free outdoor screening of the first two episodes of the award-winning HBO miniseries *Band of Brothers*.

With World War II veterans dying at an alarming rate, there is some urgency to preserve the firsthand accounts of their experiences before it's too late. The National World War II Museum has a staff of five full-time historians who are in the field doing oral histories. They have collected more than 7,000. These narratives are incorporated into everything the museum does. In the exhibits, visitors experience oral history "at every turn," said Glendening.

"At admission you get a dog tag that looks like a credit card. You follow a citizen soldier at kiosks throughout the exhibition. Personal narrative is really important. It has an authenticity that rings true, and that carries over into the commemoration events." For the 70th anniversary of the D-Day event, the Oral History Showcase in the museum's orientation center featured stories from veterans who participated in the D-Day invasion.

"This is the biggest story in human history," Glendening said. "It is filled with universal human stories, ideals, and beliefs. We recognize that there is still a living memory, and there will be for some time. Even when the last veteran passes, there are still orphans who were the first college graduates on the GI Bill and Japanese Americans who will never forget their internment. It's important that we recognize that [World War II] is emotionally important to people, and it helps them frame their view of civilization and culture."

The Gardiner Museum of Ceramic Art, Toronto, Ontario, Canada

In 1984 George and Helen Gardiner donated their world-class private collection of pottery and a building to the people of Toronto. The original donation included Ancient American pottery and European pottery and porcelain from the fifteenth through nineteenth centuries. Over the years, the collection has doubled in size, and attendance has grown to seventy thousand visitors per year.

As part of its 30th anniversary celebration, the Gardiner hosted an exclusive gala called The 18th Century Comes Alive. "In a city saturated with fundraising galas, it is difficult to stand out," said Lauren Gould, development and programs manager. "The intimate gala for 140 truly did bring the eighteenth century to life."[6] The front steps of the museum were decorated with two large groupings of lit white pillar candles. Guests entered through the museum's front doors, which were fitted with a giant "3" and "0" on the glass.

The menu, décor, invitations, and entertainment were all rooted in eighteenth-century history, but with a twist. "We had eighteenth century music, dance and opera, which then transformed into contemporary dance and music with each performance," said Gould. "Similarly we had a giant croquembouche tower which was paraded around the room, but was actually served in a more modern style in a serving dish with chocolate drizzle and gold dust. Historically, it would have been cut off from the tower to be served. It was truly about creating a few unique moments for the evening."

In her experience, Gould said the creativity of the committee can make or break a special event. The group thought outside the box to create a very memorable favor for guests. "It was common to have ceramic figures decorating the table in the eighteenth century, so we commissioned a contemporary artist to create something quite strange that everyone got to take home with them at the end of the night," Gould said.

The Gardiner also presented Spring Awakening: Gardiner in Bloom during the anniversary year. For one April weekend only, the museum presented large-scale floral arrangements by some of Toronto's most sought after floral designers alongside signature pieces from the permanent collection. Ten floral designers created the dazzling arrangements, inspired by a specific object from the permanent collection, which were displayed throughout the museum galleries. The museum promoted the event as "bringing the Gardiner's collection to life in an entirely new way." Spring Awakening included a members' day all day on Friday, an opening champagne reception Friday evening, workshops on landscape and floral design on Saturday, and a moderately priced Family Day on Sunday. Although this event had been done in the past, the museum presented it as an additional benefit for patrons during the 30th anniversary year, and added Hermes as an upscale partner for the event.

During the summer of the 30th anniversary year, the Gardiner also hosted a series of themed summer parties, called Scene on the Plaza, for five consecutive Friday nights in June and July. Marketed as an after-work social with music, food, drink, and art, the Gardiner's executive director and CEO Kelvin Browne said, "Scene on the Plaza combines art and a fantastic social experience in one of the most beautiful buildings in Toronto. People can enjoy great music, drinks and food, along with our world-renowned ceramics collection. There's no other place like this in Toronto."[7] Themes included Summer Camp, True Patriot Soul, Cantina Remix, Love Boat, and British Invasion. (See appendix C: Gardiner Year at a Glance)

The Museum at Bethel Woods, Bethel, New York

For three days in August 1969, five hundred thousand young people converged on the small upstate New York town of Bethel to celebrate "peace and music" at what would become the defining music festival of a generation. After enjoying music from some of the greatest musicians of the era—including the Grateful Dead, Jimi Hendrix, Creedence Clearwater Revival, the Who, Joe Cocker, Janis Joplin, and many others—the enormous crowd dispersed and the town of Bethel was quiet once more.

Fast forward to 1996. Entrepreneur Alan Gerry had just sold his cable television company to Time Warner and was looking for a way to revitalize his native Sullivan County. The Catskill region had been home to a vibrant tourism industry, but by the late twentieth century the once thriving resorts were gone. At the urging of his daughter, Gerry purchased the thirty-seven-acre site of the original Woodstock festival with the intention of turning it into a performing arts center. On July 4, 2006, the New York Philharmonic became the first musical performance in the new venue. Two years later, the Museum at Bethel Woods opened on the grounds with a mission to interpret the 1960s ideals of "peace, respect, cooperation, creativity, engagement, and a connection to the planet we live on and all the people who inhabit it."

Although the Bethel Performing Center for the Arts is about much more than one three-day concert in 1969, honoring Woodstock remains a key focus of the facility's programming. The museum does not host a large scale anniversary event every year, but they do plan something special for the "five" and "ten" year increments.

In 2009 the museum celebrated the 40th anniversary with a concert called Heroes of Woodstock, including the Levon Helm Band, Jefferson Starship, Ten Years After, Canned Heat, Big Brother and the Holding Company, Mountain, Tom Constanten, and Country Joe McDonald, all of whom performed at the original concert. Since the 1969 event was a "music and art festival," the museum also organized a juried art show for the 40th anniversary, featuring over thirty artisans. In a press release for the event, director of marketing Matt McNeil said, "Bethel Woods is excited about bringing so many of the original performers back to the original festival site to celebrate the 40th anniversary. We find that whenever we book bands that played here in 1969, it's a special kind of homecoming for both the performer and the fan; having so many of the original acts here to commemorate the anniversary will be something quite special."[8]

In 2014 the museum celebrated the 45th anniversary with a special free screening of the four-hour Oscar-winning documentary *Woodstock: The Director's Cut* on the site of the original festival called Back to the Field. The museum promoted it as "once-in-a-lifetime opportunity to see it WHERE IT HAPPENED!" "We showed the movie for one thousand people outside under the stars," said CEO Darlene Fedun. The event was free with a $5 suggested donation to help preserve the historic site where the concert took place. Prior to the screening, Associate Producer Dale Bell gave a lecture titled "Woodstock: The Film That Was Almost Never Made." The museum served as a partner on the re-release of the documentary, which originally came out the year after the concert. The DVD featured a promotional piece for the museum.

The museum invited Richie Havens to perform his song "Freedom" on the field at noon on the anniversary, which was streamed live on the internet to 11 million people. "We had a private event for dignitaries and guests before we opened," said Wade Lawrence, museum director and senior curator. "Havens was exceptional, mingling and talking to folks and taking photos with them."[9]

The museum has a built-in marketing opportunity for merchandise with the iconic bird and guitar logo on it, which always sells well. "We have very brisk sales in our museum store," Lawrence said. "They consistently exceed projections made before we opened." On average, 10 percent to 14 percent of museum visitors make a purchase in a museum store, spending $3 to $4. At the Museum at Bethel Woods, 30 percent to 40 percent of visitors shop and spend an average of $13 to $15. The music, jewelry, and fashions of the 1960s still resonate today, making the merchandise relevant to a whole new generation.

With the aging of the original Woodstock audience, the museum understands that it cannot focus exclusively on the festival and its anniversaries. "Our challenge is to communicate to people that we're not just about those three days," Fedun said. "We are about the explosion of culture that occurred in that decade."[10] The performing arts center hosts musical events of all genres, while celebrating its unique place in history and coming up with creative ways to engage a younger audience. The site recently hosted the American debut of the electronic music festival Mysteryland, which has been held in The Netherlands for twenty years. "They chose our site," Fedun said. "There is a whole new anniversary to celebrate in the future."

Smithsonian National Museum of American History, Washington, DC

In 2014 the Smithsonian's National Museum of American History (NMAH) launched a program called Raise It Up! to celebrate the 200th anniversary of the Star-Spangled Banner. As the largest repository of American history in the country, there are endless opportunities to celebrate anniversaries at the museum every year. But the Star-Spangled Banner is special. "Some anniversaries might be an interesting American moment, but we don't have collections expertise," said Amy Bartow-Melia, associate director for programs and strategic initiatives. "But the flag was a given."[11]

"Anniversaries are more than milestones," wrote Elizabeth MacMillan director John Gray and board chairman the Honorable Nicholas Taubman, both of NMAH. "They are crossroads at which we decide whether to live in the past or use our experiences to inform and empower our future." The Star-Spangled Banner's 200th birthday provided a perfect opportunity for the museum to launch a national conversation about these ideas. "The Smithsonian is a safe place to convene and bring people together," said Bartow-Melia. "Anniversaries are a great opportunity to look at the past and bring it to where we are now."

G. Wayne Clough, secretary of the Smithsonian at the time, described the flag's significance in an article previewing the museum's celebration plans in the March 2014 issue of *Smithsonian* magazine: "The Star-Spangled Banner, the flag that inspired Francis Scott Key to write the lyrics to our national anthem in 1814—its appearance above Fort McHenry proving that the American garrison had survived the British bombardment—has been a signature object at the National Museum of American History since the museum opened in 1964."[12] It is one of the most-recognized artifacts in the permanent collection. The flag rests in a low-oxygen chamber that is closely regulated for temperature and humidity. The museum had recently completed a major conservation project on the flag, so celebrating its birthday was a logical conclusion to that endeavor.

The museum itself was also celebrating its 50th anniversary that year. Exhibitions exploring science and technology developments in 1964 included a baby-blue 1965 Ford Mustang, which was built and debuted in 1964, and an IBM System/360 mainframe. Other exhibitions examined cultural issues in 1964, such as the March on Washington and spaceflight. Raise It Up! was part of a larger institutional effort to recognize both anniversaries.

In recent years, the Smithsonian's mission has shifted to focus more on helping people to understand the past. Across the board the staff's programming efforts began to explore ways to bring people together. This idea was a key component in planning the "Raise It Up!" event. "We want to use history to inform where we are today," said Bartow-Melia. "What can we as participants in our democracy do to make the world a better place? We wanted to bring attention to what the museum was doing in a really meaningful way."

Flag Day (June 14) is the traditional start to what Bartow-Melia calls the "patriotic season" in Washington, DC, so the major Raise It Up! event was planned for that day. The United States Postal Service released a new Star-Spangled Banner stamp in March. The museum used that event to announce its plans for Raise It Up!

"We wanted to build an audience nationally and internationally by making this a social and participatory event digitally," said Bartow-Melia. "We asked people to have their own parties around the country, which was the first time our museum has convened like that. It was really exciting that each site interpreted it in their own way." For example, Biscayne Bay National Park in Florida celebrated by holding a naturalization ceremony. "We learned that we could put something out there with lots of suggestions, but the real beauty of it was that people brought their own ideas to it." Almost all fifty states and several American embassies and military bases around the world participated. The museum encouraged people to register their parties online so everyone was celebrating across the country at the same time.

The Star-Spangled Banner is unique because it's not only a flag, it's also a song. "We were interested in using this as an opportunity to create new art and musical expressions inspired by our collection," said Bartow-Melia. "We wanted to use music and theater as a way to engage people. We asked celebrity artists to create new renditions of the Star-Spangled Banner. It was a great way to engage new audiences. They brought their own followers to the table." A live concert was a major component of the "Raise It Up!" event.

Initially the planning team pursued the idea of getting into the Guinness Book of World Records for the most people singing the Star-Spangled Banner at the same time. "We spent a lot of time in the early part of the planning trying to make that work," said Bartow-Melia. "We thought it would help draw attention if we could say we were going for a world record." In the end, it proved to be more of a challenge to pull off than the team originally expected. In order for an event to be officially certified, there has to be a representative from Guinness at each sing-along location. The budget and timeline did not provide enough resources to make that happen. "It turned out, we didn't need it as much as we thought we might," Bartow-Melia said. People wanted to participate anyway, even without the World Record component.

Much of the support for Raise It Up! came from in-kind partnerships that helped spread the word. The museum solicited national organizations, such as the Girl Scouts and the United States Chamber of Commerce, to join the celebration. Partners received a social media guide to help promote Raise It Up! through sample tweets, hashtags, a special graphic, and a partners-only blog series that outlined the tools each partner could use to easily share information with its own membership. The following campaign goals were listed in the social media guide:

- Generate excitement about Raise It Up!
- Motivate audiences to tune in, sing along, and get involved.
- Increase participants' knowledge of the history of the Star-Spangled Banner, Flag Day, the national anthem, the Battle of Fort McHenry, the War of 1812, and related topics.

The guide requested that partners tag or mention the museum on social media, providing links to accounts on Twitter, Facebook, YouTube, Pinterest, Instagram, Flickr, and Google+. The guide also shared a very important point with the partners: "Social media posts that include images tend to be more widely shared than those that don't." Partners had access to several images of the flag through the museum's Flickr account.

On the day of the event, the National Museum of American History had a full slate of programming. The Fort McHenry Guard Fife and Drum Corps shot a period cannon and performed songs from the War of 1812 twice during the day wearing period costumes. Docents gave tours of the museum's most popular exhibitions. The event culminated with the "Anthem for America" concert on the National Mall, featuring the U.S. Air Force Band, Smithsonian Folkways' Little Bit A Blues Band, Smithsonian Jazz Masterworks Quintet, country singer-songwriter Carlene Carter (daughter of June Carter Cash and Carl Smith), electric guitar phenom Kristen Capolino, and a choir of four hundred voices from across the country. The concert was streamed live on YouTube, ESPN3, and on the website (http://anthemforamerica.si.edu), and televised on C-SPAN. Macy's department store broadcast the concert live on screens in the teen departments of more than four hundred stores across the country, organized by Chorus America and the John F. Kennedy Center for the Performing Arts. In a promotional interview for the event, Bartow-Melia said, "We are asking all Americans to stop and sing at 4 o'clock EDT and really reflect for a minute on what it means to be an American living in this great country. Stop and sing the anthem, and then of course take pictures and video and share that back with us so we can share that back out across the nation."

Francis Scott Key's original manuscript for the Star-Spangled Banner, on loan from the Maryland Historical Society, was on display alongside the flag itself. This marked the first time the manuscript and the flag were in the same place at the same time. Key jotted down some notes on a letter he had in his pocket when he was still onboard the ship. Later he went back to his hotel and wrote the four stanzas that would become our national anthem. "The marriage of that tiny document in Key's own hand and the giant flag in the Smithsonian's beautiful flag chamber is a once-in-a-lifetime thrill," said Maryland Historical Society president Burt Kummerow in his remarks at Raise It Up! For a limited time, the Vera Wang gown that opera singer Renee Fleming wore when she sang the National Anthem during the 2014 Super Bowl was also on display. Bartow-Melia said these artifacts are so important to us collectively because they are a "physical manifestation of our ideals."

Behind the scenes, the museum also used the Star-Spangled Banner's anniversary to evaluate its condition since it was conserved. According to the Raise It Up! highlights report, "[t]he flag was carefully assessed in February [2014] for the first time since its painstaking seven-year conservation treatment was completed in 2006. To ensure a safe environment for preservation, oxygen levels are kept low in the state-of-the-art flag chamber, which was comparable to working at a ten-thousand-foot elevation during the flag's examination. The Star-Spangled Banner's fibers proved to be in a condition similar to when last tested—welcome news during such a momentous anniversary year."

Later that year, to appeal to the younger millennial audience, the National Museum of American History, in partnership with the Smithsonian Channel, also used the Star-Spangled Banner's anniversary to inspire an event called "Raise a Glass to History," which included a cocktail contest and a gala event. "Piggybacking on the fifteen stars and stripes, we asked bartenders in fifteen cities to create a signature cocktail [inspired by the flag]. We went to each city and recorded the bartenders creating their drinks. Then we invited those bartenders to come to DC for a big event." The event helped to launch a new Smithsonian initiative called the Smithsonian Food History Project.

The signature cocktail event also included an opportunity for ordinary people to send in their own cocktail recipes, which were evaluated by a panel of celebrity judges. Marianne Britt Duvendack of Swanton, Ohio, won with her creation Gunpowder Cream:[13]

Gunpowder Cream

1 oz. pure maple syrup
1½ oz. amber, aged rum

2–3 oz. unsweetened English Breakfast tea, chilled

¼ ounce fresh lemon juice

2 tbsp. whipped cream

Dash finely ground cinnamon

Cinnamon stick

Chill a 6 oz. Martini glass. Mix whipped cream with ground cinnamon, and set aside. In a martini shaker, mix rum with iced tea and ice cubes. Shake well, set aside. Carefully pour maple syrup all over the inside of the glass. Slowly pour the tea and rum mix into the glass, straining out the ice. Float the whipped cream on top of the tea/rum mix, add a dash of ground cinnamon to the top. Swizzle with a cinnamon stick.

Cocktail Story:

The War of 1812 led to the longest, international, peaceful border in the world. As a Ranger at Perry's Victory and International Peace Memorial, I am honored to tell this story daily. One of the best parts of my job is that I also get to work with Parcs Canada Rangers. Last summer, during our Bicentennial activities, Rangers from our sister park, Signal Hill National Historic Site, and several others treated us to a Rum Ceremony. One of the drinks was called Rum Gunpowder. My cocktail takes a bit of the history of the Canadian rum traditions and adds the sweetness of maple syrup (which my family makes here in Ohio), and adds a sweet dollop of cinnamon infused whipped cream. As you drink the cocktail, you start with the rum and tea (a very traditional Newfoundland evening drink), and end with the creamy, sweetness of maple syrup. Before dinner, after dinner, you can't go wrong. And celebrating 200 years of Peace over a cocktail with great friends is indeed a wonderful thing.

Duvenback was flown to DC to participate in the Star-Spangled Banner Gala Event on September 12, 2014, where all the mixologists showcased their "Star-Spangled Banner-inspired" cocktails. According to the Raise a Glass to History website, guests "toasted the flag two hundred years after Battle of Baltimore began during the War of 1812, when this fledgling country held back a British attack and the flag inspired Francis Scott Key to write the song that became our national anthem." The event included cocktail-related artifacts from the Smithsonian's collection, mixology demonstrations, and cocktail historian David Wondrich. Music was provided by the Smithsonian Jazz Masterworks Quartet and DJ Will Eastman.

The Raise a Glass to History website includes a blog series called "Tales from the Collection," featuring stories inspired by documents and artifacts in the Smithsonian's collection. Posts include in-depth articles written by curators at American history on topics such as these:

- Tales from the Collection: A Bartender's Guide to Medicinal Wine
- Tales from the Collection: A Bartender's Guide to Patent Medicines
- Tales from the Collection: Is This George Washington's Still?
- Tales from the Collection: The Armistead Punchbowl

- Rye Is This So Hard?
- Sherry: America's First Wine
- Origin Story: Mint Juleps
- Origin Story: Cocktail Shakers
- Origin Story: The Martini
- Origin Story: Cocktail Umbrellas
- Bibulous Bios: Carrie Nation
- Bibulous Bios: Jerry Thomas
- Loophole Liquor: Five Drinks You Could Legally Have During Prohibition
- A Bootlegger's Dictionary: The Lexicon of Prohibition
- Say Can You Drink?
- Myths and Muses: Who Is the Gibson Named After?
- Myths and Muses: Who Is Harvey Wallbanger?
- A Thirst for Independence

Unlike many anniversary celebrations which tend to be "one off" events, the museum wanted this event to last beyond the 200th birthday of the flag. "How can we use this opportunity in a bigger way to inform something we do on an annual basis?" Bartow-Melia said. "We didn't want it to just go away." A website was created to provide a lasting "digital home" for the event, which includes an interactive musical timeline of the Star-Spangled Banner created by the education department. "People are always accessing and using the website," said Bartow-Melia, particularly during the patriotic holidays. "It's something that lives on."

The museum collaborated with the Smithsonian Channel to create a documentary, *A Star Spangled Story: Battle for America*, based on research done by the museum and its curators. According to the official description of the show on the Smithsonian Channel's website, "The Star-Spangled Banner is known by all, treasured for its powerful melody and stirring lyrics. And yet, only about 40 percent of U.S. citizens know all the words. And even fewer know their meaning. Join us as we travel back to 1814, when Washington D.C. was under British attack during the "Second War of Independence," and the very bricks and mortar of American democracy were reduced to smoking rubble. We examine the battle that inspired witness Francis Scott Key to immortalize its final moments, then reveal how his poem transformed into an anthem."[14]

The museum also used this project as an opportunity to welcome new citizens. On June 17, 2014, former Secretary of State Hillary Rodham Clinton and fashion icon Ralph Lauren helped the museum welcome fifteen new U.S. citizens as fellow Americans. Lauren was presented with the James Smithson Bicentennial medal to honor his lifetime contributions to American entrepreneurship, artistry, and creativity. Clinton delivered the keynote address.

Raise It Up! has become the basis for an annual themed event, based on the flag itself. According to the project's website, "[e]very year the Smithsonian's National Museum of American History will bring people together to *Raise It Up!* and explore who we are, how we got there, and how together, we shape a more humane future, inspired by the enduring principles embodied in the "Star-Spangled Banner."[15] Themes include America Innovates, America Participates, Becoming US, and Creating Culture. A Raise It Up! campaign brochure outlines what the project is moving forward:

- A national moment convened by the Smithsonian, led from the National Mall
- Strategic social and participatory experiences for digital audiences across the United States and the world
- New art and musical expressions, inspired by the national collections, that tie our history to our future
- New blockbuster exhibitions exploring compelling ideas and ideals of American history
- Star-studded involvement from leaders in American business, government, music, entertainment, and arts
- Participatory, innovative, and newsworthy

The success of Raise It Up! led to a significant funding opportunity and the project has now transformed into a ten-year initiative titled "America Now" that will explore these themes with audiences in collaboration with two other Smithsonian museums, the National Portrait Gallery and the Smithsonian American Art Museum.

In total, more than 150 people worked on this project in some capacity, earning the team the Smithsonian Secretary's Award for Excellence. Planning began eighteen months ahead of time, and events were finalized in January 2014. "Coordination is really important," said Bartow-Melia. "In an attempt to keep people coordinated but not have a lot of meetings, we created a small core team who was looking at the whole project. Other project leaders met once a month. We didn't have everybody in every meeting, and that worked out really well." The project generated 2.7 billion worldwide media impressions, and more than one hundred anthem-themed parties registered across the globe.

Like many of the ideas shared in this book by major museums throughout the world, the scale of Raise It Up! may be difficult to replicate at your museum. However, what the National Museum of American History did to celebrate its signature artifact's anniversary can certainly inspire smaller institutions to reach new heights with their own celebrations. Everyone has a special artifact in the collection that resonates in the community, and it is about to have an anniversary you can celebrate.

National Corvette Museum, Bowling Green, Kentucky

Rather than celebrate only on a "round" number anniversary, the National Corvette Museum celebrates its anniversary every year. After more than a decade of planning, the museum opened its doors on September 2, 1994, in Bowling Green, Kentucky, home of the Corvette Assembly Plant. Its mission is to promote the restoration, preservation, and conservation of America's sports car, including the printed technical materials and historical information relating to the Corvette.

The annual anniversary celebration has become "a meeting place for guests to reconnect year after year and celebrate the continued success of the museum and the Corvette itself," said Karen Renfrow, events manager at the National Corvette Museum. "It does increase attendance, which in turn brings in more money for the museum, through registration, new memberships, Corvette Store sales, and Corvette Café sales."[16]

Each year's celebration is different, but successful activities have included seminars, car shows, road tours, and the annual Corvette Hall of Fame induction ceremony, which honors those who have been influential in making Corvette a success. "Our objectives are to promote the National Corvette Museum as well as recognize and thank our members who support us all year long," said Renfrow. Planning is a full team effort and begins just after the conclusion of the previous anniversary event. "We make notes as to what worked and what didn't," she said. "We listen to ideas and comments from our participants. Customer service is #1 for any event!"

Even though the anniversary celebration is an annual event, every five years it is kicked up a notch when caravans of Corvettes come rolling in from all 50 states. "It increases our attendance as much as 10,000 people," said Renfrow. The museum usually utilizes about one hundred volunteers during a "regular" anniversary, but every five years they need 250 to 300 volunteers to pull off the extra-large celebration. Coordinating the national caravan requires additional volunteers and planning. "We relied heavily on a network of caravan leaders that were stationed throughout the United States," Renfrow said. "Members of this group, led by the chairman selected by the museum, each organized a plan on how to gather and lead the participants from their area to the museum. As distant caravans got closer to the museum they joined other caravans, eventually arriving in a several hour long parade of Corvettes around the museum. Our local hotels hosted entertainment and vendor type meals outside their establishments to better connect with our participants as well."

The 20th anniversary in 2014 was particularly significant for the museum. "Many participants were museum members who had not been able to come to the museum recently, but the event provided an opportunity to bring them back into the 'family' and introduce them to the newest generation of Corvettes," Renfrow said.

The museum's location provides some unique experiences for Corvette enthusiasts. "We are very fortunate to have a 3.1-mile road course here at the museum that we have access to for our visitors" said Renfrow. "During events we frequently offer Parade laps (low-speed laps in the participant's personal Corvette), Hot laps (high speed laps with a professional driver in a provided vehicle), and Autocross."

Renfrow feels that many of the events she and her colleagues plan are possible to host at other sites, especially the road tours. "Any location that had a large enough parking area to stage twenty to thirty cars would be adaptable as a starting spot for a caravan to a local attraction or popular lunch spot." In 2015 the museum planned a road trip to the Kentucky State Police's Trooper Island, a summer camp for Kentucky's underprivileged youth who are introduced to policemen as a positive influence. "We try to maximize our economic impact with the locations that we visit," Renfrow said.

The Andy Warhol Museum, Pittsburgh, Pennsylvania

To celebrate its 20th anniversary, the Andy Warhol Museum planned a black-tie gala with a sit-down dinner on May 17, 2014, for 650 guests from around the world. The event was held in an outdoor tent at the museum and was sold out before a single formal invitation was sent. The event's honorary chair was Theresa Heinz, and the honorary cochairs were Diane von Furstenberg and Jane Holzer.

The Andy Warhol Museum's gala had a "jet setting" theme, complete with 1960s-era flight attendants. The Andy Warhol Museum, Pittsburgh, Pennsylvania. Photo by Renee Rosensteel.

"From the very beginning, the organizers thought creatively," said Jessica Warchall, assistant communications manager. "The branding of the event as a 'jet-setting' celebration was new and exciting for the museum."[17] The gala tickets looked like passports, and the community opening of the newly rehung permanent galleries was ticketed with a "standby" ticket that looked like a boarding pass. The free public opening was held at midnight, after the gala.

Historic New England, Boston, Massachusetts

To celebrate its 100th anniversary in 2010, Historic New England planned two distinct events: a Centennial Gala and a Birthday Bash. "For several years prior to 2010, Historic New England held its fundraising gala in January, a time of year that donors and key constituents had come to expect this annual celebration," said Diane Viera, executive vice president and chief operating officer. "The centennial year was no exception. The 2010 Historic New England Gala was themed as a centennial celebration. During our centennial planning process, it was decided that the centennial gala must be balanced with a celebratory event with a lower ticket price for members and supporters who don't attend the gala. The Historic New England Birthday Bash was held in April, the actual month of Historic New England's incorporation, attracting a wide audience. Refreshments at the Birthday Bash celebrated foods that originated in each of the New England states—from Fluffernutter sandwiches to clam chowder."[18]

North Andover Historical Society, North Andover, Massachusetts

Anniversary celebrations are not only for big museums. With just one full-time and three part-time employees, the North Andover Historical Society used the 100th anniversary of its organization in 2013 to modify its annual fundraising event High Tea at the Ridge. "Downton Abbey was in its late teens/early 1920s season and we took that as an appropriate tie-in with our 1913 founding date," said Carol Majahad, executive director. "Our objective, besides a new style event, was to engage our membership and supporters in a new and fun way. The event included a challenge to dress the part—at least to wear a hat for the afternoon. Most people complied and many enjoyed the costume party feel. Our subsequent events—a 1920s house party and a World of Mad Men Party—continued this component. The costume angle for the High Tea, while not new, was new for us and it worked to increase interest in future fundraising programs."[19]

The Rolling Ridge Conference Center approached the North Andover Historical Society about a partnership for a restyled event. The 38-acre property that would become Rolling Ridge was purchased by Ethan Allen, a wealthy New York wool merchant, in 1899. In 1915 plans were made to build a home and landscaped gardens. The property was sold to the New England Conference, United Methodist Church in 1948, which continues to own and operate it as a conference center today. The historic site was an idyllic setting for the North Andover Historical Society's event, with in-kind support. "Our costs for the meal were kept to a minimum ($14 per person) as a courtesy for this first year," said Majahad. "The active involvement of the conference center's staff saved us considerable expenses for this event." Tickets for the High Tea were $50 per person, which included a $25 donation. Proceeds were used to build a new History Discovery Room.

Planning began six months in advance. In addition to the event coordinator at Rolling Ridge, the staff asked members of the fundraising committee, as well as members who represented both the historical society and the Historical Commission, to help plan the event. "Sometimes what you don't plan is as important was what you try and control," Majahad said. "For the Tea, someone brought an antique car and we made that part of the event at the last minute."

Just before the event took place, the historical society was approved for a $396,000 Community Preservation grant. "I believe that our success, public money approved by the public for a non-public entity, was due in part to the publicity for our 100th anniversary," Majahad said.

In 2015 the historical society had the opportunity to celebrate another milestone in its history: the 300th anniversary of the historic Parson Barnard House. Built in 1715 by ministers of the North Parish Church of North Andover, today the home retains many of its original architectural details. The North Andover Historical Society purchased it in 1950 to preserve it and open it to the public.

"The Parson Barnard House anniversary seemed like a natural celebration," said Majahad, "and we scheduled it to coincide with our participation with the Essex County 17th Century Saturdays. By extending the day and hosting period music, reenactors, members of the Garden Club and a local poet, we attracted a large and mostly new audience to the house. Proclamations from the state legislature also added to the ceremony, which was capped by birthday cupcakes and a showcase Parson Barnard cake."

The "Birthday Bash" was held over Labor Day weekend. There was no budget for the event. "All the expenses were taken on by donors who are very attached to this house," said Majahad. "There was no income as it was offered as a free event to the community. The

300th birthday party was also a thank you for the town for voting for us to receive the Community Preservation grant."

The anniversary event opened new marketing opportunities as well. "The local cable TV station came out and did a segment on the event for their local monthly news journal," Majahad said. "This was the beginning of a new History segment that we now do monthly, increasing our exposure throughout the town. Staff also created companion exhibitions for both events afterwards, including photographs of participants. "People enjoyed seeing themselves and their friends in the case, creating a real feeling of being part of the institution's history."

Celebrating both of these milestones provided a chance for the North Andover Historical Society to reconnect with its community. "Anniversaries remind us of where we have been as institutions and help guide us in where we are going," said Majahad. "They connect with people in a very special way, helping the present generation bond with the people from the past who shaped the institution, or built and lived in the historic site."

South Bend 150, South Bend, Indiana

When the city of South Bend turned 150 in 2015, the city celebrated all year long. But by far, the biggest event planned was its Birthday Weekend celebration held in May. It was the largest event held in South Bend in decades, drawing large crowds. "The three-day bash sealed off many city blocks as over sixty thousand guests explored South Bend's history, art, food, music, games, and examples of innovations happening in the city today," said George Garner, curator at Indiana University South Bend Civil Rights Heritage Center. To help visitors navigate the many activities available during Birthday Weekend, Force 5, a local marketing communications firm, created a free app that included a color-coded map, transportation and parking information, and opportunities to buy tickets to some of the events.

According to the *South Bend Tribune*, the festival kicked off with an "Olympic-style" opening ceremony, which included a flaming torch run. Other highlights included fireworks, a zip line across the St. Joseph River, hot air balloon and helicopter rides, a champagne and jazz brunch, Taste of South Bend with fifty food vendors, and local, regional, and national musical performances. "Recording artist Ben Folds played a concert to end the first evening, dressed in an I (heart) SB t-shirt given to him by South Bend Mayor Pete Buttigieg, himself a somewhat accomplished pianist," said Garner. "And Mayor Pete, as he is affectionately referred to here, even had the honor of playing a song with Ben Folds!"[20]

In order to pull off such an ambitious anniversary celebration, SB150 solicited volunteers to assist. The following information about becoming a volunteer was shared via the SB150 website:[21]

ALL volunteers will need to attend one of these four mandatory Volunteer Orientation Sessions. It is required by our insurance company that all volunteers and staff attend them, so that everybody is informed of safety procedures and knowledgeable about the event in general.

These sessions will also help you and/or your group to feel more comfortable and prepared when you arrive for your shift, and will go over any and all questions you may have, such as where you should park, what you should wear, where you need to check in, etc.

This event is slated to be the biggest party South Bend has ever seen, which is a huge undertaking. There will be a lot of information to go over, but we will make it fun and keep the meeting around forty-five minutes—no longer than an hour.

Volunteer shirts will also be distributed at these meetings, and only at these meetings. It is important that anyone wearing this shirt during Birthday Weekend be able to answer questions that guests may have, such as where the restrooms are, what to do if they have lost a child, etc. This is another reason that these meetings are mandatory for everyone—so that guests can have complete confidence in the ability and knowledge of the SB150 Volunteer Team.

Note—there is no need to RSVP for a session, and if you are with a group, it is not necessary that all members of your group attend the same session.

If you are unable to make any of the orientation sessions, you can still assist with the cleanup and teardown shift on Sunday evening. Just show up at the Volunteer Headquarters—Howard Park Senior Center—at 5:30 p.m. Sunday. The shift will run until about 9 p.m.

Thank you in advance for your contribution to SB150!

When planning a large-scale event, it is important that your volunteers are well informed and organized. Members of your volunteer corps, as well as new volunteers, should attend meetings such as this in order to learn more about their specific responsibilities and the event in general. You should also plan for more help than you need. In spite of detailed training, approximately 40 percent of the volunteers who registered did not show up for their shift during Birthday Weekend, placing additional strain on the rest of the volunteer staff.

While most of the responses to Birthday Weekend were positive, there were a few negative reactions. During the event, an eight-block by four-block section of downtown South Bend was effectively closed off. Because of security concerns, there were only three entry and exit points allowed. The businesses inside this section had vastly different experiences. For example, a bar or a pizza shop inside the cordoned-off zone saw a huge increase in business for three days, but for a business like a frame shop it was a massive disruption. Most people, however, had positive feedback for the celebration. "Almost everyone else saw the benefit to the city and made accommodations," said Garner.

Morris-Jumel Mansion, Manhattan, New York

Built in 1765 as a summer villa for Colonel Robert Morris and his wife Mary Philipse, the Morris-Jumel Mansion is the oldest surviving home in Manhattan. "The Mansion's 250th anniversary was a milestone not many historic houses, let alone museums, could celebrate," said Carol Ward, executive director. "So we knew right away we wanted the year to be a grand culmination of the past 250 years of the house, but also looking forward to the next phase of the mansion's life as a museum. We hoped to achieve a threefold objective: fundraising, increased visibility, and heightened attendance."[22]

The Mansion's first event was a benefit performance of the hit musical *Hamilton*, fusing "traditional Broadway style" with hip hop, for a unique look at one of the most significant individuals in the development of our government. The Mansion has deep roots in both colonial America and the early republic, making this musical an ideal match for the anniversary celebration. Alexander Hamilton was once a dinner guest at the home, dining with George Washington, John Adams, Henry Knox, and Thomas Jefferson on July 10, 1790. There is a second Hamilton connection as well; Aaron Burr, who killed Hamilton in a duel, later lived in the Mansion.

"The creator, Lin-Manuel Miranda, was the guest of honor at our inaugural CAFé," Ward said, "and in chatting with him I asked what his next project was. He mentioned that it was going to be a hip-hop musical about the life of Alexander Hamilton. So I joked with him that if he ever wanted to write some of the songs in Aaron Burr's actual bedroom, that would be fine with us. Which he did and we became involved in the creation and then initial launch of the show at the Public Theater. The timing could not have been more perfect to open our celebration with a musical which honors the past but brings it into contemporary society, exactly what the Mansion aims to do," said Ward.

The benefit performance not only included tickets to the musical, but also a pre-show cocktail reception and a post-show Q&A session with Miranda and the show's director Thomas Kail. Ticket packages included various elements of the experience:

Exclusive: Tickets in the back half of the theater and an invitation to the Q&A event ($250)

Premiere: Tickets in the front half of the theater and invitations to both the pre-event cocktail party and the Q&A event ($375)

VIP: Tickets in the first two rows, invitations to both the pre-event cocktail party and the Q&A event, and a one-of-a-kind VIP gift ($500)

A special $90 ticket price for the show only was made available to students and Manhattan residents. Tickets were sold through the website www.brownpapertickets.com.

The Morris-Jumel Mansion's second event was the 4th Annual Culture and Arts Festival (known as CAFé), branded in 2015 as the 250 Edition. Advertised on the museum's website as "One of New York City's most beloved cultural events," the event featured the best artists Manhattan has to offer, including performances of opera, jazz flute, storytelling, and swing dancing; watercolors, oil paintings, ceramics, bespoke hats and headdresses, and children's clothing for sale; and food vendors. A guided tour of the Mansion was offered as part of the CAFé. There was no charge for the event, which attracted more than six hundred attendees.

Through planning these signature events, Ward learned that you can't start too early. "You have to get all the stakeholders on board early as each individual event within the anniversary celebration took a lot of time and effort to plan and execute," she said. "Map out the whole year well ahead of time. We did this and it was a great roadmap whenever we started losing track. Also, be sure to secure funding (or at least ask) well prior to the event.

Lastly, set very clear goals (scope, fundraising, etc.) so that you don't kill yourself and that the other stakeholders know what the end goals are and should be."

Chesapeake Bay Maritime Museum, St. Michaels, Maryland

To mark its 50th anniversary in 2015, the Chesapeake Bay Maritime Museum kicked off a yearlong celebration in May with a festival called Party on the Point: Celebrating 50 Years on the Bay, which included an exhibition opening for *A Broad Reach: 50 Years of Collecting* and a bell ringing ceremony. "A 50th anniversary is a significant milestone," said Tracey Johns, vice president of communications, "and we wanted to leverage the occasion to engage more donors, sponsors, members, and the public in the museum. Our objectives were to build awareness of the museum and engagement in programs, festivals, and philanthropy."[23] The museum celebrated their anniversary for one year, from May 2015 to May 2016.

At the Ringing of the Bells ceremony, bell buoys from the Chesapeake Bay were rung 50 times by individuals who had played significant roles in the museum's history. Bell ringers included Senator Addie Eckardt; Joanne Clark, president of the Town of St. Michaels, Maryland Commissioners; Larry Denton, president of the Talbot Historical Society; John Valliant, former president of the Chesapeake Bay Maritime Museum; Lisa Morgan from PNC, the museum's lead sponsor for the 50th anniversary; Kelley Cox, executive director of the Phillips Wharf Environmental Center; Rick Carrion from the Classic Yacht Restoration Guild; Robbie Gill from the YMCA of the Chesapeake; Pete Lesher, Chesapeake Bay Maritime Museum's chief curator; and several volunteers, emeritus board members, and family of the staff.

Party on the Point, which was free for members, featured scenic river boat rides on the 1920 buyboat *Winnie Estelle* and other historic boats from the museum's floating fleet. The first 500 guests received a commemorative ditty bag with a small gift, coupons, and other goodies from local merchants. The Classic Yacht Restoration Guild offered dockside tours of the 1888 yacht *Elf.* The festival also included live music, regional food, children's activities, and craft vendors.

The museum also used the Party on the Point to launch the #Snapshots2Selfies campaign, which became the basis for the "community curated" online exhibition Snapshots to Selfies: 50 Years of Chesapeake Summers the following year. Community members were asked to submit personal photos of fishing, sailing, lounging on the beach, catching crabs, and enjoying the summer in the region. The festival also kicked off a community time capsule program which lasted for the entire yearlong celebration.

The Party on the Point was held on a Saturday, and two area businesses extended the festivities for the entire weekend. The Crab Claw Restaurant, which was also celebrating its 50th anniversary in 2015, held a special event on Friday evening, and Patriot Cruises offered special cocktail river cruises on Sunday.

For the Chesapeake Bay Maritime Museum, it is important to evaluate what works and what doesn't work after every event. "We are always looking to improve our festivals by seeking input from staff, vendors, and partners on ways to improve our events and have great things to offer," said Johns. "After an event, we hold a 'Stop, Start, and Continue' meeting. It's a great way to wrap up a festival or any initiative and improve for the next year."

The Paul Revere House, Boston, Massachusetts

When the Paul Revere House celebrated its 100th anniversary as a historic house museum in 2008, staff spent about a year planning 1908 Day to commemorate the occasion. The celebration included a large cake in the shape of the Paul Revere House, costumed reenactors portraying key figures from the past, and musical performances by local school children. One school group recited Longfellow's poem "Paul Revere's Ride," and another group sang patriotic songs. The staff incorporated many 1908-themed ideas into the celebration, including the admission price to the event. "We 'threw-back' our prices before #TBT was a thing," said Emily Holmes, education director. When the museum opened, admission was 25 cents per person. "We expected visitors would like the idea of paying only a quarter but would be so surprised at the 'low' price that they would tell our staff to keep the change. In fact most people waited patiently for their $0.75 in change."[24] The invitation to the 2008 event was inspired by the 1908 invitation to the grand opening of the museum.

Dignitaries were also invited to come to the event. "The City of Boston sent a representative who read aloud the proclamation signed by the mayor declaring it Paul Revere House Salutation Day," said Holmes. "Some of our fellow museums sent good wishes and/or included articles about the anniversary in their own publications. Aaron Michelwitz, representing the Massachusetts Speaker of the House's office, also attended. This was particularly nice because he grew up in the neighborhood and had stories about his interactions with the Revere House as a kid."

Leading up to the event, staff used *The Revere House Gazette*, the museum's quarterly publication, to promote the event and get their core audience reenergized about the site. "We carried articles and mentions of the anniversaries that led up to 1908 Day," Holmes said, "marking the formation of the Paul Revere Memorial Association, the restoration process, etc. In the Spring 2008 issue, which coincided with 1908 Day, we reprinted articles in the Boston newspapers chronicling the opening of the museum in 1908, along with an invitation to attend the 100th anniversary. In the Fall 2007 issue we had 'primed the pump' by running an article about the world in 1907–1908, hoping to put the celebration in context, and get our members and friends in the mood!"

Holmes identified several aspects of 1908 Day that could be easily replicated at other institutions. "Having a large cake made in the shape of *anything* eye-catching and representative of your site would be replicable by the right bakery," Holmes said. "We're lucky to have access to a great one but the explosion of reality TV baking shows since then surely means lots of other areas of the country would also have choices."

First-person interpretation opportunities are also a great way to bring history to life for event participants. "We asked two reenactors, who we had worked with previously on developing other first-person interpretations of real people, to portray the two Revere great-grandchildren who were primarily responsible for saving the house and turning it into a museum," Holmes, said. "Each of them did research using our resources and created a persona, and then they worked together to establish a dialogue appropriate for the occasion, as if we were seeing them opening the house to the public for the first time. Obviously this was very site specific, but the concept could be adapted to another site with different storylines."

A centerpiece of the Paul Revere House's anniversary celebration was a cake shaped like the house. Paul Revere House, Boston, Massachusetts.

"Community involvement was very important to us," said Holmes, "and there are so many ways this can be done. We involved our local schools and local government in the program, but we also asked students near and far to compete in an essay contest and made the awarding of the prizes part of the big day's event. We also chose to highlight the 100th aspect of the day by giving a prize basket to our 100th visitor on that day."

1908 Day also provided a significant opportunity for publicity. "The event generated some national and local media attention, which no doubt prompted some new or returning visitors to seek us out that week and throughout that year," said Holmes. "In fact we set a (then) record for annual attendance in 2008. But more important was the goodwill and positive feelings generated amongst our various stakeholders—board members, former staff, colleagues, schools, local community groups, etc. And of course the opportunity to introduce our Anniversary Fund and the idea of significant fundraising, which we later relaunched/rebranded as our Capital Campaign."

Holmes learned a lot from the process of celebrating the museum's centennial and has some advice for those who are embarking on a similar project. "Prepare for the unexpected," she said. "And expect to be *exhausted* at the end of the day. Also plan as far out in advance as you can, and think about how each element will relate to the message you want to get across to your audiences. You can never go wrong with bunting. When in doubt, order the bunting. It makes the whole place more festive. Try to have something 'eye-catching' like a giant cake in the shape of an iconic house, for instance, that will grab media attention!"

George Washington's Mount Vernon, Mount Vernon, Virginia

In 1999, George Washington's Mount Vernon commemorated the 200th anniversary of Washington's death with a yearlong series of events and programs. The 1999 Annual Report begins, "Some said it could never be done—a full year of commemorative events and programs marking still another bicentennial. This time, it was a bicentennial that was not celebrating someone's birth, but commemorating someone's death. Two major public relations firms told us that death was a 'downer,' and that our expectations should be modest, at best. But the 'someone' in this case was George Washington, and the time seemed right. As a new millennium was approaching, Americans were looking to the past as well as to the future. . . . The *raison d'etre* for the George Washington Bicentennial was a simple one. We wanted George Washington's leadership and character to continue to inspire new generations of Americans well into a new century."[25]

A highlight of the bicentennial of Washington's death was a reenactment of his funeral at Mount Vernon. The staff meticulously researched the details of the original funeral, knowing that they needed to get it right to create an authentic reenactment. According to the 1999 Annual Report, "If our scholarly research failed to uncover not just what happened, but when

For the 200th anniversary of his death, George Washington's bedroom at Mount Vernon was set up to replicate his deathbed in 1799. Courtesy of Mount Vernon Ladies' Association.

The exterior of Mount Vernon was shuttered and draped in mourning during the 1999 com-memoration of George Washington's death. Courtesy of Mount Vernon Ladies' Association.

and how, we recognized the event itself would be much more fiction than fact. . . . If we did not treat the event in the most dignified fashion, the results could be corny or trivial, rather than moving and meaningful."

Behind the scenes, the tribute to Washington's death began at the very moment he died two hundred years earlier:

> At ten o'clock in the evening, we gathered in Washington's bedroom the descendents of those who were in the room in 1799. John Augustine Washington and Martha Custis Peter represented the families of George and Martha Washington, while Stephen Lear stood in the position of his ancestor Tobias Lear [Washington's secretary and friend]. Mike Bible, Master of the Alexandria-Washington [Masonic] Lodge No. 22, assumed the position of Dr. Elisha Cullen Dick, who was the master of the lodge 200 years ago. And near the fireplace stood Zsunnee Kimball Matema, whose great-great-great-great grandmother Caroline, one of Mrs. Washington's most devoted servants, provided a shoulder upon which to lean—and perhaps to cry—during Washington's final hours. For the first time, the clock from the master bedroom, which, according to Masonic tradition, had its pendulum cut the moment Washington died, was returned to its proper place. As John Augustine Washington noted, "Washington died just as he had lived—with dignity and grace."

Following the 200th anniversary of the exact time of his death, Mount Vernon's collections staff "began immediately to transform the mansion into a place of mourning, tying the shutters shut with black ribbon, draping the dining room windows in black, and covering

A highlight of the 200th anniversary of George Washington's death was a reenactment of his funeral. More than 250 people participated in the event, which aired live on C-SPAN. Courtesy of Mount Vernon Ladies' Association.

all reflective surfaces with white fabric." The next morning, visitors arrived to find a "representation of Washington's draped body on a makeshift table in the large dining room." A great deal of time was spent researching "mourning customs in general and what was done at Mount Vernon in particular," said Mary Thompson, research specialist.[26] Thompson's research allowed her to create a program on mourning customs, as well as a paper for the planning committee about how the mansion should be outfitted to reflect a well-researched and historically accurate funeral.

The funeral reenactment was aired live on C-SPAN and is still available for viewing and purchase today. According to C-SPAN, "Over 250 reenactors at Mount Vernon, including descendants of Washington and his slaves, recreated the funeral of George Washington to mark the 200th anniversary of his death. Several participants read remarks by Washington's contemporaries expressing sympathy for his death, while others, dressed in period clothing recreated the remarks made at the funeral. Before and after the funeral, guests commented on the ceremony and telephone lines were opened for audience comments and questions."[27] The entire C-SPAN presentation is nearly three and a half hours. Highlights of the event included an Episcopal and Masonic funeral service, an authentic re-creation of his coffin, and the closing of his tomb, which had recently been restored. More than four thousand people attended the event.

The 1999 Annual Report summed up the event by saying, "Clearly there existed a renewed admiration for Washington and his accomplishments. And though there were many tears shed, the event proved to be more uplifting than depressing. In an age where there are far too few experiences that elicit a true sense of patriotism, Washington's funeral demonstrated that Americans still possess a sense of history, of place, of togetherness."

Thompson suggests institutions start planning any anniversary event earlier than you think necessary—and be prepared for glitches. "Start acquiring or booking anything needed for a reenactment, if you choose to do one (such as costumes, wigs, etc.), well in advance of when they are needed. For example, by the time we got around to ordering clothing and wigs for the funeral reenactment, the best products made by the best companies had already been booked by the production company doing the Mel Gibson movie *The Patriot*, which left us with really bad wigs, among other things." But such matters did not tarnish the event, which was widely hailed as an amazing success. Vincent Hawkins, a reenactor who portrayed Honorary Pallbearer Colonel Charles Sims, best summarizes the reverence and honor of the occasion: "As a history reenactor, that moment will rank as the greatest and most significant event of my reenacting life. From this point forward, when I'm asked what was the best reenactment I ever participated in, I will honestly be able to say, without reservation or further thought, 'The day I helped escort General Washington to his final rest.'"[28]

Minneapolis Institute of Art, Minneapolis, Minnesota

When the Minneapolis Institute of Art (Mia) celebrated its 100th anniversary in 2015, the staff wanted to plan something big to celebrate. They came up with an innovative and ambitious plan to unveil fifty-two surprises—one every week—during the Birthday Year. "It wasn't about a one off big party," said Katie Hill, audience engagement specialist. "It was about the community and celebrating them. Our intention was to leverage this moment in time as a launch pad for the next one hundred years, gain new audiences, increase aware-ness, and engage current audiences in new and surprising ways." Surprises included pop-up musical performances, art installations, tours by local celebrities, and free treats for visitors. Revealed one at a time, Mia has archived the announcement of each surprise on a special page of its website:[29]

1. Mia Kicks Off Its 100th Birthday with a Bang!

We're thrilled to announce the long-term loan of the Myron Kunin collection, widely considered to be one of the most important privately held collections of American art in the world, with a special exhibition, American Modernism: Selections from the Kunin Collection, on view for the entire Birthday Year. As *Star Tribune* notes, "Planned in secret, the unannounced exhibit is an eighty-piece sample of more than 550 paintings, sculptures, prints, drawings and photos on loan from the Kunin family, with the hope it will become a permanent part of the museum."

2. Happy (actual) Birthday, Mia!

January 7th is Mia's official date of birth, and we are celebrating today with surprise sweet treats from Glam Doll Donuts for visitors all day long.

3. Mia Unveils the First of Three Mystery Masterpieces

Widely regarded as one of the greatest artists ever, Johannes Vermeer painted only thir-ty-four known works. Starting at 10:00 a.m. today, you can walk into Mia and see one of these rare paintings, *Woman Reading a Letter*, visiting from the world-renowned collection of the Rijksmuseum in Amsterdam, up close and personal, for free.

As part of Masterpiece in Focus, an unprecedented series of surprise exhibitions pre-sented in celebration of the museum's 100th Birthday Year, preeminent European museums are lending Mia three of the world's most influential paintings for the enjoyment of the people of Minnesota.

Stay tuned for the next two Masterpiece in Focus reveals throughout the 2015 Birthday Year.

4. Scott Seekins Leads Surprise Tour at Mia

Worlds collided when two Minnesota icons came together unexpectedly, in celebration of art! On Saturday, January 24, at 2:30 p.m., Mia hosted a special #BDayMia free public tour of the museum, led by none other than local artist (and living legend), Scott Seekins.

5. Mia Presents "Of Us and Art: The 100 Videos Project"

In conjunction with its Birthday Year festivities, Mia is making movies, one hundred of them to be exact. "Of Us and Art" is a year-long series of films exploring the museum, its collection, and people's experiences with art.

The films are short, and the subjects are varied, but ultimately the series tells the story of the how Mia connects the community with art. Because—let's face it—without the community it serves, Mia would not be where it is today, looking forward to the next one hundred years.

New films will be launched regularly throughout the year on Third A/V, Mia's video portal. Stay tuned for fresh content that just might put a unique twist on what it means to be a classic art museum.

6. See Mia as It's Rarely Seen: Empty

Every day (except Mondays, of course), Mia is full of visitors, artists, students, and families . . . and we like it that way. But there's a certain magic in the air when the museum is empty—a creative hum that reverberates into infinity when no one's there to catch it. With that in mind, we took a tip from our friends at the Metropolitan Museum of Art, and invited members of the local Instagram community into the empty museum to capture what's there when no one else is.

Follow along on Instagram with hashtags #BDayMia and #EmptyMia as the journey through the empty halls of Mia unfolds.

7. Mia Announces Partnership with Mall of America

As part of its mission to expand the museum's footprint beyond its walls and bring art into the greater community, Mia is pleased to announce a new partnership with Mall of America. Merging art with fashion and entertainment, the two Minnesota institutions are excited to offer the community artful new programming, activations, and installations debuting throughout the year.

The multi-faceted partnership launched with a twirl. On Friday, February 13, guests visiting MOA were delighted with a surprise pop-up Viennese waltz performance by dancers from USA Ballroom Dance. The performance, co-organized by Mia and MOA, celebrated Mia's exhibition The Habsburgs: Rarely Seen Masterpieces from Europe's Greatest Dynasty, which opened Sunday, February 15.

The two organizations will continue their partnership throughout the year. In addition to Mia having a strong presence at the opening of the new MOA Grand Front Entrance, guests can look for the museum's Family Day programming at Toddler Tuesday events and digital art installations at the Mall facilitated by Mia.

The organizations are also eager to launch a very special project this spring: artist-designed t-shirts for sale to the public. Evocative and inspiring, the exclusive, limited-edition shirts will be available at both MOA and the Store at Mia in celebration of the museum's 100th Birthday Year.

8. Mia Celebrates The Habsburgs Opening Day with Surprise Carriage Rides and a Pop-up Musical Performance

To celebrate today's opening of The Habsburgs: Rarely Seen Masterpieces from Europe's Greatest Dynasty, Mia is surprising visitors with horse-drawn carriage rides around the block and a pop-up performance of music by Mozart, performed by the Musical Offering.

9. Mia Presents Public Ice Sculpture near Lake Calhoun

Continuing in its quest to surprise and delight, and bring art outside the museum walls and into the community, Mia has created a giant ice sculpture of a dragon to display in the public space next to Lake Calhoun in Uptown, starting this Friday, February 20, and running through March 4.

A uniquely Minnesotan expression of what it means to inspire creativity and wonder in a place that is frozen for a significant part of the year, the dragon also symbolizes Mia's world-renowned Asian art collection.

Truly a one-of-a-kind installation of public art, this sculpture will only be around for a limited time (thank goodness!), so be sure to see it before it melts away.

10. Doctor Fink Leads Surprise Tour at Mia

On Saturday, February 28, Grammy-award-winning keyboardist, record producer, and songwriter Matt Fink led a special #BDayMia tour of the museum. Matt is better known by the stage name Doctor Fink, and as a leading member of Prince's band, the Revolution.

11. A Late Night with the Habsburgs for 100 Mia Members

Sisi, Maximilian I, Rudolph II, Franz Joseph I, Maria Theresa—Which Habsburg Are You? This week's #BDayMia surprise asked Mia members to take the BuzzFeed quiz and report their results on Twitter or Facebook. The first one hundred members to disclose their inner royal personality earned themselves (and a friend) free after-hours access to "The Habsburgs: Rarely Seen Masterpieces from Europe's Greatest Dynasty." There haven't been so many "Habsburgs" in one place since 1854!

12. Mia Presents Surprise Party, an Unexpected Installation by Aaron Dysart

Last year, Mia invited the artist community to propose surprise projects to help celebrate the museum's one hundred years of wonder and counting. This installation by Aaron Dysart is the first of several artist-designed birthday surprise projects to happen throughout the year.

Animating the Fountain Court with zillions of disco-light sparkles, it's an immersive installation that, like the museum itself, only comes alive with your participation. When you pass through the room, an infrared sensor detects your movement and triggers LED lights to blast the slowly rotating twenty-four-inch disco ball suspended from the ceiling.

13. Mia Announces Major Gift from the Mary Griggs Burke Foundation of World-Renowned Japanese Art

Of the over one thousand objects going to both the Minneapolis Institute of Art and the Metropolitan Museum of Art in New York, approximately seven hundred are becoming part of Mia's Japanese collection. This addition brings the Japanese collection to seven thousand objects, making it one of the most significant encyclopedic collections of Japanese art in the nation. With this gift, as well as a recently established endowment for Asian art programming and the addition of key staff positions in Japanese art at Mia, the museum is poised to become a leading center for the study of Japanese art.

"This is a transformative gift," Matthew Welch, the deputy director and chief curator of Mia, told the *New York Times*. "Curators throw that word around, but this is staggering."

Mia will showcase more than 170 of these masterpieces in Gifts of Japanese and Korean Art from the Mary Griggs Burke Collection on view from September 26, 2015, through April 2016.

14. Jamie Yuccas Leads Surprise Tour at Mia

On Saturday, March 28, WCCO This Morning anchor Jamie Yuccas will lead a special free #BDayMia tour of the museum. A Minnesota native, experienced journalist, and novice museum tour guide, Jamie will share what she finds intriguing about art and give her fresh take on pieces in the galleries.

Join in the celebration and meet Jamie in the lobby at 2:30 p.m. for an hour-long tour on Saturday March 28!

15. Mia Celebrates 100 Seasons of Spring with a Pollinator Seed Giveaway

Happy Bee-Day Mia! The museum has kept beehives on its roof since 2013 with help from the U of M Bee Squad. Mia bees are ambassadors of bees worldwide that have recently suffered devastating declines, threatening the global food supply. This week's surprise giveaway is intended to celebrate the art of nature and the arrival of spring, plant the seed for an upcoming surprise this fall, and help feed the bees everywhere!

"Bee" one of the first one hundred visitors to Mia on Saturday, April 4 to receive a special surprise pollinator seed pack in celebration of spring!

16. Mia Offers Free Screening of *The Royal Tenenbaums*

In honor of the Habsburgs: Rarely Seen Masterpieces from Europe's Greatest Dynasty, Mia invites you to get to know a similarly quirky, though not technically "royal," family with a free screening of Wes Anderson's cult classic *The Royal Tenenbaums* on Friday, April 10. (Bonus, the film features a score by Mark Mothersbaugh, the musician and visual artist whose work will be on view at Mia this summer in a unique retrospective.)

Doors to the auditorium will open at 6 p.m. and the screening will begin at 6:30 p.m. Arrive early to enjoy Wes Anderson movie trivia hosted by Trivia Mafia and, of course, popcorn! Feel free to sport your favorite track suit, tennis outfit or polo dress in honor of your favorite Tenenbaum.

The screening is free, but tickets are required.

17. Mia Presents *Lifetime of Wishing (100 Birthdays)*, a Film Installation by Ben Moren

Last year, Mia invited the artist community to propose surprise projects to help celebrate the museum's one hundred years of wonder and counting. This installation by Ben Moren is one of several artist-designed birthday surprise projects happening throughout the year.

Moren's unique short film documents one hundred people, ages 1 to 100, blowing out their birthday candles—a surprise installation to celebrate Mia's 100th Birthday. Moren, a Minneapolis-based media artist working at the intersection of filmmaking, performance, and technology development, compiled footage from appropriated home movies onto Super 8mm film.

Come experience one hundred years of birthday wishing for yourself—on view in the Target Wing through May 21, 2015.

18. Mayor Hodges Leads Surprise Tour at Mia

On Saturday, April 25, Minneapolis Mayor Betsy Hodges will lead a special #BDayMia tour of the museum.

A Minnesota native, accomplished public servant, and arts enthusiast, Mayor Hodges will share her favorite pieces in the collection and what she finds inspiring about art. When she's not governing the city of Minneapolis, Mayor Hodges works on staying physically fit, writes, reads poetry, and enjoys seasonal viewings of *Die Hard*, her favorite movie.

Join in the celebration and meet Mayor Hodges in the lobby at 2:30 p.m. for an hour-long tour on Saturday, April 25!

19. Mia Launches Pop-Up Museum Around Town

Get ready to see Mia's collection in a whole new light—outside!

As part of our Birthday Year commitment to bring art experiences out of the museum and into the community, we created high-quality reproductions of four of our iconic paintings, that were installed at surprising outdoor locations throughout the month of May 2015, which is Minnesota Museum Month. In a unique twist, a museum docent was stationed at each painting from 1:30 to 3:30 p.m. every Saturday, weather permitting, to share insights and stories about the paintings and answer questions people may have about the works.

Leading into the first week of May, stunning, full-scale reproductions of Rembrandt's *Lucretia*, Monet's *Grainstack, Sun in the Mist*, Van Gogh's *Olive Trees*, and Soutine's *Carcass of Beef* popped up outside Bobby and Steve's Auto World in Minneapolis, U.S. Bank in Uptown, Hennepin County Library—Minneapolis Central, and Kramarczuk's in Northeast, respectively. Halfway through the month, the paintings popped up again to turn heads and cause double-takes at Wedge Table, Loring Park, the Stone Arch Bridge, and the Strip Club Meat and Fish.

Never before has Mia undertaken a project like this, and after May it won't happen again. All were invited to stop by and visit the reproductions, especially while a docent was present, and to share the enthusiasm for surprising public art moments with others by snapping a pic and sharing it using #BDayMia.

20. Mia Launches Campaign to Acquire Eros, a Monumental Outdoor Sculpture for the Community

In celebration of Mia's 100th Birthday Year, our curators searched for a monumental outdoor sculpture that would reference the museum's historic art collections and be a new masterpiece for the community. Handsome, mysterious, and poignant, *Eros* is sure to become an icon for the museum and Minneapolis.

To mark the Birthday Year, Mia raised funds from the community to purchase this remarkable contemporary sculpture. Inviting the public to play a tangible, meaningful role during the museum's centennial celebration, as this new work has changed the face of the "people's museum" for generations to come. We've met our goal to raise at least $1 million to bring this work into Mia's collection. Donations large and small were happily accepted.

21. Mia Debuts a Birthday Surprise in Honor of Art in Bloom

Even Mia's Guardian Lions are celebrating spring and Mia's Birthday Year! To commemorate the museum's 100th year, the two lions who guard Mia's entrance, opening for the season today, are decorated in full floral regalia. The adorned lions kick off Mia's 32nd annual Art in Bloom, presented by Friends of the Institute.

The Guardian Lions were donated to Mia in 1998 by Ella Pillsbury Crosby in honor of her husband. In turn, Ella's daughter Lucy (Bob) Mitchell has donated the floral arrangements for the lions in memory of her mother and in celebration of Mia's Birthday Year.

22. Mia Marches in May Day Parade with Chihuly-Inspired Float

Mia is proud to participate in the 41st annual May Day Parade, the Minneapolis rite of spring marked by larger than life puppets, creative costumes, and a public celebration of the community. The museum is excited to present a community-created "Sunburst" float inspired by Mia's iconic work of art by Dale Chihuly in the parade.

A team of artists, led by Amy Ballestad, worked together with about three hundred people in the community through the Art in the Park program to create the five hundred "flames" on the bicycle-powered float. The mobile collaborative sculpture is made out of recycled plastic bottles, aluminum foil, and tissue paper.

Watch for the Sunburst float in the "We Rise" section of the parade on Sunday May 3, 2015!

23. Mia Unveils the Second of Three Mystery Masterpieces

Raphael, together with Michelangelo and Leonardo da Vinci, form the holy trinity of great masters of the Renaissance period. Starting today at 10 a.m., you can walk into the museum and see one of Raphael's masterpieces, *Madonna of the Pinks*, visiting from the world-renowned collection of the National Gallery in London on view for a limited time, for free.

This jewel of a painting, originally produced as a devotional image, depicts the Mother and Child in a dark interior, a bedchamber, exchanging a sprig of pink carnations. The artist captures in their affectionate and natural playfulness the tender emotions one might expect between a young mother and her child. Raphael's unique and beautiful vision of this popular subject set a new precedent that would be imitated by artists for centuries.

As part of Masterpiece in Focus, an unprecedented series of exhibitions presented in celebration of the museum's 100th Birthday Year, preeminent European museums are lending Mia three paintings by three of the world's greatest artists for the enjoyment of the people of Minnesota. Stay tuned for the third and final reveal later this year.

Surprise #24 during the Minnesota Institute of Art's 100th anniversary celebration was wrapping three water towers in the area with iconic art. The water tower featuring Frank Stella's Tahkt-I-Sulayman Variation II was located in Minnetonka. Minneapolis Institute of Art, Minneapolis, Minnesota.

24. Mia Wraps MN Water Towers with Iconic Art

Just in time for summer road trips and to lighten the mood for many daily commutes, Mia has adorned three Minnesota city water towers with works of art as a continuation of the museum's Birthday Year commitment to bring art experiences into the community in surprising ways. Check out renditions of Vincent van Gogh's *Olive Trees* in Chisago City, Katsushika Hokusai's *Under the Wave off Kanagawain*, New Hope, and Frank Stella's *Tahkt-I-Sulayman Variation II* in Minnetonka. We couldn't think of a more delightful surprise to spot from the road, so enjoy the view from Memorial Day Weekend through September.

Share in the fun and snap a photo (from the passenger's seat, of course!) and tag #BDayMia @artsmia.

25. Mia Unveils 2015 Photography Commission by Cinthya Soto

In conjunction with 100+: A Photograph for Every Year of the Mia, an exhibition that celebrates Mia's 100th Birthday Year with photographs from every year since the museum's founding in 1915, the museum has commissioned international photographer Cinthya Soto to capture a local place in her unique photographic style to represent the year 2015.

Soto, who splits her time between Costa Rica and Switzerland, captures everyday public and private settings with large-scale gridded analog camera techniques. This new work, *Dahl Violin Shop*, captures the intimate interior of the downtown Minneapolis violin repair shop. The artist's interest in the passage of time and the price of progress focuses her work on documenting independent businesses that are disappearing with the expansion of globalization. Cinthya is a new artist to Mia's collection and this piece rounds out the representation of one hundred years in the exhibition. 100+: A Photograph for Every Year of the Mia is on view through October 18, 2015.

26. Mia presents Artist Statements, Limited-Edition T-Shirts

Ready to wear art on your sleeve? Mia is proud to launch an exclusive, limited edition run of artist-designed t-shirts in honor of the museum's 100th Birthday Year. In partnership with the Mall of America and working closely with five artists in the museum's collection, Jenny Holzer, Alec Soth, David Rathman, Kota Ezawa, and Chris Larson, Mia has created an unforgettable and highly covetable collection of wearable art. Read more about the artists here.

These t-shirts will be available for $25 at the Store at Mia and the Mall of America, while supplies last.

27. Mia Presents "HB2U: A Northern Spark Birthday Surprise" by Alyssa Baguss

Last year, Mia invited the artist community to propose surprise projects to help celebrate the museum's 100 years of wonder and counting. This Northern Spark project by Alyssa Baguss is one of several artist-designed birthday surprises happening through the year.

Indulging in special things is at the heart of what makes birthdays so happy: tearing open beautiful wrapping paper, eating the corner piece of cake and partying for the sake of your existence on this planet. This project extracts the essence of birthday and traps it inside a hot air balloon you walk into at Northern Spark 2015. Party hats, horns, and confetti provided, along with art-inspired cake decorating and a surprise party photo booth!

Alyssa Baguss's practice explores mediated natural environments through drawing processes, interactive installation and playful public programming.

Join us for Northern Spark on Saturday, June 13 from 9 p.m. to 2 a.m. to experience this once in a lifetime installation first hand.

28. Mark Mothersbaugh Surprise Performance at Myopia Opening

Founder of punk rock band Devo, composer of Wes Anderson film scores, and extremely prolific visual artist Mark Mothersbaugh is full of surprises! "Mark Mothersbaugh: Myopia," a retrospective of Mothersbaugh's work, features a dynamic combination of cultural criticism and personal expression through his drawings, films, paintings, sculpture, music, and plenty of postcards. The artist will surprise the crowd at the exhibition's opening night on Thursday, June 18, 2015, with a special performance on his unique instruments called Orchestrions.

Please join us at the museum for the exhibition opening night festivities at Third Thursday on June 18, 6–9 p.m., FREE!

29. Free Admission to Leonardo da Vinci Exhibition for Dads on Father's Day

This #BDayMia surprise is just for dads. In honor of Father's Day and the opening day of the Leonardo da Vinci, the Codex Leicester, and the Creative Mind exhibition, dads will receive free admission to the show on Sunday, June 21, 2015.

Engineer, inventor, scientist, artist: Leonardo da Vinci embodies the ideal of an innovative mind who uses his vast intellect, powers of observation, and boundless curiosity to explore the world around him. This rare exhibition presents one of Leonardo's original notebooks, a vital tool in his creative process, and examines how his renaissance thinking is shared by some of today's most visionary artists, engineers, and designers.

Leonardo da Vinci, the Codex Leicester, and the Creative Mind opens on Sunday June 21 and runs through August 30, 2015.

30. Mia Commissions Crop Art Inspired by Van Gogh

In a continued effort to bring art outside the museum's walls and into the community in new and surprising ways, the Minneapolis Institute of Art has commissioned renowned crop artist Stan Herd to create a planted version of the beloved van Gogh's *Olive Trees* painting.

Minneapolis Institute of Art commissioned renowned crop artist Stan Herd to create a planted version of the beloved van Gogh's Olive Trees painting as Surprise #30. Minneapolis Institute of Art, Minneapolis, Minnesota.

For Surprise #32, Minneapolis Institute of Art and the Minneapolis Parks and Recreation Board teamed up to plant art-inspired plots at Lyndale Park Gardens, near Lake Harriet. Minneapolis Institute of Art, Minneapolis, Minnesota.

Planting began this spring and the final piece has revealed itself! It has been exciting to watch it grow and it will remain intact through the fall of 2015! The field location was chosen specifically so that the growing art can be seen from many flights coming and going from MSP airport. If you spot it, snap a pic and share it with #BDayMia #vangrow!

Special thank you to Thomson Reuters for sharing their field with the museum in celebration of the Birthday Year.

31. Mia Commissions Handsome Cycles to Create Art-Inspired Bikes

Together with Handsome Cycles, the Minneapolis Institute of Art is excited to announce a partnership that merges art and bikes!

Launching at the museum's popular Bike Night event on July 16, 2015, three custom bikes inspired by works of art from Mia's permanent collection, including paintings by Claude Monet and Frank Stella, and the 1948 Tatra T87 sedan, were unveiled. The artful bikes were created in celebration of the museum's Birthday Year. Additionally, the two Minnesota brands will offer an exclusive line of Mia bikes available for purchase through the Store at Mia and Handsome Cycles' website.

32. Planted Paintings Pop Up at Minneapolis Park

In celebration of our 100-year partnership, the Minneapolis Institute of Art and the Minneapolis Parks and Recreation Board have teamed up to plant art-inspired plots at Lyndale Park Gardens, near Lake Harriet. Garden Designer Rachel DeVries took inspiration from paintings in the museum's collection for a spring tulip garden and a summer installation of annuals.

Head over to Lyndale Park Gardens and see the beautiful collaboration in bloom! Snap a photo and share with #BDayMia @artsmia to join in the celebration.

33. Surprise Grown-Up Field Trips

Adding a surprising twist to a typical Minneapolis Institute of Art experience, the museum thanked some of its generous corporate partners this week with grown-up field trips. Over the lunch hour, groups of employees from 3M, Thomson Reuters, and Fredrikson and Byron, PA boarded yellow school buses, headed to the museum for a special tour of Leonardo da Vinci, the Codex Leicester, and the Creative Mind, and enjoyed a grown-up boxed lunch courtesy of Agra Culture.

The Minneapolis Institute of Art is grateful to all of our sponsors for helping us to inspire wonder through the power of art.

34. Mia Unveils the Final Mystery Masterpiece

For our third—and final—surprise masterpiece, a bouquet of iconic *Irises* by Vincent van Gogh. Starting today at 10 a.m., you can walk into the museum and see this visiting masterpiece from the world-renowned collection of the Van Gogh Museum in Amsterdam. It's on view for a limited time, free in our Cargill Gallery.

As part of Masterpiece in Focus, an unprecedented series of exhibitions presented in celebration of the museum's 100th Birthday Year, preeminent European museums are lending Mia three paintings by three of the world's greatest artists for the enjoyment of the people of Minnesota.

35. Mia Presents Art Cars by Korrin Lohmann and Sarah Holm

Last year, Mia invited the artist community to propose surprise projects to help celebrate the museum's 100 years (and counting!) of inspiring wonder through the power of art. This project by Korrin Lohmann and Sarah Holm is one of several artist-designed birthday surprise projects happening throughout the year.

The artists have designed two Mia-collection-inspired art cars that will make their debut this Saturday at the Minnesota State Fair Art Car Parade. The cars were inspired by Nick Cave's Soundsuit and the Modernism Gallery (G378). Members of the public got a sneak peek at the cars during Mia's BDay Block Party on August 9, 2015, when they were invited to help paint the designs. Korrin Lohmann is a furniture and home goods designer and maker, educator, and artist with an emphasis on community involvement. Sarah M. Holm is the owner and maker of fine leather goods at Black Spoke Leather Co., a clothing designer, and a mixed media artist.

Keep an eye out for the Mia art cars in the State Fair Parade this Saturday, August 29, at 2 p.m. and around town after that!

36. Robyne Robinson Leads Surprise Tour at Mia

On Friday, September 4, Robyne Robinson will lead a special #BDayMia tour of the museum.

Robyne Robinson has been a well-known personality in the Twin Cities for more than 20 years. An award-winning pioneer in Minnesota broadcasting and state politics, Robinson was the first black prime time news anchor in the Minneapolis–St. Paul TV market and only the second African American to run for lieutenant governor of Minnesota. She's also known as a staunch advocate for Minnesota arts, as well as an international jewelry designer. Robinson currently serves as arts and culture director of the Airport Foundation MSP at Minneapolis–St. Paul International Airport. She will share her favorite works of art in Mia's collection on this special Friday night tour.

Join in the celebration and meet Robyne Robinson in the lobby at 6 p.m. for an hour-long tour on Friday, September 4!

37. Art Shanty Projects Pop Up at Mia

Typically found on a frozen lake in February, Art Shanty Projects (ASP) popped up at Mia from September 10 to September 13, 2015.

As one more way to engage with local artists and the community in celebration of the museum's 100th Birthday Year, we partnered with one of Minnesota's favorite creative organizations to bring a taste of the frozen fun off the ice and onto Target Plaza in the museum's backyard. Mia and ASP brought selected shanties and performers to the museum to transform Mia's communal space into an artist-driven temporary community. We expanded the notions of art and artistic practice with the ASP Board Shanty, dICEHOUSE Shanty, Ambient Tarp Shanty, and Dance Shanty, while engaging with Plein Air Painting from Outdoor Painters of Minnesota, a life-sized polar bear puppet, and family-friendly DJs, including Flipstyle TC.

38. Chef-Inspired Surprise Etsy Pop-Up Shop at Mia

Announcing Mia + Etsy: The Chef's Table, an artisanal pop-up shop inspired by the museum's exhibition Ferran Adrià: Notes on Creativity (September 17, 2015–January 3, 2016) and featuring independent Etsy sellers from all over the world. You'll see natural and organic washed linens, kitchen tools made from beautiful woods, metals and porcelain, and handmade stationery, journals, and maker kits. This unique partnership will continue through the holiday season, so visit often to see the different products available.

Treat yourself, and the chefs you love!

39. Mia Presents The Art of Wonder

"If you look at art long enough, it begins staring back at you." —David Carr

In celebration of the Minneapolis Institute of Art's 100th birthday, the museum asked some of the United States' most talented writers, photographers, and illustrators to muse about art, creativity, and inspiration in this newly released publication. What they conjured is a work of art itself: fiction, essays, photojournalism, and illustrated stories, by turns delightful and reflective.

Contributors to this surprising publication include the late New York Times journalist David Carr, renowned photographers Alec Soth and Ann Hamilton, National Book Award–winning author Pete Hautman, illustrator Eric Hanson, hip-hop artist and author Dessa, and graphic novelist Kevin Cannon. The Art of Wonder also features personal reflections from the curators of the Minneapolis Institute of Art on the objects of their affection and wonder.

See a sneak peek of Alec Soth's photo essay of the museum guards via the New Yorker's Photo Booth and get your copy of the book at the Store at Mia!

40. Mia Offers Surprise Touch Tours

Yes, please touch the art! Register for one of the special touch tours offered in October in honor of Art Beyond Sight month. These tours are free and open to the public. And we'll provide the gloves.

October is Art Beyond Sight month when arts and cultural organizations around the world promote the engagement of people with visual loss and other disabilities. During the month of October at the Minneapolis Institute of Art, you can experience selected works of art through touch. These free public tours will be held on October 13, 15, 20, and 22 at 2 p.m. Please call (612) 870-3140 to register, children 10 and up are welcome.

Mia also offers private verbal description and touch tours by appointment. Service animals are welcome. Please note that guided access tours are free of charge, but require advance registration. Contact the Tour Office at (612) 870-3140. Read more information about accessibility at Mia: http://new.artsmia.org/visit/services-for-visitors-with-disabilities/

41. Mia Presents Community Mural

In keeping with Mia's 100th Birthday Year theme of bringing art outside the walls of the museum and engaging with new audiences and communities, we're excited to present a creative collaboration between Mia and Centro Tyrone Guzman.

This intergenerational project allowed a group of women and teens to identify pressing issues affecting their lives and create a visual representation in mural form. For the past three months, both groups worked with a facilitator and a mural artist to collect and share stories; they took field trips to mural sites across the city to get ideas; and visited the museum to get inspiration and learn basic painting techniques in the studios. This mural, located on Centro's Chicago Avenue facade, was conceived of by the women's group and contains imagery important to them, alongside a message of hope for the future: a woman's face is turned to the right, looking toward a section of blank wall, which will be painted by the teens next summer.

42. Mia Displays Delacroix Like Never Before

Three major special exhibitions have anchored this 100th Birthday Year celebration at Mia, and so for the last of these exhibitions, we're presenting the star of the show, Eugène Delacroix, like you've never seen him before—on our front steps!

Opening Sunday, October 18, the exhibition Delacroix's Influence: The Rise of Modern Art from Cézanne to van Gogh focuses on this exceptional French artist and his expansive influence on modern art as we know it.

Take advantage of this opening weekend opportunity to enter the museum through the seasonal 24th Street classical facade entrance and take in Delacroix's self-portrait one step at a time.

43. Jack Farrell Leads Surprise Tour at Mia

On Sunday, October 25, Jack Farrell, chairman and CEO of Haskell's, Inc., will lead a special wine, beer, and sake themed #BDayMia tour of the museum.

In addition to leading one of the largest retailers of fine wines in the country, Mr. Farrell is known publicly for his twenty-six years of radio broadcasting for WCCO's "Entertaining Ideas" and "Dinner Tonight." As a buyer and connoisseur of wine, he has conducted over thirty tours of Europe with special emphasis on food and wine, served on panels with Julia Child and James Beard, and consulted with the White House on food and wine pairings.

During this special tour, Mr. Farrell will share his insight and stories on food, wine, beer, and sake as it relates to objects he's selected from Mia's collection.

Join the celebration and meet Jack Farrell in the lobby at 3 p.m. for an hour-long tour on Sunday, October 25!

44. 100 Carved Pumpkins: A Halloween Birthday Surprise

Trick-ART-Treat! Mia showcases the art of pumpkin carving on the seasonal 24th Street entrance in honor of the 100th Birthday Year. After inviting artists, community members, museum partners, staff and volunteers to create artful gourds inspired by art and artists in the collection, the museum is proud to present one hundred jack-o-lanterns on the steps, on view Thursday, October 29–Saturday, October 31.

Stop by Mia this weekend and check out the amazing examples of human creativity in the galleries as well as on the steps before the seasonal entrance closes and share your artful pumpkin creations with #BDayMia @artsmia.

Special thanks to all the artists and community members that participated, including Thomson Reuters, Made to Create, Twin Cities Public Television, Friends of the Institute, and Minneapolis College of Art and Design.

45. Mia Presents Selfie Mural by Lys Akerman-Frank

Last year, Mia invited the artist community to propose surprise projects to help celebrate the museum's one hundred years (and counting!) of inspiring wonder through the power of art. This project by Lys Akerman-Frank is one of several artist-designed birthday surprise projects happening throughout the year.

Lys Akerman-Frank joined Mia's Community Arts program this summer at various workshops and events in the Twin Cities, inviting people to take selfies to be included in this mural project. The invitation was extended worldwide through social media as well. As the artist states, "The Selfie Mural idea came to me, not only as a personal challenge, but also collaboration between myself, and everyone willing to 'donate' their self-image to the mural. The intention of the project is to show that the community is Mia. Our faces are part of the museum; we are part of the art that is shown here." Brazilian American Lys Akerman-Frank has lived in Minnesota for over twenty years and is a mom, artist, picture framer, business owner, puppet designer, and beginner puppeteer.

Come see yourself and many others in the Mia Community Selfie Mural, installed in the Community Corridor on the first floor of the museum November 3, 2015–January 24, 2016.

46. Mia Hosts 100 Musicians in the Galleries

This surprise is a feast for the senses! Experience the galleries in a whole new way as the halls of Mia fill with music of all kinds.

On Sunday, November 15, from 12:30 p.m. to 4 p.m. Mia will host over one hundred musicians from MacPhail Center for Music continuously performing all over the museum. Wander through the galleries and get inspired by the thoughtful pairings of musical performance styles and the art that surrounds the performers. Performances range from harp ensemble to African drumming to a woodwind quintet to vocal soloists, and everything in-between, so join us for an afternoon of wonder and delight in the experience of live music in the galleries as diverse and engaging as the museum's global collection.

47. Surprise Collaboration with Faribault Woolen Mills

Together with Faribault Woolen Mills, the Minneapolis Institute of Art is excited to announce a special #BDayMia surprise collaboration that brings together two classic Minnesota institutions.

Launching on Black Friday, November 27, the Store at Mia will unveil a limited edition Mia blanket and scarf. Inspired by the classic, clean lines of Faribault Woolen Mill's heritage craft pieces and in celebration of the museum's 100th Birthday Year, these specialty items are only available for purchase at Mia.

48. Mia Presents Unvending by Caitlin Warner

Last year Mia invited the artist community to propose surprise projects to help celebrate the museum's 100 years (and counting!) of inspiring wonder through the power of art. This project by Minnesota-based book artist Caitlin Warner is one of several artist-designed birthday surprise projects happening throughout the year.

Since 2012, Caitlin Warner's Unvending project has been installed in many gallery and non-gallery spaces throughout Minnesota. Unvending machines are ordinary vending machines that have been refurbished and repurposed to dispense nothing but art! Warner creates playful pieces to dispense from her machines—producing take-home art products that try to give form to life's little intangibles and questioning the nature of important artwork.

These fully functional Unvending machines are Art Experience Supplement vending machines, specialized for an "Art with a Capital A" museum setting, but surprisingly found in the restrooms in the Community Corridor, on the first floor of Mia.

49. Mia Plus: A New Way to Engage in the Galleries

People experience the museum in many different ways. When you visit, we want you to feel comfortable and welcome, no matter your entry point. As part of Mia's 100th Birthday Year, we're excited to introduce Mia Plus, a new gallery experience that's both enjoyable and educational.

Mia Plus offers more opportunities to gather, converse, contemplate, and experience the art on display in a manner that is friendly and inviting. In the museum, you'll find comfortable seating areas, generously provided by Room and Board, as well as new labels and panels that offer interesting facts and stories about artists and works of art, with a focus on human creativity.

This also marks the launch of a new digital storytelling platform, ArtStories, which is available on iPads in the galleries or on your smartphone at http://artstories.artsmia.org. ArtStories offers an interactive experience that provides deeper insight into the art objects, including videos, photography, audio and additional context as well as surprising narratives about the works of art.

50. Surprise "Candlelight" Tours of the Period Rooms

Surprise! Mia is offering a special "candlelight" tour of the period rooms in conjunction with the Living Rooms project. Curators will take a limited number of people through the rooms after the museum has closed and the modern lighting has been turned off, illuminating the history and context of these beloved museum installations as they originally existed.

The surprise candlelight period room tours will take place on Thursday, December 17, from 9–10 p.m. Sign up here (http://artsmia.org/candlelight-tours) to experience the wonder of Mia's Living Rooms in a whole new light!

51. Staff Favorites: Now on View at Mia

In closing out the year of celebration for the Minneapolis Institute of Art's 100th Birthday, we've invited Mia staff to call out their personal favorite works of art. These are marked in the galleries with special temporary labels and will be on view through the end of the year. Much like you'd find in a wine shop or bookstore, we wanted to share the variety of perspectives, beyond the purely curatorial, illuminating why different people like different works of art. There's no right or wrong way to experience the museum or appreciate art, and with a collection as diverse and broad-reaching as Mia's, there really is something for everyone.

52. Thank You for a Great Year!

As the Minneapolis Institute of Art brings the exciting yearlong 100th Birthday celebration to a close, we thank you for making it all possible.

To conclude our year of fifty-two surprises, we are delighted to announce the gift of more than four hundred works of art from fifty-eight individual collectors, including longtime supporters of the museum, current and past Mia trustees and donors, as well as new patrons and nationally known collectors.

These new gifts include paintings, sculptures, works on paper, and decorative arts in all areas of Mia's permanent collection. You'll find the new works on view in the galleries at Mia, denoted with a special 100th Birthday marker.

Read more about the Birthday Year art gifts in the *Star Tribune*.

Thanks to you, we were here one hundred years ago, we're here now, and we'll continue to be here in the next century and beyond, inspiring wonder through the power of art.

According to Hill, ideas came from "all-staff brainstorming sessions, planning for the last 5–10 years as an institution, artist-proposed projects, curatorial opportunities, inspiration from other museums/institutions, inspiration from non-museums/outside the field, and a huge drive to do something completely different." As a result of the Birthday Year initiatives, Mia had its highest attendance ever with 850,000 people in 2015.

Memorial Art Gallery of the University of Rochester, Rochester, New York

Emily Sibley Watson founded the Memorial Art Gallery (MAG) in 1913 as a memorial to her son, architect James Averell. Originally located on the university's campus, the University of Rochester moved to a new location in 1930 and 1955, leaving the art museum to function more independently as a community art museum.

To celebrate its 100th anniversary in 2013, the gallery created a nineteen-member Centennial Celebration Steering Committee, including board, staff, and community members. The Library/Archives staff began digitizing materials that would be needed for the celebration five years before the anniversary began, but planning began in earnest two years ahead of time.

A highlight of the festivities was a black-tie Celestial Centennial Gala. Highlights of the evening included a treasure hunt throughout the collection, an exhibition of 1913 costumes, a caricature artist, "savory hors d'oeuvres and luscious desserts," first viewing of Memory Theatre 2013 (MAG's centennial exhibition), and live music. Designed by the students of the Rochester Institute of Technology's School for American Crafts and inspired by the Gallery's collection, the Centennial Charms Collection also premiered at the Gala. They were produced by Richards and West, a jewelry design company in East Rochester, New York. The invitation included an announcement about the collection, with a detailed description of each design and its significance to the Gallery:

- MAG's original emblem, lappet of lace acquired in 1913 (in honor of members and donors)
- Teke necklace from central Africa (in honor of staff)
- Todd McGrain's sculpture *Passenger Pigeon* (in honor of docents and volunteers)
- Fritz Trautmann's painting *Galaxy* (in honor of Creative Workshop teachers and students)
- Ancient Greek Wreath of Oak Leaves (in honor of MAG's volunteers)

The invitation noted that the Centennial Charms Collection would be "the evening's only fundraising effort." The preorder cost per set was $290, and payment could be made along with your reservations. Guests could attend a cocktail reception and dinner at the Genesee Valley Club before the Gala at the Gallery for $350 per person ($600 as a benefactor), or the Gala only for $150 per person. The invitation tempted guests with the phrase, "Be unique . . . be surprised . . . be moved . . . be charmed . . . be there!"

The Memorial Art Gallery also collaborated with Douglas Lowry, dean of the Eastman School of Music, to present the world premiere of *The Polite Abductress*, an original operetta by Lowry that takes place in Paris, circa 1913. The evening included a patron dinner, a cocktail reception with Parisian entertainment, and a cabaret performance by the Rochester City Ballet. Intermission for the operetta included a complimentary coffee bar and sweets. A live auction featured three packages:

An assortment of Fine French Wines (value $600)

A Theatre and Spa Getaway (value $700)

Dinner for Eight at Restaurant Good Luck (value $1000)

More than two hundred people attended the event.

In addition to the gala and the operetta, museum supporters Robert and Joanne Gianniny commissioned Jeff Tyzik to compose a piece of music to honor the gallery's 100th anniversary. *Images: Musical Impressions of an Art Museum*, a forty-minute orchestral suite based on seven works in the collection, "was enthusiastically received by the audience and critics alike," according to MAG's Centennial Report.

Notes

1. Personal interview with author, July 15, 2015.
2. Personal interview with author, July 7, 2015.
3. Personal interview with author, July 1, 2015. All quotes in this chapter are from the same interview.
4. Personal interview with author, July 1, 2015. All quotes in this chapter are from the same interview.
5. Personal interview with author, July 15, 2015. All quotes in this chapter are from the same interview.
6. Personal interview with author, July 31, 2015. All quotes in this chapter are from the same interview.
7. "Scene on the Plaza: Outdoor Summer Art Party Series launches at the Gardiner Museum for Five Friday Evenings Only," Gardiner Museum, http://www.gardinermuseum.on.ca/news-and-media/pressreleases/sceneontheplaza, updated June 17, 2014.
8. "Bethel Woods Center for the Arts Celebrates the 40th Anniversary of the Woodstock Music and Art Fair," Bethel Woods Center for the Arts, July 23, 2009, http://bethelwoodscenter.s3.amazonaws.com/doc/07.23.09_AnniversaryRelease.pdf.
9. Personal interview with author, July 30, 2015. All quotes in this chapter arc from the same interview.
10. Personal interview with author, July 30, 2015. All quotes in this chapter are from the same interview.
11. Personal interview with author, August 20, 2015. All quotes in this chapter are from the same interview.
12. G. Wayne Cough, "Previewing the Smithsonian's Plans for the 200th Anniversary of the Star-Spangled Banner," *Smithsonian*, March 2014.
13. The "Raise a Glass to History" portion of the Smithsonian's website is no longer live.
14. "A Star Spangled Story: Battle for America," Smithsonian Channel, accessed August 30, 2015, http://www.smithsonianchannel.com/shows/a-star-spangled-story-battle-for-america/0/3407072.
15. "Raise It Up!," Smithsonian National Museum of American History, accessed August 30, 2015, http://raiseitup.si.edu/about/.
16. Personal interview with author, July 9, 2015. All quotes in this chapter are from the same interview.
17. Personal interview with author, October 19, 2015.
18. Personal interview with author, October 30, 2015.
19. Personal interview with author, November 23, 2015. All quotes in this chapter are from the same interview.

20. Personal interview with author, November 18, 2015 and February 8, 2016. All quotes in this chapter are from the same interviews.
21. "South Bend Celebrates 150 Years," SB150, accessed February 8, 2016, http://www.sb150.com/.
22. Personal interview with author, December 7, 2015. All quotes in this chapter are from the same interview.
23. Personal interview with author, December 17, 2015. All quotes in this chapter are from the same interview.
24. Personal interview with author, December 18, 2015. All quotes in this chapter are from the same interview.
25. George Washington's Mount Vernon, *1999 Annual Report*.
26. Personal interview with author, December 28, 2015. All quotes in this chapter are from the same interview.
27. "Reenactment of George Washington's Funeral," C-SPAN, December 18, 1999, http://www.c-span.org/video/?154157-1/reenactment-george-washington-funeral.
28. George Washington's Mount Vernon, *1999 Annual Report*.
29. "52 Surprises," Minneapolis Institute of Art, accessed October 30, 2015, http://new.artsmia.org/100/52-surprises/.

CHAPTER 2

Programs and Tours

EDUCATIONAL PROGRAMS and tours can be an important part of your anniversary celebration. Whether you plan a traditional lecture, workshop, reenactment, or fictional play, use your anniversary as an opportunity to offer something out of the ordinary for your visitors.

McKinley Presidential Library and Museum, Canton, Ohio

When the McKinley Presidential Library and Museum celebrated the 100th anniversary of the completion of the McKinley National Memorial (also called the McKinley Monument) in 2007, it was natural to schedule behind-the-scenes tours to highlight its history. A behind-the-scenes tour is particularly engaging and can be done at almost any institution. When staff has regular access to places that are restricted to the public, they tend to forget how appealing it is to get a peek behind a locked door. A behind-the-scenes tour is a great way to showcase what makes your museum unique. In a historic house, you can show people the attic, the basement, or other areas that are not part of the regular tour. Every museum has a collection storage area that people will love to see. A sign shop, design studio, or other workspaces are also surprisingly interesting on a behind-the-scenes tour. The possibilities are endless!

For the 100th anniversary of the McKinley Monument, director of education Christopher Kenney focused on tours of its basement. "The Nooks and Crannies tour gave us the opportunity to offer a unique experience for our visitors," said Kenney.[1] While the monument itself is open seven days a week from April through November for self-guided tours, guided tours are offered on a limited basis to keep the experience "exclusive." The basement is not open to the public and is only accessible through a guided Nooks and Crannies tour. Kenney planned several tours during the anniversary year, including ten tours during the 100 Hours Celebration for 446 people, but has offered them at least annually since then.

"People are going to sign up to go where they can't usually go," said Kenney. "It makes you feel special when you get to do something that not everyone gets to do. People like to say, 'I got to go behind the scenes. I got to go into collections storage. I got to see an artifact that wasn't on display.'" In the McKinley Monument's basement, visitors get a chance to see the support structure that holds up the double sarcophagus where the President and First Lady's caskets reside. They can also see some of the 2 million locally made bricks used to build the foundation.

In addition to showing off secret spaces, the Nooks and Crannies tour highlights the monument's history, construction, and design. "By getting people to look closely at the details and the symbolism of the monument, it's our hope that they will understand, appreciate, and take ownership of the site," said Kenney. While working on his book, *The McKinley Monument: A Tribute to a Fallen President*, Kenney researched architect Harold Van Buren Magonigle, which later helped him create the tour. "Researching the architect himself gave me a more personal connection to the building. His own description of the site gave me a better understanding of what he was trying to convey through his design." Kenney's tour also includes plenty of facts and figures, including dimensions, how much it cost to build it then, and what that sum equates to now.

Many of the details people hear on a Nooks and Crannies tour aren't easily shared through signage or exhibition labels. "A guided tour provides much more information," said Kenney. "It also gives people a chance to ask questions. It's the extras, the anecdotes and stories, and the personal attention that make a tour special."

During the anniversary year in 2007, Kenney scheduled a tour on the exact date of the dedication ceremony in 1907. "It was really awesome," he said. "We were standing right where all of the dignitaries, like President Theodore Roosevelt and Supreme Court Justice William R. Day, stood exactly one hundred years earlier and all the sudden you're now part of its history. You became part of its story." To make that particular tour extra special, museum staff served anniversary cake that day.

Shaker Heritage Society, Watervliet, New York

Sometimes the best events are the easiest to plan. In celebration of the 100th anniversary of the Church Family Barn Complex, the Shaker Heritage Society hosted a country picnic on the grounds. "It was simple and engaging," said executive director Starlyn D'Angelo. "The intent of the picnic was to get people to the site to enjoy the grounds. We plan to hold it again as an annual event because it went so well."[2] Almost everyone who came was a first-time visitor, and the museum picked up some new members and volunteers.

Staff organized "silly lawn games," such as three-legged races, that were not necessarily from the 1915 time period. With buildings from many different time periods on site, historical accuracy was not the primary focus. A food truck was on site to feed hungry guests. Tables with red and white tablecloths provided just the right note of country charm. A popular local band played music in the barn, and other musicians strolled the grounds.

"It was great," said D'Angelo. "I was pleasantly surprised. I thought we didn't have enough activities going on. But it was low key. We let people relax and explore on their own."

The Gardiner Museum of Ceramic Art, Toronto, Ontario, Canada

In 1984 Toronto philanthropists George and Helen Gardiner donated their entire world-class ceramics collection—and a building to exhibit it—to the people of Canada. In 2014 the Gardiner Museum of Ceramic Art celebrated its 30th anniversary. "The Gardiner saw this as an ideal opportunity to highlight the museum's history while looking to its future," said Lauren Gould, development and programs manager. "This milestone presented an important and unique opportunity for the Gardiner to showcase the objects and collectors that have shaped the first three decades of the museum's history, and set the new direction for its future—to present ceramics in a diverse and expanding context. Our primary goal was to increase the number of visitors and people engaging in public programming, instilling a love for the Gardiner Museum and its collections that will draw repeat visitors in future years."[3]

A major piece of the celebration was a special series of six lectures given by experts from around the world:

- Professor Timothy Wilson from the University of Oxford presented a program on Italian maiolica titled "From Things for Villas to Princely Gifts: Maiolica for Renaissance Dukes and Duchesses of Urbino." The lecture explored the ways in which gift giving between women often drove commissions. The lecture also highlighted objects from the museum's maiolica collection.
- Cynthia Volk of Sotheby's presented "Blue and White Chinese Porcelain: Social Currency Past and Present." Before joining the Sotheby's staff, Volk was a gallery director for the Chinese Porcelain Company and Berwald Oriental Art, both in New York City, and ran her own business specializing in Chinese ceramics, sculpture, and art.
- Dr. Paul Atterbury, former curator of the Minton Museum, gave a talk titled "Memorable Minton" in which he explored the "inventive, artistic, skillful, ambitious and hugely successful" British potter. He believes Minton helped to define Victorian taste through its approach to "art, design and manufacture," according to the Gardiner Museum.
- In his program "Shopping with Dr. Wall," popular antiques expert John Sandon took participants "on a very special shopping trip, traveling back in time to the 1750s and visiting a new china shop in London," according to the museum's promotional materials. "A remarkable price list of Worcester's China Warehouse has survived and we can identify everything that was on sale and how much it all cost."
- Dr. Dorie Reents-Budet from the Museum of Fine Arts Boston spoke on "The World of Style: Ancient Maya Ceramics and Power." The lecture examined "the myriad roles played by these ceramic creations throughout ancient Mesoamerica, focusing on artistic style and its implications for exploring the social, economic, and political dynamics of authority," according to the museum.
- Nicole Coolidge Rousmaniere discussed "The Importance of Being Kakieman: The Origin and International Impact of Japanese Kakieman Style." Rousmaniere

is curator, Department of Asia at the British Museum, and a professor of Japanese Art and Culture at the University of East Anglia.

Each lecture focused on a topic that related to pieces in the permanent collection, creating a series that celebrated the museum's mission. In your anniversary year, "choose to do a few meaningful things really, really well," Gould said, "and have a series that runs throughout the year that closely aligns with programming that would have happened anyway." The museum hosts lectures every year, but for the 30th anniversary staff chose to package them as an International Lecture Series.

Eiteljorg Museum of American Indians and Western Art, Indianapolis, Indiana

In the mid-1980s, a convergence of events led to the establishment of the Eiteljorg Museum of American Indians and Western Art in Indianapolis. The city was experiencing an economic and cultural renaissance and was looking for a "compelling project" to anchor its new master plan; the Museum of Indian Heritage was on the verge of closing and desperately needed a new home; and Harrison Eiteljorg was looking for a home for his extensive collection of American Indian art. As a result of these and other factors, the Eiteljorg Museum opened on June 24, 1989, to great fanfare, both locally and regionally.

The Eiteljorg Museum celebrated its 25th anniversary in 2014 with a series of programming aimed at a variety of audiences. The museum partnered with Storytelling Arts of Indiana to bring Choctaw author and storyteller Tim Tingle to present Coyote This and Rabbit That: Native Trickster Tales for families. Josephina Day, inspired by American Girl doll Josephina from New Mexico, was a celebration of Mexican culture with folk dance performances, papel picado demonstrations (an elaborate perforated paper craft), loteria games (a Mexican game similar to Bingo), tortilla making, and a grand prize raffle drawing for a Josephina American Girl doll. Other programs during the year included actor Rochelle Coleman performing the one-man show I, Nat Love: The Story of Deadwood Dick, which chronicled the story of Love's life from a Tennessee slave to fame as a cowboy in the West. The museum's regularly scheduled Native American Storytelling program with Teresa Webb was performed at the museum, in local schools, and at the children's wing of the Riley North Hospital.

Museum staff provided pre-opera programming for the Indianapolis Opera's performance of Puccini's *Girl of the Golden West*, including historical context and a screening of an early film version of the opera. The Indianapolis Women's Chorus performed their own 20th anniversary concert in the museum's Clowes Ballroom. The museum screened the film *Bidder 70*, a film documenting Tim DeChristopher's environmental activism in the West, twice during the month of April for Earth Day.

Attendance in the anniversary year outperformed expectations by more than 20,000 people. Facebook and Twitter interactions increased 55 percent and 54 percent, respectively. Membership increased from 2,403 in 2013 to 3,160 in 2014.

Mackinac State Historic Parks, Mackinaw City, Michigan, and Mackinac Island, Michigan

Mackinac State Historic Parks, administered by the Mackinac Island State Park Commission, includes five sites located in the Mackinac Straits region of Northern Michigan: Mackinac Island State Park, Fort Mackinac, Colonial Michilimackinac, Old Mackinac Point Lighthouse, and Historic Mill Creek Discovery Park. From 2012 to 2015, Mackinac State Historic Parks commemorated the bicentennial of the War of 1812 with several projects focused on Fort Mackinac.

Fort Mackinac was active from 1780 through 1895, and the current reenactment period is the final phase of the fort's history in the 1880s. There are fourteen restored buildings within the fort, each with period furnishings or exhibitions relating to the history of the site. Regular seasonal activities at Fort Mackinac feature daily cannon and rifle demonstrations, a court martial reenactment, musical performances, a guard mount ceremony, and drilling activities. In honor of the anniversary, new interpretive programs at Fort Mackinac included costumed interpretation focusing on the British occupation of the fort during the War of 1812. According to the fort's website, "In July 1812, in the first land engagement of the War of 1812 in the United States, the British captured the fort. In a bloody battle in 1814 the Americans attempted but failed to retake the fort. It was returned to the United States after the war."[4] A special anniversary event reenacted the capture of Fort Mackinac with

The 200th anniversary of the War of 1812 at Fort Mackinac included reenactors. Mackinac State Historic Parks, Mackinaw City, Michigan.

invited reenactors on the actual date when the battle occurred. It was free and open to the public. When planning an event that commemorates something of this scale, it is important to keep in mind the availability of those you would like to participate. "We hoped to attract more reenactors to the battle events," said deputy director Steven Brisson. "Part of the issue was burnout among these volunteer groups on account of the various commemorations going on throughout the country."[5]

Other reenactments included the Battle of 1814, which was held on the site of the original battle on August 2, 2014. The brig *Niagara* was part of the event, with a special sail and a reception on board the ship. The transfer of Fort Mackinac to the Americans in July 1815 was reenacted on the same date, at the same time, as the original transfer.

Historic New England, Boston, Massachusetts

Historic New England used its 100th anniversary in 2010 to launch a series of initiatives to strengthen its mission and position itself as forward-thinking cultural organization. "The centennial was not a series of self-focused activities that took place in one twelve-month period," said Diane Viera, executive vice president and chief operation officer.[6] "Instead, all centennial initiatives were designed to have broad and long-lasting impact. Consistent with our vision of creating the best heritage organization in the nation, we committed to the following goals for centennial activities:

- Celebrate Historic New England's legacy and contributions, yet focus on the future
- Be externally directed, strategically advancing Historic New England's mission of public service
- Be region-wide, serving all six New England states
- Engage Historic New England with new constituencies
- Engage Historic New England with new partners
- Be inclusive of each of Historic New England's five key program areas for serving the public
- Encompass projects and organizations both large and small
- Be a theme of current as well as new activities throughout the year
- Positively impact the region and inspire efforts beyond the centennial year

Historic New England collects and preserves buildings, landscapes, and objects dating from the seventheenth century to the present. It owns and operates thirty-six historic sites in Connecticut, Massachusetts, Rhode Island, Maine, Vermont, and New Hampshire. Its collection includes more than 110,000 objects, creating the "most comprehensive and best documented collection of New England decorative arts and household furnishings in the country," Viera said. "These collections, which date from the mid-seventeenth to the twentieth-first centuries, include the whole range of goods needed for day-to-day life, from furniture and clothing to cooking and heating equipment." Innovative educational programming is a focus of the organization as well. "Historic New England's school and youth programs, serving fifty thousand students each year, receive national attention for the creative ways in which they use historical resources to enrich learning. The programs are fun and multi-disciplinary, encouraging learning through a variety of approaches, including hands-on activities and role playing," Viera said.

Throughout 2010, the 100th anniversary activities were the focus of all the staff at every Historic New England site. "Historic New England's centennial initiatives were not done in addition to the 'regular' work of the institution," Viera said. "Using the centennial to advance our vision and strategic agenda goals was the work of Historic New England in 2010."

Planning for the centennial began in 2003. The slogan "Toward 2010" provided motivation and drive for the staff as activities were brainstormed, conceptualized, and ultimately carried out. It was "our shorthand for our vision of being a more public institution and the national model for regional heritage organizations," Viera said. Brainstorming for specific public programming began in 2007, with ideas coming from staff teams throughout the organization. "These new initiatives were carefully vetted against the centennial goals, and complemented our ongoing, successful programming—all of which was looked at through the lens of 'centennializing' every public touch point," Viera said.

As a vast regional organization, the annual planning process is quite in-depth, even in a non-celebratory year. First, the leadership team defines the focus and priorities for the fiscal year that will advance the previously established goals of the five-year strategic agenda, which is approved by the board of trustees. Next, each Historic New England team conducts planning sessions with staff to brainstorm and propose work for the upcoming year. Teams include administration, business services, collection services, development, external affairs, preservation services, property care, and visitor experience. "Team leaders develop the institution-wide annual plan based on this input," said Viera. "The plan is then approved by the president. Once approved, each staff member works with his or her supervisor to develop personal objectives for the year to complete the work in the annual plan. In developing the centennial year focus and priorities, and annual plan, the centennial goals were the priority."

Although the entire staff was working toward the centennial goals, one staff member was selected as the centennial project manager to coordinate projects, programs, and activities. His responsibilities included the following:

- Ensuring that all initiatives were successfully completed on schedule and within budget to meet goals. Working collaboratively throughout the organization, and effectively communicating progress and results to the leadership team, staff and the public as appropriate.
- Leading the 100 Years, 100 Communities initiative to collaborate with partners large and small in all six New England states on mutually beneficial projects to collect, preserve, and disseminate twentieth-century history.
- Overseeing coordination of activities and programs created specifically for the centennial to maximize impact for the public. Maintaining clear channels of communication among staff and teams on all activities.
- Coordinating the "centennializing" of ongoing programs among Historic New England staff and teams.

All programming for the 100th anniversary was designed to have an impact in the organization far beyond 2010. Historic New England used the celebration as an opportunity to redesign its website, which had originally launched in 1998. "Although the original website had been improved and expanded over the years, it was past time to replace it with a freshly designed, contemporary site," Viera said. "Work began on the website fundraising and redesign in late 2008 with the goal of launching a new HistoricNewEngland.org for the centennial year. One of the most significant features of the new site was the introduction of Collections Access, online access to Historic New England's unparalleled New England decorative arts and archival collections."

Historic New England also created new web-based school resources to enhance learning among school children. "A web-based school program that highlights our institutional belief that everyone's history matters was launched with the new website," Viera said. "Inspired by our popular Family Ties program, education staff developed an interactive school program aimed at New England's elementary and middle school students. Rich in primary source material and graphically exciting, the program guides students through new ways of exploring their own family and neighborhood histories."

Since historic preservation is an important aspect of Historic New England's work, a symposium called Looking Forward was part of the activities. "Working with the next generation of professional preservationists is important to Historic New England," said Viera. "This symposium was held in partnership with Roger Williams University to engage undergraduate and graduate students in a dialogue about historic preservation in the twenty-first century. Focusing on the built environment, students explored what should be preserved and potential ways the field will continue to evolve in a world faced with challenges very different from those encountered by our founder William Sumner Appleton a century ago. We continue to hold symposia for emerging preservation professionals."

The centennial goals also included an expansion of the magazine *Historic New England*, a popular benefit of membership with the organization since 2000, to thirty-four pages. "Content throughout the year included a series of feature articles on the 'state of preservation' written by guest authors working in the preservation field in each New England state," Viera said, "and a selection of articles by well-known guest authors on their favorite items in Historic New England's collection."

For several years staff had envisioned a passport program visitors could use to record visits to all thirty-six historic properties of Historic New England. "In celebration of the centennial, the *Historic New England Passport* was launched and provided to all members," said Viera. "Each of our historic sites has a custom-designed passport stamp featuring an iconic motif from the property. Each property has its own page in the passport which is stamped when a member visits. The *Historic New England Passport* is very popular and continues to be issued to new members when they join."

Historic New England created a new Annual Prize for Collecting Works on Paper, modeled after the successful Annual Historic New England Book Prize. The prize recognizes "a collector or dealer who has assembled or helped save a significant collection of historical material related to New England that might otherwise have been left unrecognized or lost." Two prizes are awarded annually. Honorees have included Charles Burden, who collects maritime materials relating to Maine and the temperance movement; Nelson Dionne, who collects materials about nineteenth and twentieth century industrial heritage in Salem, Massachusetts; Mehmed Ali, PhD, who collects materials relating to the diversity of

Lowell, Massachusetts; M. Stephen Miller, who collects Shaker ephemera; and Nina Heald Webber, who collects material related to the history of the Cape Cod Canal. The prize is $500 and a Historic New England membership.

The most significant centennial initiative to come out of the centennial was the program 100 Years, 100 Communities, which continues today as *Everyone's History*. "During our centennial planning process, we thought hard about what we could do to serve all six New England states, especially communities we have not served before," said Viera. "Partnerships and a focus on New England stories that could be lost were identified as key components of the effort. Thus launched 100 Years, 100 Communities, a multi-year initiative begun in our centennial year to partner with one hundred communities throughout New England to save and share twentieth-century history before it's lost. We defined communities broadly—they could be geographic locations, professional associations, common interest or affinity groups, etc. Likewise, the projects on which we partnered could be broad as well. Some were smaller public programs, others were much larger, like documentary films."

The pilot project for 100 Years, 100 Communities focused on the town of Berlin, New Hampshire:

At the River's Edge: An Oral History of Berlin, New Hampshire
Partners: Berlin and Coos County Historical Society, Timberlane Regional High School

Nestled in the Great Northern Forest of New Hampshire, the city of Berlin was once the world's leader in paper production. Generations of Berliners worked in the mills of the Brown Paper Company, once the centerpiece of the community. The closing of the mills in the late twentieth century had significant impact on Berlin's economy and social atmosphere, and forced the city to shape and redefine its future without losing site of its proud past. Working with our partners, Historic New England produced a documentary incorporating oral histories with residents from 24 to 92 years of age, and historic images to tell the story of the rise and fall of the paper industry and its impact on the region. The documentary premiered at the local movie theater in Berlin with four sold-out show-ings to 500 people. Over 250 people also attended a celebration at a community center following last showing. The New Hampshire Chronicle television program was on hand for the premiere and aired a piece on the project. At the River's Edge won an American Association for State and Local History Leadership in History Award.

With such a successful pilot program behind them, Historic New England went on to work with one hundred community partners during the centennial. "It was just the tip of the iceberg," said Viera. "We realized there are so many diverse stories that would be lost if this effort didn't continue. Building on the success of 100 Years, 100 Communities, Historic New England continues its work today with communities throughout the region through the Everyone's History initiative." So far projects have included the Haymarket Project; Back to School: Lessons from Norwich's One-Room Schoolhouses; Claiming a Piece of the American Dream: African American Vacationers in New England; Woolworth's: Remembering Haverhill's Shopping District; and Connecting the Threads: Overalls to Art at the H.W. Carter and Sons Factory. The projects are available on Historic New England's website.

Stan Hywet Hall and Gardens, Akron, Ohio

To celebrate the centennial of its Manor House in 2015, Stan Hywet Hall and Gardens created a special guided tour called Blueprints to Bricks: An Estate in the Making. This tour "showcased the story of how the house was conceived, created, and constructed between 1911 and 1915," said July Frey, director of museum services.[7] The museum's website describes the tour as follows:

> This specialty tour focuses on Stan Hywet Hall from conception to creation. Guests will learn about F. A. and Gertrude Seiberling's desire to build a lavish country estate for their family and friends to enjoy. The tour highlights how the estate was planned, beginning with the search for land and architects, trips to England and France for inspiration, and an in-depth look at the planning and construction of the Manor House, services buildings, and gardens. This tour lasts approximately two hours and includes a modified Guided Manor House and Guided Garden Tour, Self-Guided Manor House Tour with booklet, Self-Guided Gardens, Gate Lodge and Corbin Conservatory.[8]

"The tour was so successful that it was decided to continue it past the anniversary year," said Frey.

A highlight of the centennial year was Community Day, which began as a birthday party but soon evolved into a more elaborate celebration. No admission was charged, but pre-registration was required so staff could anticipate attendance. Community Day "highlighted all that Stan Hywet Hall has to offer, our variety of volunteer organizations, and how you can become engaged at Stan Hywet Hall," said Frey. The event included a formal dedication ceremony, musical performances, plein air painters in the gardens, guided tours with the artist who created the Bloom! outdoor exhibition, historic automobiles, a vintage baseball game, geocaching and questing, facepainting, games, and free crafts for kids sponsored by craft store Pat Catan's. Throughout the day Goodyear Blimps circled over the property, in honor of Frank Seiberling who built Stan Hywet and founded Goodyear. "Community Day engaged people who had never been before but were interested because the admission was free," said Frey.

The anniversary was also used as an opportunity to increase the museum's profile. "Our marketing department strategically outlined an aggressive plan throughout the season including billboards, print media, social media, TV spots on local news, and radio advertisements during key events," said Frey. "We definitely felt we saw a return on this investment throughout the season. Attendance numbers for daily tours and admission to the property far exceeded projections."

The Paul Revere House, Boston, Massachusetts

When the Paul Revere House celebrated one hundred years as a historic house museum in 2008, the staff looked for ways to incorporate the yearlong celebration into regular activities and offerings. "For example, we always had two exhibits in the 'closet' spaces in the Paul Revere House," said Emily Holmes, education director. "That year they were themed to reflect the anniversary, 'Saving the Paul Revere House' and 'Restoring the Paul Revere House.'"[9] Elements from the museum's signature event 1908 Day were also used again later in the year. "The two reenactors we worked with to create the characters of Revere's great-grand-children, John Philips Reynolds, Jr., and Pauline Revere Thayer, reprised their program: 'Rescuing the Revere House' in September and October on days when we normally offer similar programming." The museum's annual September Lecture Series, held at Old South Meeting House, was titled "Historic Preservation During the Colonial Revival" in honor of the anniversary and examined "significant preservation projects and the personalities involved at the turn of the twentieth century."

George Washington's Mount Vernon, Mount Vernon, Virginia

With the bicentennial of George Washington's death approaching in 1999, the staff at Mount Vernon wanted to present the mansion with a "special look" for that year. According to the 1999 Annual Report, "Our goal was to make the atmosphere in Washington's home more authentic and more alive, while at the same time focusing on Washington's death—a subject that can be both awkward and compelling."[10]

Research specialist Mary Thompson was in charge of two of the redesigned room set-tings. "I was responsible for the dessert setting in the Large Dining Room," she said. "The initial idea was to re-create a dinner in that space, but we did not have the original china and glassware to be able to pull that off, so I suggested a dessert course. I was also assigned the task of making Washington's bedroom look like he had just died in that room. This involved making fake blood for use in a bleeding bowl and on bloody rags near the bed. All of the 'food' and 'blood' was made in my office over the course of a few weeks. A colleague who walked in while all of this was in progress started laughing and said that my office looked like an abattoir!"[11]

Of course, Washington's bedroom was the most significant reimagined space. According to the 1999 Annual Report, "The most talked about room was the bedchamber shared by the Washingtons for some 25 years, where we sought to stop the clock at a little after ten o'clock on the evening of December 14, 1799, when Washington drew his final breath. The most advanced medicines of the day—incredibly crude by our standards—clutter Martha's small desk, while bleeding instruments rest ominously on the bedside table. Visitors reacted with horror and fascination when they learned that doctors drained about a third of Wash-ington's blood, making him weaker and more susceptible to a rapidly spreading throat in-fection. They shared a sense of loss and frustration, knowing that what seemed like a simple sore throat proved fatal to America's strongest and greatest hero in a matter of 48 hours."

In addition to the reimagined spaces inside Mount Vernon, visitors could take a forty-five-minute walking tour of the original funeral procession route, complete with black armbands, three times a day throughout the bicentennial year. There was also a multimedia presentation available called "Washington Is No More," based on an account of his final hours by friend and secretary Tobias Lear, according to the *New York Times*. Described as a "more lighthearted" program, Mount Vernon also offered a patriotic musical revue called "An American Celebration in Music" on Friday and Saturday evenings from April through August.

The bicentennial commemoration also included programs specifically aimed at kids. In May, 1,400 high school students came to Mount Vernon for a capstone experience to a yearlong program called We the People, a national conference focused on leadership and government. A first-person interpreter dazzled the students with tales of Washington's life from his own perspective, earning a rousing standing ovation at the end. In partnership with Boy Scouts of America, Mount Vernon also created a new patch to honor Washington's life. In November almost one thousand scouts and troop leaders camped out on the George Washington's lawn for the weekend and participated in activities such as surveying, eighteenth century crafts, and historical lectures.

Memorial Art Gallery of the University of Rochester, Rochester, New York

To celebrate its 100th anniversary in 2013, the Memorial Art Gallery (MAG) hosted several programs and lectures to commemorate the occasion. A yearlong monthly Sunday afternoon lecture series called What's Up focused on the gallery's history and collections, with speakers from the MAG staff and the community. A total of 599 people attended the lecture series.

Two Centennial Lectures in November 2012 and 2013 featured prominent guest speakers. In 2012 Dr. Eric Kandel, Nobel Prize–winning neuroscientist, discussed his new book *The Age of Insight: The Quest to Understand the Unconscious in Art, Mind, and Brain, From Vienna 1900 to the Present*. Sponsored by university president Joel Seligman, the lecture drew a crowd of 285 guests. In 2013 the Memorial Art Gallery welcomed Dana Gioia, poet, professor of poetry and public culture at the University of Southern California, and former chair of the National Endowment for the Arts. She gave a lecture titled "Why the Arts Matter," sponsored by the Office of the Provost on behalf of the UR Arts group.

Another program, "Art Reflected: The Inspiration of 100 Years," featured new and original artwork by more than forty artists that reinterpreted one of the top-100 works in the MAG's collection. The pieces were on regional view for approximately six weeks and were sold to benefit the Gallery.

The Solomon R. Guggenheim Museum, New York, New York

The Guggenheim Museum celebrated its 50th anniversary in 2009 with a spectacular series of events, including musical performances, members-only parties, and the debut of a new annual arts awards program. Mayor Michael R. Bloomberg declared May 15, 2009, Solomon R. Guggenheim Day in New York City, and the following day the museum moved its popular Pay-What-You-Wish hours from Friday to Saturday evenings. The Guggenheim also hosted the opening ceremonies of the 2009 Museum Mile Festival on June 9, which included a ribbon-cutting ceremony led by Cultural Affairs commisioner Kate Levin. The event featured live music and art activities in connection with the 50th anniversary.

Many anniversary programs featured music. To mark the summer solstice, Make Music New York offers free concerts across the city. For its anniversary year the Guggenheim participated in the event by presenting *ORBITS* by Henry Brant, an "acoustical spatial" composer, including soprano voices, an organ, and eighty trombones. This marked the first time the piece was performed on the East Coast. In the fall, the museum launched a new live music series called It Came from Brooklyn, featuring bands, writers, and actors from Brooklyn to highlight the borough's musical renaissance.

In September the museum hosted a performance by Rafael Lazano Hemmer called Levels of Nothingness. "Inspired by Vasily Kandinsky's *Yellow Sound* (1912), Mexican-born Rafael Lozano-Hemmer creates an installation where colors are automatically derived from the human voice, generating an interactive light performance," wrote Eleanor Goldhar, former deputy director of external affairs, on the museum's website. "Actress Isabella Rossellini will read seminal philosophical texts on skepticism, color, and perception while her voice is analyzed by computers that control a full rig of rock-and-roll concert lighting. Audience members will have the opportunity to test the color-generating microphone."

When the Solomon R. Guggenheim Museum celebrated its 50th anniversary in 2009, the staff created a large photo-op board for visitors. The Solomon R. Guggenheim Museum, New York, New York.

One of the most popular events for the 50th anniversary of the Solomon R. Guggenheim Museum was Free Day on October 21, 2009, the museum's exact anniversary date. The Solomon R. Guggenheim Museum, New York, New York.

To celebrate the exact day the museum opened on Fifth Avenue, the Guggenheim waived admission fees on October 21, 2009. The day featured tours offered in several different languages and many family-friendly programs and activities. That same day the Empire State Building was lit with red lights in honor of the museum's anniversary.

During the 50th anniversary celebration, the Guggenheim unveiled a new arts awards program in a style reminiscent of a Hollywood awards ceremony with live performances. Awards were presented to individuals and projects that made a "significant impact" on contemporary art. Categories included Curator of the Year, Artist of the Year, New Artist of the Year, Writer of the Year, and Solo Show of the Year. Winners were announced during dinner at the Guggenheim, followed by an after party. The anniversary festivities also included a members-only evening preview event and three private morning viewings of the exhibition *Frank Lloyd Wright: From Within Outward*.

Ohio Civil War 150, Ohio History Connection (formerly the Ohio Historical Society), Columbus, Ohio

Many different organizations participated in the sesquicentennial of the Civil War in a variety of ways, including reenactments on the battlefields, special exhibitions, and public programming. Some states, including Ohio, created a program to organize and coordinate Civil War–related events. "The Ohio History Connection decided to create and spearhead the Ohio Civil War 150 initiative because the Civil War was a transformative event in the state and the nation's history," said Amy Rohmiller, program coordinator, local history and AmeriCorps. "Ohio contributed the third largest number of troops to the Union behind New York and Pennsylvania. Many prominent Civil War figures (including U.S. Grant, William T. Sherman, Edwin Stanton, Rutherford B. Hayes, James Garfield, William McKinley, etc.) were Ohioans. Ohio played an important role on the Underground Railroad in the abolition movement, yet was also the home of Copperhead leader Clement Valandigham. These complex Civil War stories (and more) point to relevant issues that Ohioans still wrestle with today, and we wanted to bring them to new generations of audiences. The Local History Services department was charged with implementing the commemoration."[12]

On April 27, 2009—the birthday of Ohio-born General Ulysses S. Grant, a Civil War hero and two-term U.S. president—Ohio Governor Ted Strickland issued an executive directive to create the statewide initiative. According to a press release announcing the move, "the directive aims to help Ohioans rediscover the many ways in which Ohioans contributed to Union success and how the Civil War shaped contemporary Ohio and American society. The Ohio Historical Society has been designated to lead the statewide memorial effort."

The Ohio Civil War 150's objectives were as follows:

- Tell a more complete, diverse story than the centennial celebration, giving voice to the stories of African Americans, women, and those who served on the home front among other underrepresented groups.

- Be the facilitator and supporter of a statewide commemoration by coordinating, providing resources for, and support of local commemorative efforts around the state. Help build regional and state partnerships and networks.
- Create a commemoration of "lasting value." Provide new and lasting interpretation and education; improved access to collections, especially through digitization; build capacity of Ohio's local history organizations.

As part of CW150, the Ohio History Connection worked with Shomer Zwelling & Associates to create an "interpretive framework" for the commemoration. The introduction of the document explains the purpose of such a document: "An interpretive framework organizes diverse information and perspectives on a topic in history, culture or nature. It organizes these materials into an integrated, meaningful and useful instrument for the development of engaging and relevant public programs that are firmly rooted in high quality, contemporary scholarship." The Interpretive Framework was funded in part by the Ohio Humanities Council. (See Appendix A: Ohio Civil War 150 Interpretive Framework.)

The Ohio History Connection started planning by creating an advisory committee that guided all four years of the commemoration. "In selecting advisory committee members, we strived to get a wide variety of voices at the table (informally "thinkers" and "doers")," said Rohmiller. "We had academics—professors who studied the Civil War, the abolition movement, and African American history during the Civil War period. We had museum and local history professionals from large (Western Reserve Historical Society, National Underground Railroad Freedom Center) and small (Peninsula Foundation, Greene County Historical Society) institutions. We included reenactors, the Sons of Union Veterans, high school history teachers, and dedicated bloggers/publishers. We also had liaisons to other organizations in the state including the State Library of Ohio, the Army National Guard, the Ohio Tourism Division, and the Ohio Humanities Council." From December 2009 to December 2011, the project had one full-time and one part-time employee. From 2012 through the end of the commemoration in 2015, one part-time employee served as coordinator for the initiative, with the assistance of other Ohio History Connection employees as needed. Everyone outside of the Ohio Historical Connection staff served voluntarily.

The advisory committee convened for the first time in January 2010, one year before the launch of the Civil War's 150th anniversary, and continued to meet quarterly through the summer of 2015. "Before the first meeting, the Ohio History Connection had already laid some groundwork, including surveying Ohio's history organizations, libraries, Civil War buffs, etc. to get a sense of what they would like from the sesquicentennial, setting the big objectives, developing the interpretive framework, and creating a website," Rohmiller said. "The survey informed the first parts of the planning process—respondents asked for a speakers' bureau and a small traveling exhibit, so those became high priority items and were rolled out early in the commemoration in spring and summer 2011."

The rest of the planning process took place in two stages. "The advisory committee first created a marketing/PR subcommittee, an education subcommittee, and a programming subcommittee," said Rohmiller. "This structure ensured the creation of the CW150 Facebook page, some of the early education materials like those produced by the State Library of Ohio, and the planning and implementation of the kickoff event in 2011. In late 2011 the structure and planning process changed. As a whole, the advisory committee looked at significant dates in national and Ohio Civil War history and used those dates to generate yearly themes." These themes were included:

- Emancipation (2012)
- Ohio's Role in the Civil War (2013)
- The Homefront (2014)
- Coming Home/Legacies (2015)

"The committee then generated ideas for programming each year based on the theme and the skills and interests of advisory committee members," said Rohmiller. "In general, committee members would decide in the late fall of the previous year / early winter of the year what they wanted their major project to be and then the rest of the year would carry that out. For instance, the subcommittee for 2012 was made up largely of teachers and museum educators, so the major project for that year was developing a toolkit for teachers of resources they could use to effectively teach the Emancipation Proclamation to their students. The majority of the planning was done at quarterly committee meetings, with one day-long retreat in the summer to hash out the details of the toolkit. Then, individual members were assigned homework (activities they were responsible for) and sent them in to me (the CW150 Coordinator) to be compiled and put on the website. It was available and ready for teachers by the beginning of the 2012–2013 school year."

In 2013 and 2014, Ohio Civil War 150 issued a list of monthly themes within the yearly theme:

Ohio Civil War 150 Advisory Committee Themes for 2013

Theme of the Year: Ohio's Impact on the War
    Monthly Themes:

- January—Emancipation
- February—Ohio Generals
- March—Medal of Honor
- April—The Costs of War (wounded, relief societies)
- May—Ohio Civil War Road Trips
- June—United States Colored Troops
- July—Ohioans in Battle
- August—Ohio's Regiments and Militia
- September—Political Leadership
- October—Immigrants in the Civil War
- November—Why They Fought
- December—Supplying the Military

Ohio Civil War 150 Advisory Committee Themes for 2014

Theme of the Year: Ohio's Homefront
    Monthly Themes:

- January—Ohio's Economy
- February—Veterans (ex: furloughs and Veterans Corps)
- March—Medal of Honor recipients
- April—Children
- May—Sanitary Fairs/Soldiers Aid
- June—100 Day Regiments
- July—Ohioans in Battle
- August—POW Camps
- September—Women in the Home Front
- October—Wounded Soldiers/Hospitals
- November—Politics (ex: Election of 1864)
- December—Letters and Photographs Home

The bottom of each list included possible ways to incorporate the themes into your programming: speaker series, book discussions, blog posts, exhibits/displays, and tours highlighting sites in your area.

A highlight of the Ohio Civil War 150 initiative was a traveling exhibition, which was one of the priorities identified in the statewide survey conducted prior to the anniversary. "It was booked for the vast majority of the four years of the commemoration (2011–2015) and went to all kinds of different places from small library branches to the Ohio State Fair" Rohmiller said. The exhibition, titled Ohio and the Civil War: 150 Years Later, was developed in partnership with the Ohio Humanities Council and American Electric Power. The panel exhibition was tailored for smaller institutions that aren't usually able to host traveling exhibitions due to cost and space limitations. The exhibition explored three themes—Democracy, Transformation, and Memory—to "reveal Civil War stories that impacted Ohio in the 19th century to the present day," according to the Ohio Civil War 150 website. "Through the lens of these themes, the exhibit explores topics such as civil rights, political dissent, pacifism, religion, and popular culture and reveals patterns in our country's response to such topics throughout history."[13] One of the goals of the initiative in general, and the exhibition specifically, was to broaden the story of the Civil War beyond the traditional military and battle-centered stories. "I think we succeeded in this goal," said Rohmiller. "The traveling exhibit included stories of abolition and the Underground Railroad, popular culture of the time period, Quakers, and others. The committee [also] held a one-day symposium in 2014 that focused on the stories of the Civil War home front, mostly women's stories."

Part of the initiative was to create a website as the "digital headquarters" for the project. Originally the advisory committee wanted it to contain a great deal of user-contributed material, including digitized items from personal collections, student essays on Civil War topics, and an active discussion forum. "These never really caught on with the public," said

Rohmiller, "and eventually the user-contributed forums and 'exhibit' items were shut down after being repeatedly hacked." The website did, however, provide a wealth of resources for both institutions and individuals, such as self-guided routes for Civil War Road Trips throughout the state, the Ohio Civil War 150 Speakers Corps, and a number of classroom resources for teachers.

Through the Ohio Civil War 150 project, the Ohio History Connection strengthened and initiated partnerships with the Ohio Humanities Council, the State Library of Ohio, the reenactor community, local history organizations around the state, and history educators. "Perhaps the biggest result of this 'friend making' is that the State Legislature appropriated money to the Ohio History Connection to also lead statewide commemorative efforts for World War I," said Rohmiller.

Several aspects of the Ohio Civil War 150 initiative are easily adaptable at other sites. For example, a blog post series could be replicated anywhere, on any topic. "The committee picked subthemes for each month related to the yearly theme and/or tied to a major event in the war," said Rohmiller. "Then, they divided up to write one blog post a month about some aspect of the theme. Many advisory committee members used this as a chance to tell a wider audience about their own historical interests. For example, one member wrote her blog posts on women's history or what was happening during the war in Greene County. One member used the opportunity to do his own research about Civil War pensions. The blogs were posted on the website and shared via the Facebook page. Several were picked up and shared by places like the Smithsonian Civil War 150 Twitter. Any site or organization that has a website or a Facebook page could adapt this idea for their own commemoration. Just pick themes members are excited to explore and write about. The trick is making sure someone follows up consistently to get the content."

Ohio Civil War 150 also created an awards program to "recognize people and organizations who had done outstanding work saving and sharing Civil War history well before the commemoration started and who continue to keep it up long after the commemoration ends" said Rohmiller. "We recognized people who had built exhaustive websites, created amazing programming for school kids, and brought the John Hunt Morgan Heritage Trail to life, among other ideas." The awards program could be easily adapted at other sites. "The committee wanted to formally recognize the great work other people were doing, and it was an easy program to put together," Rohmiller said. "The committee decided on a set of criteria for who and what could be recognized, then solicited nominations from themselves and from the larger community using Survey Monkey. Then, the committee voted on the nominations, got plaques for the winners, and presented them in a ceremony once a year, or presented the award at the time or place of the winner's choosing. Winners were thrilled someone was recognizing their work and it was a way for the committee to recognize that other people and organizations had been doing Civil War related activities. Again, this would be easy for a small organization to adapt to whatever celebration is going on. It could be an opportunity to recognize local historians or outstanding school teachers or supportive city council members in a fairly low-budget way."

The Ohio History Connection also built upon partner activities that already existed. "For example, every two years the State Library of Ohio creates Choose to Read Ohio Toolkits for a selected set of books," Rohmiller said. "In 2011–2012, several selected books for this program had a Civil War theme. The Ohio Humanities Council added Civil War speakers to its popular speakers' bureau program for the duration of the commemoration. In addition, the Ohio History Connection created a "resources" page on the Ohio Civil War 150 website that brought together all existing Civil War programs, activities, etc., into one easy to find place."

Some of the activities created during the anniversary celebration resulted in permanent commemorations that will last long after the end of the project. "As a result of the Civil War 150th, there is a permanent Morgan's Raid Heritage Trail in southern and eastern Ohio tracing the route of John Hunt Morgan's raid through Ohio in 1863 and Buffington Island received new, permanent interpretation," said Rohmiller. "The Ohio Historical Markers program also offered all local sponsors the option to include an Ohio Civil War 150 logo on any Civil War related markers that were erected during the commemoration. These markers are permanent in their local communities. The website and all the resources available on it continue to live on, even though the commemoration is over. The Ohio History Connection created new Civil War exhibits that are still up. The AmeriCorps program that was originally created to give history organizations some manpower to commemorate the Civil War continues to live on, helping small organizations build capacity in other areas. One AmeriCorps member used the commemoration to get Civil War veterans buried in unmarked graves headstones from the VA."

Ultimately the Ohio Civil War 150 initiative was successful, and the staff involved learned a lot from the experience. "We learned that it's hard to sustain momentum and

Ohio Civil War reenactors cheer during the Final Civil War 150 Celebration at the Ohio Statehouse on May 17, 2015. Ohio History Connection, Columbus, Ohio.

interest across a four-year commemoration," said Rohmiller. "We learned that it helps to have more clearly defined, specific goals besides our large objectives when we need to engage partners or committee members in making programming or events happen. We had success when asking members to contribute specific things (e.g., giving a talk on a specific topic), but had less success when asking for more ambiguous contributions (e.g., help us publicize this event or develop educational programming). We also learned that it's possible to accomplish a lot with a little. We had a small amount of money, a small amount of staff time, and limited resources. By strategically thinking about what programs we wanted to take on, the impact we wanted to have, and giving existing programs a Civil War focus (either internal or partners), we were able to create a very successful commemoration."

MacArthur Memorial, Norfolk, Virginia

The MacArthur Memorial is a museum and research center dedicated to preserving and presenting the story of General Douglas MacArthur. It also honors the millions of men and women who served with MacArthur in World War I, World War II, and the Korean War. In April 2014 the MacArthur Memorial celebrated its 50th anniversary. "The event objectives were to showcase General MacArthur and the memorial, reinforce the memorial as [a] community asset to Norfolk and Hampton Roads, draw diverse audiences to the memorial, increase the memorial's profile, and freshen the permanent exhibits," said Christopher L. Kolakowski, director. "We also invited potential national and international partners to attend, to plant the seeds for future collaborations. The 50th anniversary met all of these objectives."[14]

Initial planning began in the fall of 2013. "I started as memorial director on September 16, 2013," said Kolakowski. "My third day on the job, the staff came to me with a general concept for the event. I reviewed and refined it at a meeting on September 25, and after socializing it with key partners in the City and Foundation, began moving forward. We defined the concept and timeline, and tracked specific preparatory tasks over the 120 days prior." Monthly meetings started in December 2013. Marketing efforts included a banner on an overpass, flags around the city, and appearances on several television stations. The MacArthur Memorial purchased advertising in the *Virginian-Pilot*, and in turn the newspaper ran a front-page story about the memorial two days before the anniversary events.

"We brought in all partners and stakeholders early in the process, and gained support of city hall for our efforts and objectives," Kolakowski said. "This thorough planning, combined with good communication and coordination between everyone on the day of execution, ensured a smooth course of events on April 11 and 12." Three months ahead of time, staff worked to secure a chaplain, color guard, and music for the ceremony; created souvenir invitations; and developed 50th anniversary merchandise and staff uniforms. Two months before the event, staff began sprucing up the exhibitions and secured a caterer. One month beforehand staff ordered books for the Author's Form event; created press packets including a 50th anniversary brochure; and completed exhibition upgrades. Ten days out staff wrote speeches, cleaned up the grounds, and held a press conference. (See Appendix B: MacArthur Planning Timeline.)

Norfolk Mayor Paul R. Fraim lays a wreath at the base of the MacArthur statue, with the Mac-Arthur Memorial in the background. The MacArthur Memorial Museum, Norfolk, Virginia.

The anniversary commemoration began on April 11, 2014, with a public ceremony at 11:00 a.m. Uniformed JROTC cadets from Oak Ridge Military Academy in Greensboro, North Carolina, served as ushers. The schedule for the event included the following:

- Welcome from Kolakowski
- Presentation of the Colors by the Norfolk State University Army ROTC
- Pledge of Allegiance
- Invocation
- Posting of the Colors
- Remarks from the Chair of the General Douglas MacArthur Foundation, the Mayor of Norfolk, and the President Emeritus of Old Dominion University
- Wreath Laying
- Playing of Taps
- Closing Remarks

"The reception décor, food, and overall presentation created an appropriate level of sophistication befitting the [MacArthur] Memorial and the occasion," Kolakowski said. "Attendees to all events on April 11 referred to them as 'first class,' and staff received many compliments about how events were executed and presented." During the event, staff observed that the VIP chairs were in the sun, while the rest of the guests were seated in the shade. Future recommendations for similar events suggested using a different space on the museum property to avoid VIP seating in full sun exposure. A special sensitive microphone was used to accommodate soft-spoken speakers, which was very successful and will be used again in the future. In addition, the ceremony was held on a Friday, which reduced attendance. Future events will be planned on weekends to hopefully increase the number of people who are able to attend.

The program for the ceremony featured a quote from General MacArthur's planned remarks for the dedication of the MacArthur Memorial on April 11, 1964 (he passed away on April 5): "Today has been for me a dream come true. For many years it has been my fondest hope that merciful providence would permit me to return to my ancestral home." The dedication turned into a public viewing and funeral, attracting a crowd of twenty thousand to the brand new site. A second quote in the program read, "Could I have but a line a century hence crediting a contribution to the advance of peace, I would yield every honor which has been accorded by war."

The ceremony was followed by an Author's Forum in the afternoon, featuring discussion and book signings with Daniel Rice, Rod Frazer, Thomas Hutson, and Mitchell Yockelson. That evening the MacArthur Memorial hosted an invitation-only reception for current and future partners. The next day featured a living history encampment, military vehicles, military miniature displays, model making for kids, and a concert by Tidewater Pipes and Drums.

The success of the 50th anniversary events inspired the staff to plan more anniversary commemorations. In the fall of 2014 the MacArthur Memorial executed a major symposium in conjunction with the centennial of the start of World War I. The museum staff planned additional World War I programming for 2017–2018 and created "Keeping the

Promise: Liberation of the Philippines," a five-thousand-square-foot exhibition commemorating the 70th anniversary of MacArthur's historic campaign:

> In early 1942 it was clear that the Philippines was doomed. With no relief in sight and with his forces trapped on Corregidor and the Bataan Peninsula, General Douglas MacArthur was ordered to leave the Philippines. Arriving in Australia, he made a public promise to return and liberate the Philippines. Two years later, with the support of President Franklin Roosevelt, this pledge was fulfilled in what would be the largest campaign of the Pacific War. This special exhibit explores the liberation of the Philippines through unique artifacts and documents from U.S., Filipino, and Japanese sources.[15]

Kolakowski believes anniversaries, in general, are important to celebrate. "Anniversaries are milestones," he said, "and they give you the opportunity to showcase where you have been and demonstrate where you are going. They also allow you to again demonstrate what you do and why it matters, while connecting to that element of your story in a way that energizes audiences."

Notes

1. Personal interview with author, July 15, 2015. All quotes in this chapter are from the same interview.
2. Personal interview with author, July 12, 2015. All quotes in this chapter are from the same interview.
3. Personal interview with author, July 31, 2015. All quotes in this chapter are from the same interview.
4. "Fort Mackinac History," Mackinac State Historic Parks, accessed August 30, 2015, http://www.mackinacparks.com/more-info/history/individual-site-histories/fort-mackinac-history/.
5. Personal interview with author, August 30, 2015.
6. Personal interview with author, October 30, 2015. All quotes in this chapter are from the same interview.
7. Personal interview with author, November 1, 2015. All quotes in this chapter are from the same interview.
8. "Tours and Attractions," Stan Hywet Hall and Gardens, accessed November 15, 2015, http://www.stanhywet.org/tours-attractions.
9. Personal interview with author, December 18, 2015. All quotes in this chapter are from the same interview.
10. George Washington's Mount Vernon, *1999 Annual Report*.
11. Personal interview with author, December 28, 2015. All quotes in this chapter are from the same interview.
12. Personal interview with author, December 3, 2015. All quotes in this chapter are from the same interview.
13. "Traveling Exhibit," CW150 Ohio, accessed December 15, 2015, http://www.ohiocivilwar150.org/resources/resources-for-organizations/traveling-exhibit/.

14. Personal interview with author, December 7, 2015. All quotes in this chapter are from the same interview.

15. "Keeping the Promise: The Liberation of the Philippines 1944–1945," The MacArthur Memorial, accessed December 15, 2015, http://www.macarthurmemorial.org/390/Keeping-the-Promise-Liberation-of-the-Ph.\

CHAPTER 3

Fundraising Campaigns

ANNIVERSARY CELEBRATIONS are a brilliant excuse to raise some much-needed funds for your organization. Whether your goal is to add to your endowment or provide funding for educational programming, seize the moment and launch a fundraising campaign in conjunction with your anniversary. This chapter provides some great ideas to get you started.

McKinley Presidential Library and Museum, Canton, Ohio

During the fundraising phase for the McKinley National Memorial in 1901, organizers collected the "pennies of schoolchildren" from across the country to help build it. In fact, a major portion of the budget to build the memorial came from this source. When the McKinley Presidential Library and Museum was gearing up for the Memorial's 100th anniversary in 2007, Museum Shoppe manager Cindy Sober conceived the Let's Do It Again! Penny Campaign.

"I had always thought it was inspiring when I heard the story about how the school children across the country collected their pennies to help build the McKinley Memorial," Sober said. "After reading some of the notes that were written at the time the donations were made, I was even more fascinated. As we approached the 100th anniversary of the memorial, I thought, 'Let's do it again. Let's have the school children across the country collect and send their pennies to help keep the memorial in good condition.' And that is how the 'Let's Do It Again Penny Campaign' got its start."[1]

Using leftover materials from other projects, the McKinley Museum's maintenance staff constructed a large box (eight feet by four feet and approximately two feet deep) to collect pennies, which was placed in the main lobby. The front of the box had plexiglass "windows" with a vinyl graphic of a penny that would become copper colored as the number of pennies grew.

Sober researched schools across the country with McKinley in their names and sent 137 letters inviting students to participate in the penny campaign. All local schools also received a letter. Many brought pennies they had collected with them on school field trips.

One inner city school in Canton used the penny campaign to create a unique project. "The students from Belle Stone elementary took the penny campaign to a whole new level," said director of education Christopher Kenney. "The teachers created a multi-disciplinary lesson incorporating math, science, and language arts. The end results were amazing and provided fantastic PR for an inner city school."[2] The teachers brought their students to the memorial to measure the dimensions of one of the 108 steps leading up to its entrance. Using their math skills, students calculated how many pennies they would need to cover an entire step. As their teacher intended, they quickly realized they would need some help in order to meet their goal. The students then wrote letters to other classrooms in their building to ask for help collecting pennies. When they had raised enough pennies to cover one step, they invited Kenney, a representative from the mayor's office, and the local newspaper to come to their school. The positive publicity was a nice change of pace from the usual negative stories coming out of inner city school districts.

The Let's Do It Again! Penny Campaign was strictly for pennies only. Sober made sure that all monetary donations were converted into pennies, going as far as to check the penny box for "silver" and trading quarters, dimes, and nickels for their equivalent in pennies. All checks were turned into pennies, and rolls of pennies were kept on hand so visitors could "buy" pennies to throw into the box. Each donor received a certificate modeled after the

The McKinley Presidential Library & Museum raised over $14,000 in pennies as part of the 100th anniversary celebration of the McKinley National Memorial. McKinley Presidential Library & Museum, Canton, Ohio.

original certificate given to McKinley National Memorial donors. A map on display near the penny collection box encouraged visitors to let a staff member know what state they were from if they donated to the penny campaign. In the end, the museum received penny donations from all fifty states. As the campaign grew, businesses and individuals began requesting an "official" penny label to put on their own containers to help raise funds for the museum.

Sober even created an event out of the Let's Do It Again! Penny Campaign called "Panning for Pennies." For $1.00 per scoop, visitors could look for special pennies to keep. A "finder's fee" of one cent for every penny kept was charged. Participants looked for pennies with birth or wedding years, wheat pennies, or other unique pennies. Any pennies from 1907—the year the Memorial was completed—were exempt from the search.

A penny campaign is a great way to raise money and awareness for your anniversary project. Pennies are in everyone's pockets and purses, and are easy to just give away. But they really add up over time. In the end, the McKinley Presidential Library and Museum collected 1,408,274 pennies or $14,082.74, which was added to the McKinley National Memorial's endowment fund. It took thirteen hours to count them all, using automatic counting machines. Although the campaign ended more than eight years ago, visitors continue to collect and donate pennies to the museum.

Another more straightforward fundraising campaign that capitalized on the anniversary celebration was the 100 for $100 campaign. The museum asked for 100 donors to give $100 each, which was also added to the memorial's endowment fund. Donors like being part of a clearly defined campaign. You can use whatever numbers make sense for your organization's anniversary to create your own unique fundraising goals.

Boise Art Museum, Boise, Idaho

As part of its 75th anniversary celebration in 2012, the Boise Art Museum (BAM) launched an ambitious fundraising campaign with many strategic initiatives. According to an internal document outlining fund development goals for the anniversary year, "Donations from individuals comprise the most significant and reliable source of ongoing revenue for nonprofit organizations. Restricted and unrestricted gifts of any size enable people throughout the community to participate in meaningful visual arts experience at BAM. However, fund development money is not just about asking for money; it is about inspiring people with a vision of change in the world and convincing them that BAM can make that vision a reality. The arts make our communities stronger and healthier, boost our local economy, enhance student achievement in our schools, and improve our quality of life. Be an advocate for this vision by forging relationships with people in our community. Listen to them. Engage them. Invite them to join you and BAM in creating this vision." BAM set a goal of meeting with seventy-five potential donors, engaging every member of the board in the process, with an average of four to five visits per board member.

The centerpiece of its anniversary fundraising campaign was the 75 for Seventy-Five initiative. A brochure described the appeal as a "portfolio of seventy-five compelling giving opportunities that reflect annual costs and examples of the ways in which your unrestricted donations may be utilized."[3] BAM created the following giving categories for donation amounts:

Modernist Circle	$150—$999
Romanticist Circle	$1,000—$4,999
Expressionist Circle	$5,000—$24,999
Impressionist Circle	$25,000—$49,999
Classical Circle	$50,000—$99,999
Renaissance Circle	$100,000 +

Two new giving initiatives included the Diamond 75 Business Circle for corporate sponsorships of $1,000 or more and the 1937 Circle for planned giving and bequests. According to an internal document outlining fund development goals for the anniversary year, "an estimated $42 trillion to $125 trillion transfer of wealth will take place in the U.S. over the next few decades. Non-profits can secure part of this wealth through planned giving; a study by the Center on Philanthropy at Indiana University found that 31% of Americans would consider a bequest to a non-profit organization, *if asked.*" The goal was to secure at least five documented commitments in any amount to create the 1937 Circle. In BAM's 2012–2013 Annual Report, board president Nicole Snyder said, "These programs will continue beyond the Museum's 75th anniversary ensuring ongoing financial stability for the organization."

The 75 for Seventy-Five brochure listed specific giving opportunities in the categories of exhibitions, education, and collections, as well as "connecting with our community" and restricted gifts:

Exhibitions

Adopt-an-Exhibition—$5,000 to $50,000

Adopt-an-Exhibition Artwork—Levels ranging from $250 to $1000

Paint—$20,000

Framing—$5,000

Vinyl / Interior Exhibition Signage—$15,000

Benches—$2,000

Carpet—$60,000 minimum contribution

Light Bulbs / Light Fixtures—$7,500

Labels—$2,000

Catalogs—$80,000 minimum contribution

Exhibition Handouts—$15,000

Preparation Supplies—$10,000

Vitrines / Pedestals—$5,000

Outside Signage, Billboard and Banners—$15,000

Opening Receptions—$12,000

Window Coverings for Sculpture Court—$8,000

Gallery Naming—Contact Museum's Executive Director

Education

Adopt-a-Day—$6,500

Adopt-a-School—$500

Studio Tables—$1,500

Art Supplies and Studio Workshop Supplies—$15,000

Adult Programs—$20,000

Community Programs—$25,000

ARTexperienceGallery—$5,000

Docent Program—$30,000

Free School Tour Program—$50,000

ArtReach Program—$50,000

Family Programs—$30,000

Teacher Training Program—$5,000

Teen Program—$2,500

Studio Chairs—$2,000

Camp Stools for Galleries—$3,000

Sign Holders—$500

Easels for Children's Art Tent at Art in the Park—$3,500

Collections

Gift an Artwork—Subject to staff approval

Conservation Supplies—$2,500

Personal Care of the Artwork—$2,500

Photography / Imaging Supplies—$10,000

Conservations Services—$10,000

Outdoor Sculpture Care and Maintenances—$2,500

Art Moving / Crates—$10,000

Connecting with Our Community

Free First Thursdays—$2,000 each First Thursday or $25,000 for a year

Spreading the Word:

Newsletter—$6,000

Museum Map—$2,000

Join Brochure / Individuals—$7,500

Sponsor Brochure / Corporations—$7,500

Annual Report—$2,000

Member Parties—$3,000 per event or $12,000 for a year

Annual Gala—$1,500 – $10,000

Art in the Park—$2,500 – $35,000

Restricted Gifts

Endowment

Planned Gift / Bequest

Exhibition Fund—$250,000 endowed fund minimum

Education Program Fund—$250,000 endowed fund minimum

Purchase Fund for the Collection—$250,000 endowed fund minimum

Building Fund—$250,000 endowed fund minimum

Outdoor Building Improvements—$40,000

Vault Expansion for Art Collection Storage—$500,000 minimum contribution

Technology—$20,000

Scholarships for Art Camps / Classes—$2,500

General Storage Space Upgrade—$75,000

Each of the above giving opportunities were described in detail in the 75 for Seventy-Five brochure. While many of the options are standard museum needs, some of the requests are unique to BAM and require additional explanation:

Adopt-a-Day: "Keeping the Museum in operation and accessible with reasonable admission prices for our community comes at a cost of $6,500 each day."

ARTexperienceGallery: "BAM's ARTexperienceGallery is an interactive space geared toward children ages 12 and under accompanied by an adult, and is enjoyed by visitors of all ages. This innovative space enables children to investigate how art is made, who makes it, and the ways in which ideas, feelings, create approaches and meanings are communicated through visual forms. The ARTexperienceGallery is a comfortable educational environment for children and adults to learn about art and life together."

Personal Care of the Artwork: "BAM's security staff is devoted to keeping the visitors and the works of art in the museum safe at all times. To make them identifiable and uniform, BAM purchases blue jackets as well as walkie-talkies for constant communication for the employees charged with safety."

Free First Thursdays: "BAM has participated in Free First Thursday since its inception twenty-three years ago. Support from the community is crucial to ensure the continuation of this important tradition so that the museum remains accessible to all through free admission on First Thursdays throughout the year."

Art in the Park: "One of the community's most treasured annual events, Art in the Park provides art enthusiasts with the opportunity to meet hundreds of artists and purchase their works. Live entertainment, park performances, wonderful food and hands-on activities for children appeal to people of all ages and interests. Art in the Park is a valued marketing opportunity to reach more than 250,000 participants."

BAM also used the 75 for Seventy-Five campaign for other initiatives. According to a special anniversary edition of its newsletter, the Museum hoped to attract seventy-five new members during the year to "build stronger relationships and increase access to the visual arts for everyone in our community." The staff also hoped to secure seventy-five "high caliber works of art appropriate to BAM's collection mission" and seventy-five significant donations from the above portfolio of giving opportunities.

A brochure like 75 for Seventy-Five not only demonstrates tangible ways in which individuals can support the museum, it also provides an accurate reflection of what each aspect of museum work costs, from conservation of art to printing costs for the newsletter, and everything in between. These dollar amounts help educate members and the public about a seemingly mysterious and secretive aspect of museum work—the budget.

Although the campaign was chock full of great ideas and clearly articulated BAM's needs, it might have been a bit too ambitious. If she could do it all over again, executive director Melanie Fales said she would have "refined our giving opportunities. It was a time consuming project and was meant to be a tool for the board to easily communicate giving opportunities, but it proved to be overwhelming for them as well as potential donors."[4]

Stan Hywet Hall and Gardens, Akron, Ohio

Stan Hywet, the home of Goodyear founder Frank A. Seiberling, used its 100th anniversary to launch a capital campaign called 2nd Century in Bloom. The staff envisioned the centennial celebration as both honoring the past and looking ahead to the future. The campaign's goal was to raise $6 million in 2015, with $2 million designated for the endowment and $4 million to be divided between four preservation projects:

- Restoration of fifteen spaces inside the Manor House
- Phase 1 of tea house and cliff face preservation/restoration
- Reconstruction of the perimeter wall
- Leaded glass window restoration across the historic buildings on the property

In a press release announcing the campaign, honorary chair Cynthia Knight said "our collective commitment to safeguarding this singular cultural icon will ensure our community retains the stature and appeal inherent to a National Historic Landmark and America's 6th largest historic home. It will also confirm our profound desire to sustain Akron's history, legacy and opportunity as a compelling home for future generations to make their own."[5] Stan Hywet produced an eight-minute video to accompany the campaign, including interviews with Seiberling descendants and museum staff describing the importance of the home to both the family and the community. Illustrated with vintage film footage of the home in action, it made a compelling case to contribute to the anniversary capital campaign.

Donations included $500,000 each from The J. M. Smucker Company and the Mary S. and David C. Corbin Foundation. Other donors included the State of Ohio, foundations, corporations and individual friends of Stan Hywet. The campaign began with a $1 million gift two years prior to the anniversary year, which was the largest gift ever received from a single individual in the museum's history.

South Bend 150, South Bend, Indiana

Fundraising for the city of South Bend's sesquicentennial (SB150) focused on funding the anniversary events themselves, rather than raising funds for a specific organization's endowment or unrelated project. The celebration was administered through Downtown South Bend, Inc., and a separate LLC was set up specifically for fundraising. Community partners were not directly involved in the fundraising efforts on their own.

One of the signature projects of SB150 was the construction of River Lights, a new public art installation by renowned artist Robert Shakespeare. Two interactive light sculptures on either side of the river create a cascade of light that visitors can control with the movement of their bodies. As a permanent landmark honoring the city's 150th anniversary, it provided a unique incentive for fundraising efforts. Donors to the SB150 campaign could choose which event they wanted to sponsor, but each donation over $150 included a permanent remembrance at River Lights:

- $150
  Engraved brick as part of the St. Joseph River Lighting project.
- $1,500
  Engraved brick; Acknowledgment on the SB150.com website.
- $4,500
  Medium-size engraved concrete block; acknowledgment on the SB150.com website.
- $7,500
  Large-size engraved concrete block; acknowledgment on the SB150.com website.
- $15,000
  Large-size engraved concrete block; acknowledgment on the SB150.com website; acknowledgment on all banners and printed materials.
- $30,000
  Large-size engraved concrete block; acknowledgment on the SB150.com website; acknowledgment on all banners and printed materials; shared sponsorship of event.
- $45,000
  Large-size engraved concrete block; acknowledgment on the SB150.com website; acknowledgment on all banners and printed materials; individual sponsorship of event.
- $75,000
  Large-size engraved concrete block; acknowledgment on the SB150.com website; acknowledgment on all banners and printed materials; shared St. Joseph River Lighting project naming rights for perpetuity.
- $150,000
  Large-size engraved concrete block; acknowledgment on the SB150.com website; acknowledgment on all banners and printed materials; individual St. Joseph River Lighting project naming rights for perpetuity.

In addition to the above options, sponsorship opportunities for Birthday Weekend, SB150's signature event, included the following:

- Main Stage: Outdoor venue for musical performances
- Tech Hub: Hands-on displays and demonstrations of new technologies
- Kid's Activity Zone: Petting zoo, bounce houses, mascots, outdoor movies, and so on
- Adventure Park: Zip lines, ropes course, mini golf, yoga, roller skating, and so on
- Taste of South Bend: Booths set up by local restaurants
- Fireworks: One show each night of the weekend
- Artisan Alley: Booths featuring artists and their work
- South Bend 150 Green: The Jefferson Street Bridge covered in sod to create a "green" gathering space
- Volleyball Tournament
- Basketball Tournament

- Island Wine and Brew Mixer: Wine, beer and spirits tasting
- South Bend Drive: An outdoor exhibition featuring the history of South Bend

Additional sponsorship opportunities for other events included these:

- Community Impact Grants: Up to $10,000 awarded to nonprofit organizations for projects
- Essay Contest: Residents invited to submit an essay describing what South Bend would be like on its 200th birthday in fifty years
- Photo Contest: Photographers invited to submit photos highlighting South Bend
- Art Birthday Cakes: Civic organizations asked to build large birthday cake sculptures
- Pay It Forward: Citywide campaign for schools, neighborhoods, and churches to "repay a good deed to others in the community
- Discover Series: Monthly themed event highlighting South Bend's past, present, or future

The campaign brochure suggested that the events above could be renamed for the donor, such as "Essay Contest Presented by 'Benefactor.'"[6]

The Paul Revere House, Boston, Massachusetts

When it opened to the public in 1908, the Paul Revere House became one of the earliest house museums in the United States. As its 100th anniversary approached in 2008, staff wanted to leverage the occasion to launch a fundraising campaign. "Having purchased a new-to-us but dilapidated [circa] 1835 row house the year before our anniversary, we wanted to mark a significant institutional milestone with a fitting celebration that would help us build enthusiasm and generate donations as we prepared to develop what would be our first-ever capital campaign to fund our expansion," said Emily Holmes, education director. "We discovered that the anniversary of an organization was not as compelling a fundraising message as we had hoped, at least not with people who were less familiar with the Paul Revere Memorial Association. So we used the idea of an anniversary fund to do some inside fundraising and then later when we launched our capital campaign, we rolled the money raised from the fund into the campaign. It was modest but it was a start."[7] The $4 million capital campaign was used for an expansion project, not only to renovate the purchased row house, but to make improvements to the Revere House itself. Part of the funds were used to make the house handicapped accessible.

Rutherford B. Hayes Presidential Library and Museums, Fremont, Ohio

When the Rutherford B. Hayes Presidential Library and Museum began planning its 100th anniversary in 2016, the staff knew they had a unique opportunity to "set the bar" as the nation's first presidential library to reach this significant milestone. The centennial planning would lead to a comprehensive revitalization and rebranding of the organization, complete with a name change, a new logo, a capital campaign, and a fresh look at President Hayes through new permanent exhibits.

The federally funded system of presidential libraries, operated by the National Archives and Records Administration (NARA), did not start until Franklin Delano Roosevelt came up with the idea during his second term in the 1930s. Any presidential library created before FDR is privately owned, state-owned, or some combination. With a wealth of papers and artifacts in his possession after his father's death in 1893, Webb Cook Hayes immediately began planning for a public memorial to his father. At the time, no presidential libraries existed for Webb to use as an example. George Washington's Mount Vernon had been open to the public since 1860 as a historic house museum, but did not have a library component. When James Garfield was assassinated in 1881, his widow built a fireproof addition to her home to house his papers and other relics, but she did not open it to the public. A key component of Webb's vision was public access to his father's legacy. Webb deeded his father's property to the State of Ohio and donated his papers and other artifacts to the Ohio Historical Society, with the requirement that a building be constructed on the estate to house the materials. When the library and museum opened in 1916, Webb thought it wasn't big enough, so he personally funded an expansion that doubled its size and opened in 1922. A second expansion in 1968 created the building visitors see today. In addition to the library and museum, the facility includes the Hayes home and burial site.

From its inception, Hayes has operated as a private/state partnership; the state of Ohio owns the property and all of the artifacts, but the museum's employees are not state employees. This arrangement has worked well overall, but the recession in the 2000s led to severe budget cuts from the state. The museum was plunged into an austerity mentality that lasted for several years.

When Christie M. Weininger became executive director of the Hayes Presidential Center in 2012, there had not been a strategic plan in place for ten years. The previous director knew he was retiring, so he wanted to let the next director's vision guide the future of the organization. In her Director's Message in the 2015 Annual Report, Weininger wrote, "When I joined the staff in 2012, the board and staff had weathered quite a financial storm and guided this institution through nearly a decade of serious budget cuts, reduced hours and salaries for all staff and millions of dollars in deferred maintenance. Despite all of that, other than closing to visitors on Mondays, services to the public were never reduced *and* the beautiful and stunningly accurate restoration of the Hayes Home was completed. That is a tremendous accomplishment, especially considering the circumstances. However we weren't growing and flourishing in the way that we wanted to. So the first thing we needed was a strategy. We spent all of 2013 planning and dreaming for the future, knowing that our centennial—what a milestone!—was a few short years away."

To begin the process, Weininger initiated a series of surveys to gather input from as many people as possible to create a strategic plan. "We used Survey Monkey and paper surveys to ask members, patrons, donors, staff, community members, and volunteers about their vision for the museum," she said. "We also conducted personal interviews with key stakeholders. We had five hundred responses in total, which was a really rich data pool to draw from."[8] The initiatives that would become associated with the museum's centennial emerged from that survey. "People's passion was with the grounds, with Spiegel Grove itself," said Weininger. "That's what really got them excited, and we didn't expect that." This observation led the staff to be sure that the words "at Spiegel Grove" appeared in the new logo, unveiled in December 2015.

Other feedback was more critical, providing the staff with concrete data to support what they already knew: their exhibits were outdated and their handicapped entrance needed drastic improvement. In order to enter the museum, visitors with mobility issues had to use a freight elevator, which opened into a back hallway. A staff member had to meet them in order to enter or exit the museum, which was far from ideal. The museum's permanent exhibition on Hayes had not changed since 1968. One particularly harsh critic said, "It looks like high school students put your exhibits together."

Designing new exhibitions and renovating the main entrance became the primary initiatives identified in the new strategic plan. "In order to do those things, we needed more money," Weininger said. "We had never done a capital campaign before. We had raised money to restore the Hayes home, but a lot of that came from Save America's Treasures and the state of Ohio. We needed to figure out how to bring more dollars into this place. We had a very healthy development portion to the strategic plan as well."

When the state cut their budget by $500,000 several years earlier, the development staff kicked into gear. "We were actually able to increase private investment during the worst years of the recession," Weininger said, "but we couldn't make it all up." The staff and board had been operating in a "cut" mentality for quite a while, so when she presented her preliminary ideas, "They were not exactly in a risk taking mood," she said.

The original plan suggested just switching out some of the exhibit panels but leaving most of the display intact. "There wouldn't be much of a change," Weininger said, "and to my mind that wasn't good enough. We had to try to find a way." The centennial was coming, and Weininger decided to capitalize on it. "This was our moment," she said. "A century of existence is huge. We won't see anything bigger in our organization in our lifetime. It was also a presidential election year, and we realized we needed to do something big. It was time."

While her new strategic plan called for an organizational overhaul, it was broken down into manageable bites that the board and staff could get behind. Weininger's first objective was to strengthen the museum's relationship with the state. "We went out and talked to some of the state legislators," she said, "particularly those who were not in our district. We explained what we were doing, and they became more interested. We're one little item in the state budget, and some didn't even know we existed. It's been wonderful to see how many have come to see what they're investing in." As a direct result of these efforts, some of their funding has been restored. The first thing Weininger did was open on Mondays again. All of the staff—including her own position as director—had been reduced from full time to four days a week when the budget was cut. It was important to restore everyone who had been full time back to their original hours because of their workload. "Because of the new strategic plan and the centennial being this galvanizing moment that we've all rallied around, we realized that we were falling behind the times. Even our computers and computer networks were archaic," Weininger said. "From the inside out, we have gone through this complete revitalization. It's been tremendous and energizing, and we're hitting our stride."

RUTHERFORD B. HAYES

PRESIDENTIAL LIBRARY & MUSEUMS

at

SPIEGEL GROVE

To better reflect its identity, the Rutherford B. Hayes Presidential Library & Museums created a brand new logo during its 100th anniversary. At the top is a blue bar with three stars. The center star is larger and red, which is a nod to Hayes's role in the Red Star Brigade during the Civil War. The bottom bar has a notch in it, which represents the unique "burgee" or swallow-tail shape of the Ohio state flag, where Hayes was born and spent most of his life. The overall design is patriotic and "presidential," using a red, white, and blue motif in an overall vertical ribbon design. The Rutherford B. Hayes Presidential Library & Museums, Fremont, Ohio.

The name and logo change was not initially part of the strategic plan. "But as we realized how we were evolving, we had outgrown our image," Weininger said. "We needed something to represent who we were becoming." Additional research revealed that their previous name, the Hayes Presidential Center, did not fully convey who they were. "We showed people pictures of what we have—the museum, the library, the home, the tomb, and the grounds—and asked them what they would expect to see at a place called a 'presidential center.' Most people expected to see the museum, but they didn't expect to see the other things. The name was meant to be all-encompassing, but it was too vague." Some of those surveyed did not even realize the name Hayes Presidential Center referred to *President* Hayes. They thought "Hayes" might be a major donor, and the center would address the history of all of the U.S. presidents.

Weininger and her staff used this information to come up with the new name Rutherford B. Hayes Presidential Library, but they struggled with the wording that should come next. In the end, they realized they were several museums under one umbrella of presidential history, so they opted for the "Rutherford B. Hayes Presidential Library and Museums." The tagline "at Spiegel Grove" in the new logo, which is not part of the official name, gives the museum a sense of place and reflects the passion for the grounds staff discovered in the initial surveys.

The previous logo was an oval with the words Hayes Presidential Library in script. The word "Hayes" was much smaller than the other words, minimizing the museum's primary mission to interpret the life and times of the 19th president. The design was ordinary, and not distinctive in any way. "Our logo should be ours," Weininger said, "and it couldn't be anyone else's. We wanted our logo to be unique to us." Designed by Peoples Creative Group, the new logo is full of symbolism that truly represents Hayes. The word "Hayes" is front and center in the largest font, with "Rutherford B." above it and "Presidential Library & Museums" below it. Even when shrunk down for smaller ads or letterhead, the name "Hayes" is clearly visible. At the top is a blue bar with three stars. The center star is larger and red, which is a nod to Hayes's role in the Red Star Brigade during the Civil War. The bottom bar has a notch in it, which represents the unique "burgee" or swallowtail shape of the Ohio state flag, where Hayes was born and spent most of his life. The overall design is patriotic and "presidential," using a red, white, and blue motif in an overall vertical ribbon design.

"We didn't want it to be change for change's sake," said Weininger. "We had had our old logo since 1981. It's scary to launch a new logo because you don't know how the public is going to react. Sometimes rebranding doesn't make sense to them. But they love it. They think it looks clean and modern." One visitor commented, "When I see this logo I hear John Philip Sousa playing in the background!"

Several years ago an architect had drawn plans for a multi-million dollar handicapped-accessible entrance, but it was cost prohibitive then—and now. The museum needed a solution that was less expensive but accomplished the same goal. The new plan replaced the old stairs with a "switchback ramp" that has stairs built into either side. "It is being done in the United States, but it is much more common in Europe," Weininger said. The new look preserves the dramatic entrance to the museum, while accommodating the needs of all visitors.

The $1.3 million capital campaign was successful in part because it was associated with the museum's 100th anniversary. "The Centennial Campaign is a huge success because people recognize the importance of the capital projects it will address," said Kathy Boukissen, director of development, in the 2015 Annual Report. Part of the campaign included gallery and artifact naming opportunities, which the museum rarely offers. In addition to the new gallery spaces, donors could name the interior entrance to the library, the café, and the museum store. Artifact naming opportunities included the Resolute Desk, the presidential

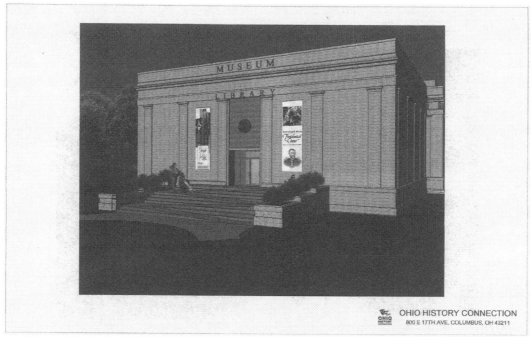

The new handicapped accessible entrance at the Rutherford B. Hayes Presidential Library & Museums features a European-inspired "switchback" ramp that achieved the goal without compromising the appearance of the historic building. The design was modified to include a series of block "benches" along the slopes that increased safety for visitors. The Rutherford B. Hayes Presidential Library & Museums and the Ohio History Connection, Fremont, Ohio.

china sideboard, the White House Carriage, a Victorian dollhouse, and several of Lucy Webb Hayes's dresses, including her wedding gown.

Notes

1. Personal interview with author, June 16, 2015. All quotes in this chapter are from the same interview.
2. Personal interview with author, July 15, 2015.
3. "75 for Seventy-Five" Fundraising Brochure, Boise Art Museum, 2012.
4. Personal interview with author, July 8, 2015.
5. "Stan Hywet Announces Major Restoration Effort Coinciding with 100th Anniversary," Stan Hywet Hall and Gardens, February 5, 2015, http://www.stanhywet.org/sites/default/files/assets/docs/SH%20News_Stan%20Hywet%20Announces%202nd%20Century%20Campaign.pdf.
6. Campaign Brochure, SB150, 2015.
7. Personal interview with author, December 18, 2015.
8. Personal interview with author, February 19, 2016. All quotes in this chapter are from the same interview.

CHAPTER 4

Exhibitions, Books, and Documentaries

FOR MOST ANNIVERSARY events, museums will focus on the traditional avenues of exhibitions and publications. There are many ways to approach these projects, ranging from large and expensive permanent installations to smaller temporary exhibitions. Publications can include anything from a lavishly illustrated coffee table book to a new brochure or booklet about your site. All of the ideas in this chapter can be adapted on a scale to fit your resources.

Cincinnati Preservation Society, Cincinnati, Ohio

When the Cincinnati Preservation Society celebrated its 50th anniversary in 2014, it had two major objectives. The first was to reconnect with its founders, who felt like it was no longer their organization after a drastic name change in 1992. The second goal was to "redefine preservation from 'don't touch' to a more active, engaged movement," said director Paul Muller, "fostering urban revitalization, thoughtful reuse, and a powerful force for bringing people back to historic areas. Plus we wanted to increase our visibility and be a fun organization to be a part of."[1] To that end, the Preservation Society created and installed an exhibition entitled Saving Buildings Together: 50 Years of Cincinnati Preservation at the Cincinnati Museum Center.

Approximately sixty thousand people viewed the exhibition between September 2014 and April 2015. There was no admission charge to view the exhibition, which is standard for most exhibitions at the Cincinnati Museum Center (unless they are "blockbuster" traveling shows like Titanic or King Tut, which usually have a separate entrance fee).

According to the organization's application for the State Historic Preservation Office awards, the major objectives of the exhibition were to "celebrate and honor our founders, increase the public's awareness of the historic resources in Cincinnati, and to provide opportunities for the public to become involved in preservation. In addition we sought to promote historic preservation as a defining feature of Cincinnati, as something that is an integral part of the life of the city."

For its 50th anniversary, the Cincinnati Preservation Society installed an exhibition called Saving Buildings Together: 50 Years of Cincinnati Preservation at the Cincinnati Museum Center. In 2015 the exhibition was recognized with a Public Education and Awareness award from the Ohio State Historic Preservation Office. Cincinnati Preservation Society, Cincinnati, Ohio.

The exhibition featured four themes: Founders and Origins, Tools of Preservation, Campaigns to Save Buildings, and Preservation Today. Each section was arranged chronologically to "help underscore the evolution of the movement from a focus on museum houses and landmark properties to today's more comprehensive view of how historic resources impact the entire city." The exhibition also helped to promote the importance of Union Terminal, the historic 1931 art deco train station where the Cincinnati Museum Center is located, in the weeks before a critical referendum vote on funding for rehabilitation of the facility.

The introductory panel introduced visitors to the establishment of the Cincinnati Preservation Society (originally known as the Miami Purchase Association for Historic Preservation), while looking forward to what lies ahead for the movement:

Fifty years ago a group of Cincinnati citizens recognized that we were losing our historic sites and buildings at an alarming rate. One highly significant archaeological site at Shawnee Lookout faced an immediate threat for a proposed transmission line at a nearby power plant. To address this crisis, they organized the Miami Purchase Association for Historic Preservation in 1964. While working to save Shawnee Lookout they also began to educate themselves and the community about the other treasures in the region.

This exhibit presents the individuals who led preservation efforts, the buildings they saved and, sadly, the many that have been lost. It also highlights the evolution of the preservation movement from its early focus on individual buildings to its current role in reviving entire neighborhoods.

The founders of MPA had to work to convince people of the value of the historic buildings. Today historic preservation is more widely appreciated and has become a central part of city planning. Cincinnati's current urban renaissance is fueled in large part by redeveloping its historic resources.

Historic buildings and sites make the world more understandable and enrich our lives. We owe a debt of gratitude to the founders and early leaders on MPA. The work they began continues today as new generations join the effort.

Most of the exhibition was presented through photographs and text panels, but artifacts included a carved wood panel from a music hall organ screen, artifacts from archeology projects the society sponsored in the 1960s, drafting tools used by historic architects, and buttons and printed materials from previous efforts to save Union Terminal.

The staff at CPS had mounted small exhibitions before, but this was the largest-scale exhibition the organization had ever attempted. Muller has exhibition experience and designed the layout and thematic divisions. The Preservation Society did its own writing and worked with a graphic designer to create the panel layout. "The museum was very supportive and provided advice on the amount of content as well as some layout suggestions to improve flow," Muller said. "They placed the objects in the cases, which added a great deal to the presentation."

Muller's favorite sections were the beginning and the end. The first section described how three women led a skeptical public to the cause of preservation. "The final section showed that preservation is now integral to all civic development, with young people leading the way," Muller said. "[We are] reinventing the city, bringing new uses and life to historic buildings, and being thoughtful about how the past can enrich our current lives."

Shaker Heritage Society, Watervliet, New York

As part of the centennial celebration of the Church Family barn, the Shaker Heritage Society in Albany, New York, partnered with three other Shaker museums in the capital region to create a major exhibition at the New York State Museum called The Shakers: America's Quiet Revolutionaries. The exhibition allowed the museums to "tell the story of the Shakers when they first arrived in Albany, which had never been done before," said Starlyn D'Angelo, executive director of the Shaker Heritage Society.[2] Staff members from the New York State Museum, Shaker Heritage Society, Shaker Museum | Mt. Lebanon (Mt. Lebanon, NY), and Hancock Shaker Village (Pittsfield, MA) worked together as part of the exhibition's curatorial team. D'Angelo spearheaded the fundraising efforts for the exhibition, securing two $5,000 grants to pay for it. It took three years to write the script, so the exhibition was on view for two years.

The exhibition explored the Shakers through six themes: Settlement in America; Shaker Theology and Religious Practice; Spreading the Faith, Keeping the Union; Comfortable Home: Being a Shaker; Shaker Made: Agriculture and Industry; and Enduring Design: The Shaker Influence on Design. The collaboration allowed three smaller historical sites to strategically partner with a larger museum to raise the profile of the first three Shaker communities in the United States. The ultimate goal of the project was to brand the region as "Shaker" in the same way Pennsylvania is associated with the Amish. Located right across the street from the region's major airport and just off a major highway, the Shaker Heritage Society is considered the "gateway" Shaker site. Shaker Museum | Mount Lebanon is thirty miles to the east, and Hancock Shaker Village is five miles farther east.

Since the Shaker Heritage Society is not a collecting institution, it would not have been able to create such an exhibition on its own. With the smallest staff and budget of the three sites, the Shaker Heritage Society was able to raise its profile in the community as well as increase visitation as a result of the exhibition. The partnership also allowed the curatorial team to pull from the three best Shaker collections, rather than just one, because each museum has its own collecting focus. For example, Shaker Museum | Mount Lebanon has a fabulous furniture collection, while the New York State Museum's focus is mostly agricultural. After working together on this project, the four museums understand each other much better now, according to D'Angelo. "We know what each museum's resources are and what we can and can't do. Working with the state museum was eye-opening; they are as understaffed as we are, just on a different scale. Pulling together made the exhibition possible. Otherwise, it could not have been done."

The partnership created a robust series of programming related to the exhibition at the New York State Museum and at the three Shaker partner sites. To complement the Shaker Heritage Society's centennial celebration of the Church Family barn, each site planned a tour of its own Shaker barn over three subsequent weekends called Shaker Barnstorming Weekends. By working together, the three Shakers sites were also able to convince a prominent Shaker scholar to come give a lecture.

Imperial War Museums, London, Manchester, and Cambridgeshire, England

The Imperial War Museums (IWM) are made up of five different museums, each contributing a unique perspective on the United Kingdom's role in conflicts since World War I. The branches include IWM London, the "flagship" museum; IWM North, focusing on people and their stories; IWM Duxford, an aviation museum and wartime airfield; Churchill War Rooms, located in Churchill's secret headquarters below Whitehall; and the HMS Belfast from World War II.

As part of the centennial commemoration of World War I in 2014, the IWM reopened IWM London after an extensive $62 million, six-month renovation. The permanent World War I galleries were redesigned and now feature 1,300 artifacts. The trench experience section was also revamped and now provides a much more realistic view of what life was like on the front. The museum's website describes the new immersion space: "Walk through a recreated trench with a Sopwith Camel plane swooping low overhead as a Mark V Tank looms above you. Explore the war at sea and campaigns in the Middle East, Africa, Gallipoli and the Western Front."[3] Another space explores the impact of World War I on the home front, with sections explaining why men signed up to fight and how women contributed to the war effort.

According to the BBC, the new four-level atrium space at IWM London features more than four hundred artifacts and artworks. Although the museum was founded during World War I to commemorate the personal experiences of that particular conflict, its mission has since expanded to collect artifacts from other wars as well. The new space incorporates artifacts that had never been on view, including the witness stand from the Lockerbie trial and a suicide bomber's vest.

IWM North, located in Manchester, opened a temporary exhibition in April 2014 called From Street to Trench: A World War That Shaped a Region. According to an IWM press release, it was "the largest exhibition ever created exploring the lives and experiences of people from the North West of England during the First World War." Over two hundred objects, photographs, letters, artworks, and sound recordings were on display. One particularly innovative interactive allowed visitors to crawl through a tunnel simulating the experience of sewer workers on a secret mission in France. The exhibition also explored the more localized story of Chapel Street, nicknamed the "bravest little street in England," where 161 men from 60 houses on the same street served in the war.

The press release quotes Graham Boxer, director of IWM North at that time, making the connection between the anniversary of the war and the exhibition: "One hundred years on, the objects we display highlight the poignancy and courage of people who shaped and were shaped by this first global conflict. Even a century later there are stories untold, experiences undiscovered and tales that will surprise."[4]

IWM also created a traveling exhibition that toured nine cities around the world during the centennial, marking the first time such an extensive exhibition based on the museum's collection left the country. Sections included The World in 1900, Shock of War, Feeding the Front, Machine of War, Trench Experience, Taking War to the Skies, Beating the U-Boat, War's End, and Making a New World. The exhibition featured more than 350 artifacts and many digital components.

Boise Art Museum, Boise, Idaho

The Boise Art Museum (BAM) mounted two distinctive exhibitions during its 75th anniversary year in 2012. First, the Museum launched its yearlong celebration with a distinctive exhibition called *Open to Interpretation*. It "invited viewers to participate in a game of discovery through the unique display of artworks from BAM's Permanent Collection," said Melanie Fales, executive director and CEO of the Boise Art Museum. "Rather than grouping the works by traditional themes, artworks were displayed so that each related to the next in one way or another, and not necessarily in the same way as the relationship of the next work of art to its neighbor. Visitors were invited to come up with their own relationships and to see if they could determine why certain works were placed near others."[5]

The second exhibition, *Nick Cave: Meet Me at the Center of the Earth*, was the centerpiece of the anniversary celebration. A special anniversary edition of BAM's newsletter provided

The centerpiece of the Boise Art Museum's 75th anniversary celebration was the exhibition Nick Cave: Meet Me at the Center of the Earth. The artist provided wearable soundsuits for community dancers to wear during an event at the museum. Boise Art Museum, Boise, Idaho.

the following description of the exhibition: "Sculptor and performance artist Nick Cave is known worldwide for his Soundsuits—eight-foot-tall, extravagant sculptures covered in vivid arrays of beads, sequins, doilies, buttons, embroidery, knitted materials, vintage toys and all manner of curious objects. These wondrous wearable sculptures evoke rich and varied associations of ritual, myth, ceremony, and identity."

The Nick Cave exhibition provided many partnership opportunities for the museum to "connect in ways that are not typical of every art exhibition," said Fales. "One of the project's greatest strengths was the widespread collaboration with a number of community partners, including arts and cultural organizations, educational institutions, area artists, and businesses. The partnerships helped ensure that the educational programs associated with the exhibition reached a wide and diverse audience, and generated tremendous publicity for the museum. Foremost among these efforts was BAM's collaboration with two dance companies, Ballet Idaho and Balance Dance Company, to present Soundsuit dance performances at the Museum and at locations throughout Boise. The five Ballet Idaho performances were set to music and choreographed. Visitors were entranced by the dancers in the Soundsuits, and gained an appreciation for the connections between visual arts and dance."

In contrast, "Balance Dance Company worked with BAM to stage flash-mob style sightings of the Soundsuits," said Fales. "The dancers created impromptu dance movements that were influenced by the Soundsuit costumes and responded to the reaction of the people around them. BAM attracted a significant social media following by cultivating a surprise element for the performances, hinting at their times and locations through Facebook and Twitter posts." In total there were seventeen spontaneous "sightings" of the Soundsuits around the city of Boise including Key Bank, Flying M, and the Boise Hawks.

Another photo showing community dancers. Boise Art Museum, Boise, Idaho.

The Gardiner Museum of Ceramic Art, Toronto, Ontario, Canada

To celebrate its 30th anniversary in 2015, the Gardiner Museum opened an exhibition and published a companion anniversary catalog called *30 Objects, 30 Insights*. The project examined thirty objects from the permanent collection that represented "its temporal and geographical breadth, as well as the universality of ceramics," according to a press release. The exhibition featured portraits of the collectors who helped to build the museum's prominent ceramics collection.

The book included thirty essays written by ceramics experts that complemented each object. "We are proud to highlight important objects in our internationally renowned collection in this superb book," says Kelvin Browne, executive director and CEO. "*30 Objects, 30 Insights* features over 100 sumptuous photographs that bring our collection to life in a whole new way, revealing the vitality and range of the medium. Readers will never look at these beautiful objects the same way."[6]

According to chief curator Rachel Gotlieb, "One of the key objectives of this volume of essays is to celebrate not only the Gardiner Museum's 30th anniversary, [but] also to show the richness and diversity prevalent in current critical writing on historical and contemporary ceramics. The authors' perspectives offer important insights on why ceramics matter in everyday life. The lively and inspired insights share distinct points of view on issues of connoisseurship, social history and consumption."[7]

It took two years from start to finish to complete the catalog, including the fundraising phase. "Objects were selected to give a broad range from the collection—from Ancient to Contemporary—and also were already known as jewels of the collection, or important artists to the development of ceramics," said Lauren Gould, development and programs manager. "I think most museums know their star objects, but it is certainly still difficult to whittle it down to thirty. Once the objects were selected, the most appropriate scholar was chosen to write the essay. They ranged from other museum directors to collectors and connoisseurs to curators."[8] All of the experts had previously worked with the Gardiner in some capacity.

A smaller exhibition called *A Tribute to George and Helen Gardiner*, honoring the museum's founders, was on view in the lobby. This exhibition served as an introduction to *30 Objects, 30 Insights* by providing historical context for the first donation that formed the foundation of its collection. "The original Gardiner collection included world-class holdings of Ancient American pottery as well as major holdings of European pottery and porcelain dating from the fifteenth to the nineteenth centuries," said Lauren Gould, development and programs manager. "Over the past thirty years, the Gardiner Museum's collection has doubled in size and expanded in scope, thanks to generous gifts from several private collectors."

A third exhibition, *Clare Twomey: Piece by Piece*, rounded out the anniversary year. The museum commissioned Twomey to "create a body of work that responds to the museum's historical collections," said Gould. "The artist interprets the past for the future through her own personal experience or 'embodied' practice. Twomey's installation investigated the intersection of making and collecting through the lens of the Gardiner Museum's seventeenth century Delftware and eighteenth century European porcelain collections."

The exhibition was a "dramatic representation of the challenges inherent in making something," according to a review in the *Toronto Star*. "In preparation for this show, Twomey worked with five other women in her London workshop," wrote *Star* fashion columnist Karen von Hahn. "They created the first 2,000 figurines from digitally scanned moulds of three 18th-century figures from the Gardiner collection: a gesturing Leda, who, in Twomey's words, is "either dancing or welcoming or saying stop"; a jauntily attired Harlequin, and a naughty Scaramouche. None would individually merit being put on a museum pedestal, but here they occupy the gallery in a lively tableau."[9]

For three hours a day, during the week, makers created more figures right in the exhibition space. By the end of the show, the number of figures grew from two thousand to three thousand. At the end of the exhibition Twomey gave the figures to museum visitors free of charge. "We gave members and patrons exclusive access," said Gould. "There was certainly a stampede when we opened it to the public, but only twenty people were permitted into the space at any one time. It was odd to see people walking through the installation to select their work." In total, the closing day attracted almost one thousand visitors.

Eiteljorg Museum of American Indians and Western Art, Indianapolis, Indiana

As part of its 25th anniversary celebration in 2014, the Eiteljorg Museum of American Indians and Western Art published a full color, 225-page catalog highlighting several pieces from its permanent collection, including paintings, sculptures, pottery, jewelry, textiles, and baskets. Funded by an anonymous donor, the catalog includes a history of the museum, a biography of its founder Harrison Eiteljorg, an examination of several collections that have been donated over the years, and museum programs and initiatives, such as the Indian Market and Festival and the Eiteljorg Contemporary Art Fellowship.

The book begins with an essay titled "Building a Museum" by president and CEO John Vanausdall, exploring how the museum was founded; the ways in which the board and staff have shaped its vision over time; the expansion of the museum's building and its mission; and building audience, community, traditions, diversity, and collections. Vanausdall ends his essay thusly:

> Quoting myself from an essay after the building expansion in 2005: "Like the collection, the Eiteljorg Museum continues to evolve. Great museums are works in progress—never finished, never complete." This remains true today as we mark the Eiteljorg's silver anniversary, and I am certain it will be true twenty-five years from now.[10]

The book not only documents how the museum has changed over time, it invites readers to contemplate what might happen in the future as the Eiteljorg continues to collect and celebrate American Indian and Western art. The catalog beautifully weaves the story of the museum and its donors throughout photographs of its world-class permanent collection.

Mackinac State Historic Parks, Mackinaw City, Michigan, and Mackinac Island, Michigan

As part of its commemoration of the bicentennial of the War of 1812, Mackinac State Historic Parks installed a new long-term exhibition in the east blockhouse of Fort Mackinac featuring an audiovisual program on the British capture of the fort and the American attempts to retake it. Since the current interpretive period for the fort is the 1880s, the museum has not traditionally focused on the British occupation of the fort's history. Mackinac State Historic Parks also published a revised and updated book on the War of 1812. Originally written in 1962 and revised in 1970 and 2004, the 2012 version included colored illustrations. The organization also added a new publication to its vignette series on the battle of 1814.

A Peace Garden, commemorating the end of the war and two hundred years of peace between the United States, Canada, and Great Britain, was created below Fort Mackinac in Marquette Park, behind and adjacent to the Richard and Jane Manoogian Mackinac Art Museum. A committee consisting of staff from Mackinac Historic Parks, a member of the Mackinac Island State Park Commission, and the head of the local arts council reviewed the entries for a bronze sculpture that would become the centerpiece of Peace Garden's design. The committee chose *Be Still* by Gareth Curtiss, featuring a male Native American figure standing on the back of a turtle between an eagle, representing the United States, and a lion, representing Great Britain.

At the Peace Garden's dedication ceremony on July 18, 2015, consulate general of Canada, Douglas George, told *Mackinac Island News* that there are important benefits to the two nations in living harmoniously as neighbors. "We solve issues peaceably, and we co-manage the Great Lakes, which is an incredibly important effort in our region," he said. "I can't think of any other two countries that have a better relationship." Brisson added, "The island was a theater of war. Action took place here, and since it is a War of 1812 site, it's appropriate to have a place that commemorates the end of the war."[11]

The Andy Warhol Museum, Pittsburgh, Pennsylvania

One of four Carnegie Museums of Pittsburgh, The Andy Warhol Museum is the "global keeper" of Andy Warhol's legacy. According to the museum's website, "The collection includes 900 paintings; approximately 100 sculptures; nearly 2,000 works on paper; more than 1,000 published and unique prints; and 4,000 photographs."[12] Highlights include commercial illustrations, sketchbooks, student work, and pop paintings of consumer products (Campell's Soup Cans) and celebrities like Marilyn Monroe and Elvis. The museum chose to celebrate its 20th anniversary "to commemorate a milestone in the museum's life and to highlight the rehang of the museum's collection on its seven floors," said Jessica Warchall, assistant communications manager.[13] It was the largest comprehensive review of the museum's collection since it opened in 1994.

The museum opened at midnight on May 17, 2014, after its black-tie gala, for a free twenty-four-hour viewing of the new exhibitions. From midnight to 2:00 a.m., visitors enjoyed music spun by New York City DJ AndrewAndrew, followed by a preview of the exhibition *Halston and Warhol: Silver and Suede*, featuring two hundred works from museums across the country. Designer Roy Halston Frowick's garments and accessories were viewed among Warhol's photography, paintings, and films. According to the museum's website, "From Warhol's Factory and Halston's Olympic Tower showroom to Studio 54, Halston and Warhol helped cultivate environments where art and fashion intersected. They shared a vision for how art, design, and business could coexist and found themselves at the very center of a new high/low culture they had helped create."[14] After its debut at the Warhol, the exhibition began traveling, with engagements at the Des Moines Art Center and the Mint Museum.

The new rehang of the permanent collection galleries displayed Warhol's artwork chronologically, with his earliest works on the seventh floor and each floor below showcasing a different decade in succession. "A new film and video gallery was created," said Warchall, "as well as the *Exploding Plastic Inevitable* [EPI] gallery, recreating the multisensory experience of the original events." The Tate Museum in Great Britain defines the EPI on its website as "a series of events that Warhol staged in 1966 and 1967, first in New York and then on tour across the United States. EPI brought together a sensory collision of live music from the Velvet Underground and Nico, multiple film and slide projectors, strobe lighting effects, and provocative dances by Gerard Malanga and Mary Woronov or Ingrid Superstar. It was what we would now think of as a multimedia experience. In 1966 Warhol was managing the Velvet Underground and actively filmmaking. It would appear that EPI was in part conceived to bring those two areas together, as one of the alternative names for the EPI was 'Disco-Flicka-Theque.'"

In July 1966, Larry McCombs reviewed the EPI in *Boston Broadside*: "It doesn't go together. But sometimes it does—suddenly the beat of the music, the movements of the various films, the pose of the dancers, blend into something meaningful, but before your mind can grab it, it's become random and confusing again. Your head tries to sort something out, make sense of something. The noise is getting to you. You want to scream, or throw yourself about with the dancers, something, anything!"[15] The experience is recreated on the sixth floor of the museum.

In addition to the premiere of the new galleries, the Warhol continued the anniversary festivities throughout the day with a community celebration that included "hands on art making and studio programs exploring Warhol's artistic practices in the Factory, the museum's studio," said Warchall. "The Factory is open to the public each day, but we created special activities for the 20th anniversary celebration. The museum's *Silver Clouds* installation is on view each day, but we brought the sculptures to our outdoor tent as well, allowing visitors to walk through the installation on their way to the event." Originally conceived in 1964, Warhol's *Silver Clouds* is a collection of helium-filled, pillow shaped "balloons" made of a shiny silver material called Scotchpak. Because of a proprietary combination of helium and air, the sculptures float around the room, and visitors can interact with them. Art Handler Matt DiClemente provided a behind-the-scenes look at taking care of the *Silver Clouds* exhibition on the museum's blog: "A Silver Cloud's lifecycle is chocked full of variables and varies greatly from balloon to balloon. Some balloons last a full seven days, while others don't make it past the inflation process. Other factors that affect a balloon's longevity include random mishaps, Clouds crashing into one another, valve malfunction, and patron interaction; the Clouds are actually quite delicate. One of the more surprising influences on the Silver Clouds are fluctuations in atmospheric pressure. Silver Clouds arrive at the museum bundled and folded in small boxes. Art handlers inflate them before the museum opens, and are changed out every Friday morning (or on an as needed basis). It takes approximately 3 minutes to inflate a new Cloud, and the new gallery holds 25 Clouds comfortably."[16]

Community Day also included a Youth Invasion Fashion Show, featuring the work of teenaged fashion designers, and a book signing with Bob Colacello, author of *Holy Terror: Andy Warhol Close Up*. A benefit auction was held in conjunction with the anniversary events, featuring work by artists who have been influenced by Warhol. The auction items were curated by Bob Colacello and Vito Schnabel, who said, "We chose these particular artists because we believe their work recognizes his influence and achievement while also moving beyond it to create art that is unique, exemplary, and of its own time. And we personally like and admire all of them."[17] The auction was administered through the online auction house Paddle8.

As part of the 20th anniversary celebration, the Warhol created an interactive digital timeline of the museum's history on its website. The timeline included descriptions of past exhibitions, events, and publications, as well as the 1996 flood that completely submerged the museum's underground level. Beneath the timeline, visitors were asked to tag their posts about the museum on Twitter and other social media with #warhol20 to "join the conversation."

Crailo State Historic Site, Rensselaer, New York

As the quadricentennial of the Hudson River Valley approached in 2009, Crailo State Historic Site seized the opportunity to reimagine itself with a host of initiatives related to the celebration. Although the site itself was not celebrating an anniversary, its location on the Hudson River and mission to preserve Colonial Dutch heritage was closely connected to the theme and purpose of the Hudson-Fulton-Champlain Quadricentennial Commission, created by New York Governor George Pataki in 2002. The introduction to the Spring 2009 edition of the *Hudson River Valley Review* describes the scope of the anniversary celebration:

> This is a momentous year in New York State and especially the Hudson River Valley. We are commemorating the 400th anniversary of the simultaneous explorations of Henry Hudson and Samuel de Champlain on the waterways that now bear their names, as well as the 200th anniversary of Robert Fulton's successful maiden steamboat voyage on the Hudson River. At the same time, we are celebrating the cultures that colonized this land— Native American, Dutch, and French—as well as the legacy of New York's Hudson-Fulton Tercentenary in 1909.

The celebration's purpose was far-reaching and included many community partners. With excitement building for local and regional history, historic site manager Heidi Hill knew it was the right time to launch her plan for the 1707 house museum. "I saw this opportunity as Crailo's one-and-only shot at moving from a quiet, forgotten historic site hidden in a residential street in Rensselaer, to a world class museum that was sought out by area residents and tourists from afar," she said.[18]

Crailo, meaning "Crow's Wood," was originally part of the estate of the van Rensselaer family. Over the years it was used as a family home, a boys' boarding school, and a church rectory. It was donated to New York State in 1924 and became a museum. Crailo's main exhibit had become dated, so it was at the top of Hill's list of objectives. She admits her plans were ambitious. "At first we thought we would just tweak the weak areas of the exhibit, but then realized that in order to make it a cohesive presentation and to introduce all the interactives we wanted, we would have to change it out wholesale," she said. "Money was an issue as this all went down during the economic downturn. We had a compelling story, however, and not only was our agency behind this, foundations and corporations were also excited about our project." The small staff of two full-time and two part-time/seasonal employees had big ideas to present to the regional administration. "They loved the ideas," said Hill, "but had doubts we would be able to accomplish all the research, writing, procuring the rights and reproductions for all the images we wanted, and generally keep on track with so many balls in the air. They kept us to a strict time frame and we met every deadline. It was high energy for a couple years straight."

The new exhibition would be called A Sweet and Alien Land: Colony of the Dutch in the Hudson River Valley. A focal point of the exhibition would be a short film that brought to life and joined together a historic court document and a Dutch-genre painting called *Keeping Order: A Fort Orange Court Record*. The court record is about a knife fight over a card game. "During the film, the actors pop off the canvas with the action," said Hill. "Both narrators are Dutch speakers so while spoken in English, the Dutch accent and inflections are there. At the end, the actors melt back into the painting. Visitors can choose just audio or closed caption and it is displayed next to a photo of the image (so you always have it for reference) and the full transcript is available in a card that can be picked up out of a holder."

According to Crailo's website, "The production, which took place near Pittsburgh, in a very cold studio, included a Dutch American, actors from local colleges, and a couple volunteers. Site staff were on hand to advise on 17th century Dutch mannerisms and costuming. While there were many tricky obstacles to overcome with the 17th century script, the most challenging aspect of the filming was the struggle to replicate the exact poses of the six actors to those of the characters within the painting." The two minute and forty-eight second film won two prestigious national awards: a CINE Golden Eagle Award and the CINE Golden Eagle Special Jury Prize for Best in Arts and Exhibits from the Council on International Non-theatrical Events.

The exhibition also included a section on archaeology, featuring an "interactive computer component that helps people understand how the historical record gets buried under many feet of earth," Hill said.

Hill accomplished most of the goals on her list, although a few projects remain to be tackled. "Reach high and know you won't achieve it all," she said, "but you will get most of what you aim for." In addition to the new permanent exhibition, Hill's plans for Crailo included the following:

- "Discover Dutch New Netherland Game Book" highlighting New Netherland and Native American/Dutch trade partners
- Restoration of the home's exterior

- New landscape look for the historic home
- New museum shop market place
- A fourteen-minute orientation film for the site
- Native American programming funded through a grant
- New exterior interpretive panels
- Develop new programming in partnership with the Albany Visitor Center

Goals they did not meet included installing a kayak and canoe dock in the Hudson River and connecting with the Half Moon, a replica seventeenth century Dutch ship.

All of the staff's hard work truly paid off. "Because of the initiatives we accomplished for 2009, the museum is really on the map now," said Hill. "We developed a great solid foundation for additional programming, new research, new exhibits that travel, and wider exposure to new audiences." Crailo saw an increase in visitation, especially people from the Netherlands, as well as invitations to speaking engagements, visits from scholars, and additional funding. The total price tag for all of their projects was $350,000. "We started with $25,000 in a mitigation fund that was received because of an energy plant going in in close proximity to the historic house's neighborhood," said Hill. They received $100,000 from a state fund called Heritage New York, as well as support from local foundations. Peebles Island, the headquarters of the Bureau of Historic Sites in Waterford, New York, provided technical services, such as exhibition design and fabrication, and staffing from curators, archeologists, and conservators. Peebles Island also funded the production of "Keeping Order: A Fort Orange Court Record."

"We had a terrific team at the site," Hill said, "and all were excited that Crailo was finally getting some attention." By aligning itself with the Hudson Quadricentennial, the site also had several marketing opportunities during other events. "We went in seventeenth-century Dutch costume to other Rensselaer city celebrations and the Albany Tulip Festival to share our news with broader audiences." Crailo is the only site in the Hudson Valley that focuses exclusively on interpreting the Colonial Dutch period.

An anniversary is the perfect time to maximize the impact of your projects. "Take advantage of the timing to make your story even more compelling," Hill said, adding that there is built-in motivation because an anniversary is a "drop dead deadline that must be met." She used her experience at Crailo to plan a second anniversary celebration at Schuyler Mansion, the other historic site she manages for New York State.

Historic New England, Boston, Massachusetts

Two exhibitions were highlights during Historic New England's centennial year in 2010. The organization was chosen to present the featured museum exhibition at the prestigious New York Winter Antiques Show in January 2010. "Our exhibition, titled *Colonial to Modern: A Century of Collection at Historic New England*, featured highlights from Historic New England's extensive collection that spans four centuries of decorative arts," said Diane Viera, executive vice president and chief operating officer. "This coveted opportunity to present the loan exhibition would be embraced in any year. The fact that 2010 was our centennial maximized the opportunity."[19]

A second exhibition for the centennial was designed to travel. "Historic New England offers traveling exhibitions for small and mid-sized museums on a range of topics," Viera said. "Typically these are panel exhibitions designed for maximum flexibility in smaller and non-standard exhibition venues. For the centennial, Historic New England developed *The Preservation Movement Then and Now* exhibition consisting of thirteen wall-hanging panels tracing the history of the preservation movement in New England, in which Historic New England's founder William Sumner Appleton played an important role. The exhibition included a panel template designed for easy use by venues to create their own customized fourteenth panel focused on important preservation stories in their communities. Six copies of *The Preservation Movement Then and Now* exhibition were created that traveled simultaneously to venues in all six New England states throughout the centennial year."

Historic New England also re-released a popular book for its centennial. "In 2000, Bulfinch Press published *Windows on the Past, Four Centuries of New England Homes*, a hard-cover book telling the stories of New England through the lives of those who lived at Historic New England's properties," Viera said. "After several years, the book was removed from Bulfinch's list. Historic New England acquired the rights and published an updated edition during the centennial year. Although published in 2010, the second edition of *Windows on the Past* did not 'celebrate' the centennial as we did not want the book to become dated. It was intended to have a long life and is still in use today."

Stan Hywet Hall and Gardens, Akron, Ohio

Built between 1912 and 1915, Stan Hywet was the home of Frank Seiberling, founder of the Goodyear Tire and Rubber Company. It is on par with the elaborate homes built by American industrial giants such as Vanderbilt and Rockefeller. The estate includes a 64,500-square-foot Tudor revival mansion, formal gardens, a carriage house, a gate lodge, and a conservatory. The Seiberling children donated the home to the Akron community as a museum in 1957.

To celebrate the 100th anniversary of the home's completion in 2015, Stan Hywet's staff began exploring ideas for outdoor exhibitions to feature throughout the grounds during the summer of 2013. Executive director Linda Conrad saw the floral sculpture exhibition Bloom! at Epcot Center at Disney World in 2014, featuring art glass by Craig Mitchell Smith. Since the mansion is known for its elaborate estate gardens, Bloom! was a perfect fit for Stan Hywet's centennial celebration.

"Our objectives were to celebrate the legacy of the Seiberling family while looking towards the next one hundred years of Stan Hywet's involvement in the Akron community," said Julie Frey, director of museum services.[20] The tag line for the year was "2nd Century in Bloom." General ideas were developed during strategic planning sessions for 2015, which took place in August 2014. Bloom! was already in development at that time.

Smith's elaborate glass sculptures are created using kiln-formed glass, with special techniques that emulate brushstrokes of paint. The exhibition was "flawless," according to Frey, and increased museum attendance and sparked exhibition-based programming. Many of the sculptures were inspired by Stan Hywet itself. According to the exhibition's brochure,

"Tudor Rose [was] installed in the Breakfast Room Garden and Butterflies of Northern Ohio feature[d] a kaleidoscope of local (glass) butterflies near the Butterfly Habitat." All of the thirty-two outdoor sculptures were for sale, ranging from $1,500 to $20,000. The purchase price included installation by the artist at a location of the buyer's choice at the end of the show. A gallery adjacent to the admissions office in the Carriage House featured smaller interior tabletop and wall-mounted pieces that were also for sale.

The floral works inspired a series of tours called Twilight and Flashlights on Thursday and Friday nights for three weeks in August and September. Visitors were invited to walk the grounds for an exclusive evening tour, where the floral sculptures were specially up-lit for the occasion. The event included food and drink, as well as live music. "We added more weeks to Twilight and Flashlights as the popularity seemed to grow as the event continued," said Frey. The success of these evenings has inspired the staff to explore similar events in the future.

New Orleans Museum of Art, New Orleans, Louisiana

Commemorating tragedies in our past can be a difficult task for museums and historic sites. Although the subject matter may be complicated to handle emotionally, it does not seem right to let an anniversary of a death or natural disaster pass without some kind of acknowledgement. Russell Lord, Freeman Family Curator of Photographs at the New Orleans Museum of Art, curated an exhibition with a unique perspective to commemorate the 10th anniversary of Hurricane Katrina:

> To begin, the word "celebrate" was one that we deliberately avoided in conceiving our exhibit "Ten Years Gone." Instead, we settled on "commemorate" as a more appropriate term to denote the recognition of a tragedy (Hurricane Katrina and its aftermath). We decided to put together an exhibition to mark the anniversary because we knew that there would be a large number of programs throughout New Orleans that directly referenced the flooding, the devastation, etc., and as the major art museum of the Gulf South, we believed that we could and should offer a different experience. It was our goal, therefore, to provide our visitors with a look at how some artists have chosen to memorialize other events, some good, some bad, in their own lives. By pulling together a group of profound works, we hoped to demonstrate that there are many ways, some direct, some more abstract, to reflect on the events in our lives. We decided finally to look for works that focused on four themes that are present in any anniversary consideration: memory, transformation, loss, and the passage of time. Some of the works were made in response to Katrina, but most were not, offering a broad look at human responses to life altering events.[21]

Lord conceptualized the exhibit two years in advance. "Many of my ideas came from studio visits with local artists, conversations with international artists, scholars, and curators," he said. "I established the idea of focusing on the four themes about a year and a half before the opening of the exhibition. I then pursued works that emphasized those themes for about a year and worked to bring those works to New Orleans to present here at NOMA."

Lord chose six artists for the exhibition. "They were all wonderful, with deeply personal, but relevant work that prompted a wide range of responses, from disbelief and frustration to admiration, and the powerfully emotional. We received amazing and wonderful comments as well as disparaging remarks on both our visitor survey and in the local press. I think that the show resonated strongly, and provoked both positive and negative responses." The exhibition was unique because it brought together works that had never been presented together, for a very short run. "Like the event it commemorated, it existed for a moment, and now is already beginning to exist only as a memory," he said.

In a review published in the *The New Orleans Advocate*, John d'Addario wrote,

> As the 10th anniversary of Hurricane Katrina approaches, expect to see media outlets and cultural institutions trotting out images of the storm and its aftermath that are likely all-too-indelibly seared on your memory already: houses, neighborhoods and lives destroyed by the floodwaters, National Guard markings inscribed like hieroglyphs on every building still standing. But the New Orleans Museum of Art is marking the occasion with a show that barely references Katrina directly at all—and is all the more engaging and powerful as a result. . . . Work by six contemporary artists exploring what Lord identifies as the four themes of the show—the passage of time, memory, loss and transformation—is used in consistently surprising ways both to reflect on the circumstances of how those concepts played out in post-Katrina New Orleans over the last decade, and to remind us how they transcend the particulars of time and place.[22]

One of the works that more directly addressed Katrina was a series of sculptures called Water Markers by Dawn Dedeaux. According to her website, these works feature "a series of images of water embedded within thick polished slabs of acrylic. The sculptures vary in height and width, and appear to contain real water samples that generate a ripple of shadow against the wall. The series refers directly to the height of flood water levels reached in neighborhoods up and down the river and canals following the levee breach. The titles of the works are drawn from overheard conversational descriptions of the flood waters, for example *Nearly Eight Feet of Water, It Topped Over Seven*, and *Had Over Five.*" Some of Dedeaux's pieces were displayed in the museum's Great Hall, but others were placed throughout other galleries, near works that also incorporate the theme of water. "I think the decision to spread the exhibition throughout the museum was one of the best decisions," said Lord. "It forced people to think about these issues in the context of other works of art from the museum's permanent collection, which I think helped people see the relevance of a museum's mission to preserve history and memory."

Christopher Saucedo's painting *World Trade Center in a Cloud* references the same human emotions through the horror of a different tragedy. Saucedo's brother was a firefighter who lost his life in the aftermath of the terrorist attacks on the World Trade Center on 9/11. The artist's work is also influenced by living through Hurricane Katrina as a resident of New Orleans, and later Super Storm Sandy when he moved back to his native New York. Having endured three of the worst tragedies in modern American history, his art helped him process his sense of loss. In *World Trade Center in a Cloud*, Saucedo painted the unmistakable silhouette of the Twin Towers in a wispy white against a backdrop of brilliant blue.

Lord told NPR imagining the World Trade Center as clouds makes something weighty feel weightless and ethereal. "And, of course, the blue paper is incredibly evocative," he said, "because we all remember the blue of the sky that day—that incredibly beautiful day against which all of these unbelievable things unfolded."

NOMA partnered with its local NPR station WWNO to bring something called the Listening Post to the museum. "It is a recording station that includes a group of questions so visitors can answer the questions and record their responses," Lord said. "The questions were based around people's experiences of anniversaries and some of their responses were aired on the NPR station. I thought that was an excellent idea that I credit to NOMA's librarian Sheila Cork, who first proposed it as tie in."

Because the exhibition was not specifically about Katrina itself, Lord expected it to be controversial. "However, I was surprised that despite our efforts to highlight and foreground that the show was not about Katrina, people still arrived at the museum expecting to see more work about destruction, etc." he said. "I think this show helped me to come to terms with how polarizing a show can be, no matter how hard you work to make it universally appealing." For any museum trying to interpret a tragic event through a different lens, Lord has some advice: "Be conscious of the deep feelings that may surround the event, be open to looking at things differently, and be willing to be controversial, as long as that controversy doesn't disparage anyone or infringe upon the rights of others," he said.

South Bend 150, South Bend, Indiana

To celebrate its sesquicentennial in 2015, South Bend 150 (SB150) wanted to fund a lasting tribute to the celebration of this significant anniversary that would outlive the festivities that year. River Lights, a new public art installation by renowned artist Robert Shakespeare, fulfilled that goal. According to Downtown South Bend, the sculpture "transforms the St. Joseph River into a canvas of living art. Color splashes from two interactive light sculptures on either side of the river, amplifying the majestic cascade of water, joined with a third sculpture highlighting the exquisite Keeper of the Fire statue, and symbolically uniting the two sides of the river. There are sensors built into the light pillars that detect motion, prompting the lights to change color or alter their pattern as a result of people moving nearby. Visitors can send a flow of colored lights across the river, and visitors on the other side can send a flow of color back." The light sculpture comes on thirty minutes before sunset and stays on throughout the night, although the interactive feature shuts off at midnight.

Planning for River Lights began in 2012. Organizers wanted to highlight the historic riverfront a way to revitalize the downtown area. In July they met with Shakespeare, a lighting designer who specializes in theater lighting and "dramatic architectural designs." In August the city installed a hydroelectric turbine that would provide green energy to power River Lights. During that month, Shakespeare also held several meetings with stakeholders in the city to discuss the project in detail. By the end of 2012, the Community Foundation of St. Joseph County had awarded a two-year special project grant for River Lights.

In January 2013, Shakespeare returned to South Bend to conduct a lighting test to see how vibrant the colors would be. A few months later, he added bridge lighting to his design.

River Lights, a new public art installation by renowned artist Robert Shakespeare, provided the city of South Bend, Indiana, with a permanent remembrance of its sesquicentennial celebration. Alexandria Lechlitner, Visit South Bend Mishawaka.

Also that year Leadership South Bend adopted River Lights as their class project, providing assistance with logistics, landscaping, and finalization of the project, as well as support for the unveiling event during Birthday Weekend. River Lights became an official SB150 project in February 2014.

Shakespeare began offsite construction in November 2014. In January 2015, he returned to South Bend to participate in the kickoff celebration of SB150, giving a talk about River Lights at an artist reception in his honor. The first shipment of pieces and parts of the sculpture arrived in late February 2015. Local volunteers, engineers, and electrical workers spent the next months assisting in the installation. River Lights debuted on May 22, the first night of the SB150's signature event, Birthday Weekend.

Creating an outdoor sculpture on the riverfront provides many benefits to a community. Downtown South Bend's website articulates the many ways in which a revitalized riverfront is a good thing for the entire community (content was created for the website by Kylie Carter, SB150 program coordinator; Kara Kelly, director of communications, Office of the Mayor, City of South Bend; Aaron Perri, executive director for Downtown South Bend, Inc., and lead organizer for SB150):[23]

Celebrates the Historical and Future Importance of the River
The St. Joseph River is the foundation upon which this city was built. It had early historical significance to both the Native Americans in this region for transportation and

agriculture, and also to the early European settlers as an important part of the fur trade route. Many years later the river powered the peak manufacturing industries that made South Bend prosper. Today, the river is being rediscovered as a source of energy and economic development.

Complements Existing Businesses

The Century Center, South Bend Museum of Art, Seitz Park, East Bank Emporium Restaurant & Shops, and the DoubleTree by Hilton are just some of the existing businesses that would see an immediate and direct impact by an invigorated, dynamic riverfront. Many other businesses in the downtown would benefit from this project that will both stabilize and enhance the economy of this corridor while increasing adjacent property values.

Spurs Public and Private Projects/Investments

The re-routing of two-way streets, a concentrated effort to revive the river walk, a focus on Howard Park revitalization, the newly created Municipal Riverfront Development District, the East Bank Village Master Plan and Howard Park Neighborhood Association plans all serve to benefit from this project, as do private housing and commercial development initiatives along the riverfront.

Attracts Visitors

River Lights is a project that will garner local, regional, and national attention. This installation will be something that will instantly attract local visitors on a consistent basis. Artist Rob Shakespeare reports that similar projects have provoked a "must-see" type sentiment for any visitors to the area. It is not difficult to imagine folks across the region asking, "Have you seen what 'they' did to the riverfront in downtown South Bend?"

Creates a Community Identity/Sense of Place

Comparable projects such as Bloomington, Indiana's "Light Totem" and Providence, Rhode Island's "Water Fire" have generated a groundswell of support from and enthusiasm for their local communities. Creating a true sense of place in a given environment, these community-galvanizing projects are the types of things for which South Bend yearns.

Preserves Public Safety

Preserving the safety of the downtown is a constant goal and one that is synonymous with development potential. A vibrant riverfront will contribute to that end. River Lights would create an environment that reclaims the riverfront from the shadows of night and provide yet another safe nighttime attraction for downtown.

Incites Geographic Development

The project area is a prime development corridor and an important geographic node to incite, complete, and complement other development projects throughout the city. First and foremost, this project would serve to connect both the east and west sides of the river, which are historically divided at many levels. This is also a high-profile link in the chain that connects downtown to the activity to the north east (East Bank Village, St. Joseph High School, Eddy Street Developments, and Notre Dame), to the south (Dining and Arts District, Coveleski Stadium, Renaissance District, and Ignition Park), to the north (Memorial Hospital), and to the west (West Washington, Near Northwest Neighborhood and Lincolnway to the Airport).

Supports Arts and Culture

The artistic nature of this lighting project will outwardly and boldly highlight South Bend as a community committed to arts and culture. The economic engines associated with arts and culture initiatives have been widely documented. Terms such as "creative economy," "creative class," and "cultural economy" are becoming more common, and the use of terminology linking culture and the economy indicates recognition of the connections among the fields of planning, economic development, and arts and culture. The American Planning Association recently released an article titled "How the Arts and Culture Sector Catalyzes Economic Vitality." The article explains how "the activities of the arts and culture sector and local economic vitality are connected in many ways. Arts, culture, and creativity can:

- improve a community's competitive edge
- create a foundation for defining a sense of place
- attract new and visiting populations
- contribute to the development of a skilled workforce."

Recreation

The backdrop of this lighting installation will immediately cement the downtown riverfront as a prime destination for special events of all varieties. It will also serve to enhance the popularity of current events which utilize the river, such as the Seitz & Sounds (the Seitz Park summer concert series), whitewater events on the East Race and special events at the Century Center Island. This project will also serve to recognize our river as a form of recreation for runners, walkers, bikers and boaters alike. Integrated into this venture is a scalability that could include various, complementary lighting installations along the entire South Bend river walk.

Perpetuates Green Initiatives

Blending a hydroelectric power source with modern lighting technology (designed to minimize light pollution) is an excellent way to educate our community on the City of South Bend's ongoing green initiatives which are broad and complex. It is also a tool to powerfully illustrate the advanced nature of our city.

A sculpture such as River Lights in a city or town with a waterway would provide all of these benefits, many of which are unique to your community.

In addition to the debut of River Lights, SB150 wanted to construct an outdoor temporary exhibition that would highlight 150 years of South Bend's history for Birthday Week-

The 150th anniversary of South Bend, Indiana, featured an outdoor exhibition covering the city's history that was on view during the Birthday Weekend celebration. Alexandria Lechlitner, Visit South Bend Mishawaka.

end. Originally conceptualized as Memory Lane, the exhibition was ultimately titled South Bend Drive. The unique nature of the venue, coupled with the large amount of material to cover, proved to be challenging. "A birthday weekend celebration was not the best place to impart an academic, in-depth, comprehensive history of the city, with an expected visitation of over fifty thousand people and a lot of events competing for attention," said George Garner, curator at Indiana University South Bend Civil Rights Heritage Center, who was in charge of the exhibition. "Even though we had virtually an entire city block, the space was in fact quite limited. The directive was to make it 'big,' thus very large panels (twenty feet wide by eight feet tall) with limited text was the best way to quickly and easily share as much of our story as possible."[24] The exhibition panels were printed on mesh vinyl with grommets every twelve inches, which were attached via zip ties to street sign posts installed by city workers for the exhibition. It was reinstalled in two additional venues after Birthday Weekend, so the organizers got some extra mileage out of the panels.

The history of the city itself dictated decisions about what was "in" and what was "out." "Looking at our 150 years, a pattern emerged of different eras and different waves of people coming in and contributing," said Garner. "That was a logical place to decide what was 'in.' A brief history of the main indigenous culture displaced by European contact, the first European "pioneer" who began transforming the area, a few of the giant businesses that emerged here, the waves of new immigrants who came and contributed (especially including African Americans coming as part of the Great Migration and the city practicing segregation as a direct result of that), the radical changes that occurred as industry transformed and left the area, and the new waves of Latino immigrants now adding vibrancy and life to our city."

When conceptualizing the idea, Garner realized an exhibition mounted in a festival setting is much different than what you would expect to see in a museum gallery. "I knew that an in-depth exploration of every era, every wave of new cultures, or every contributor was impossible," he said. "If guests left with only a brief outline of how our city evolved, I felt the project was successful. I wrote it accordingly, molding text so guests could read only titles, brief highlights, or a short paragraph and still understand something from it, as well as choosing photographs that conveyed the same message without words, such as a small log cabin, a large factory, a city building being torn down, etc." (See Appendix D: SB150 Brief Book.)

Although a streamlined approach was appropriate for the venue, Garner did not "water down" South Bend's history. "I felt it was important not to pull any punches or shy away from difficult histories, even within this setting," he said. "For example, one paragraph was entitled 'Separate, but Not Equal,' showing when South Bend practiced racial segregation. We addressed how European contact displaced the indigenous cultures that had lived here for centuries. Another was entitled 'Nuevos Poblaciones,' showing how people of Latino descent are moving into our area and becoming the latest wave of immigrants to add to our city."

Garner assembled a "review board" of local museum staff and community members to correct any mistakes, as well as to add legitimacy to the project. "Their charge was to review drafts of the brief book and offer feedback," he said, "as well as to be a resource to me when I was looking for photographs. Between the four museums/historical organizations listed—Civil Rights Heritage Center (CRHC), the History Museum, Historic Preservation Commission of South Bend and St. Joseph County, and the Studebaker National Museum—as well as the partnership between CRHC and the St. Joseph County Public Library to develop Michiana Memory, an online repository of South Bend area history, we had access to the best historic photographs in existence. It was a great opportunity to find photographs that haven't already been used a dozen times in other projects."

In addition to the exhibition, the historical section of Birthday Weekend included a virtual reality tour of downtown South Bend, circa 1925, developed by the University of Notre Dame, using Oculus Rift glasses. The display also featured some examples of the city's industrial past, such as Oliver Tractors and Studebaker cars, and historic reenactors, including a woman dressed as a player from the South Bend Blue Sox of the All American Girls Professional Baseball League.

Intrepid Sea, Air and Space Museum, New York, New York

With the 40th anniversary of the end of the Vietnam War approaching in 2015, the Intrepid Sea, Air and Space Museum decided to seize the opportunity to reinterpret its exhibitions and programming to include more about that era of the aircraft carrier's history. *Intrepid* served from World War II through the mid-1970s, actually spending more time in Vietnam, but the museum focused mostly on its World War II heritage. The staff had always wanted to do a better job telling this part of *Intrepid's* story. "As we were looking at the calendar, we realized this was a good time to tap into the general moment of reflection

The Intrepid Sea, Air & Space Museum used the 40th anniversary of the end of the Vietnam War to create an exhibition called On the Line, exploring the roll *Intrepid* played during that period of its history. Intrepid Sea, Air & Space Museum, New York, New York.

Intrepid Sea, Air & Space Museum, New York, New York.

about Vietnam," said Jessica Williams, curator of history and collections.[25] *On the Line: Intrepid and the Vietnam War* opened in October 2015.

The entire museum is located on the aircraft carrier itself, including staff offices. The museum complex also includes the submarine *Growler*, the space shuttle *Enterprise*, and a British Airways Concorde, all located off-ship but within the Museum Complex. Before this project was launched, there was a chronological permanent exhibition covering the history of the ship that covered Vietnam, but staff wanted to do more. In general, the public does not consider the naval aspect of the war, which played a large part in operations.

"We started planning in the spring of 2014," Williams said. "The team involved met weekly, including the senior vice president in charge of exhibitions, education, and public programming; two curators; an outside guest curator; education; and exhibit design." The team spent a lot of time thinking about how to present material in a balanced way, since the subject is intensely emotional and complicated. This was the first time the Intrepid Museum had hired a guest curator, but the staff felt it was important to have an objective historian who could weigh in on the controversial aspects of the topic. Through modern technology it was possible to keep in touch with a staff member working off site, but in the future they will consider creating an office space for a contracted employee. The guest curator model worked so well, they plan to utilize it for future exhibition development.

The biggest challenge with an exhibition of this scope is deciding what to include and what to leave out. The war in Vietnam is a very large topic, with many pieces and parts that are potentially controversial to various audiences. The team went back and forth between a micro and a macro approach to the subject, ultimately using *Intrepid* as a lens through which to view the bigger picture. The exhibition focuses on the experiences of *Intrepid* and its crew during its three tours of duty in Vietnam between 1966 and 1969. The Intrepid Museum's description of the exhibition on its website focuses on the sense of place it offers, which is a unique visitor experience because it is both a museum and a historic site. "Set within the very spaces where men lived and served, the exhibition focuses on the experiences of *Intrepid* and its crew 'on the line'—the periods when the ship was active in the Gulf of Tonkin, launching aircraft for missions over mainland Vietnam. This localized history serves as the starting point for understanding the larger historical landscape, including the Cold War, Operation Rolling Thunder and protests at home."[26]

The *Intrepid* has a large living history component comprised of former crew members, so the team reached out to them to collect their stories and artifacts. "A lot of them had not been asked about their own stories," Williams said. "We collected a lot of oral histories, which will be a huge resource for future interpretation. A component of the exhibition is a wall of digital photo frames featuring then and now photos from crew members. It was moving to see the faces of these guys, how baby faced they were. And now 40 years have passed." The team was not prepared for all of the interest in this project. "Our community still feels so close to this ship," Williams said. The response to their call for material was so large, they created a separate email inbox for collecting information.

According to a press release announcing the opening of the exhibition, "Over 50 artifacts are included in the exhibition, including a handwritten calendar counting down the days until the crew members' return home, letters to loved ones written on the ship, items showing the unrest and protests at home, an anti-aircraft gun used by North Vietnamese forces, and an A-4B Skyhawk that flew from *Intrepid* during the war and is painted exactly as it was during the 1966 deployment."[27] *On the Line* includes some of the more controversial aspects of *Intrepid's* involvement in Vietnam as well. "In 1967, four *Intrepid* crew members—Craig Anderson, Richard Bailey, John Barilla and Michael Lindner—deserted while the ship was on leave in Japan. Their decision was motivated by a desire to protest the United States' military policy in Vietnam."

Modern scientific advances in DNA testing are also part of the exhibition's narrative. On August 1, 1968, Lieutenant Edward J. "Barney" Broms was shot down during a strike mission on Dong Dun, North Vietnam, as part of Operation Rolling Thunder. He was declared missing in action at the time. In 1993 American investigators found remains near a crash site that likely belonged to Broms, but DNA testing at the time could not confirm his identity. Finally in 2011 technology made it possible to positively identify the remains through a DNA match with Broms's sister.

With the installation of the exhibition came new opportunities for tours, public programming, and educational experiences for students and teachers. This new guided tour and tour guide talk are listed on the Intrepid Museum's website:[28]

GUIDED TOUR
ROLLING THUNDER: INTREPID IN VIETNAM 1966–1969
In April 1966, *Intrepid* was the American aircraft carrier that seemed least likely to play an attack role in Vietnam. More than 20 years old and incapable of operating the U.S. Navy's heavier and more sophisticated aircraft, the ship was technologically and materially unprepared for much of what it would be asked to face. Learn how the crew of *Intrepid* overcame these challenges during the ship's three tours of duty in the Vietnam War. This tour will run twice daily, at 10:30am and 2:30pm.

TOUR GUIDE TALK
ONE DAY IN VIETNAM: OCTOBER 9, 1966
The day-to-day operations and stories of the Vietnam War often get lost in the big picture. Delve into one particular day in *Intrepid's* service to gain a better understanding of the U.S. Navy's role in the war and the complexity of operations in North Vietnam. Hear about the events of October 9, 1966, and the people that experienced them, including Lt. Tom Patton, who shot down a jet-powered MiG-17 from his propeller-driven airplane. This Tour Guide Talk, offered daily in hangar 1, is open to the public and free with admission to the Museum. Ask at the Information Desk for exact times.

On the Line also inspired a public program on posttraumatic stress disorder, which connects the Vietnam era to contemporary issues surrounding current conflicts in the Middle East:

MEMORY, TRAUMA AND RESILIENCE
DATE: NOVEMBER 18, 2015
Four decades after the Vietnam War, 11 percent of veterans still suffer from posttraumatic stress, and new research suggests that for some people, this condition is unlikely to go away. Learn about new research on memory and trauma in this moderated panel fea-

turing Joseph LeDoux, Henry and Lucy Moses, Professor of Science at New York University (NYU) and director of the Emotional Brain Institute at NYU; George Bonanno, professor of clinical psychology and director of the Loss, Trauma, and Emotion Lab, Teachers College, Columbia University; Charles Marmar, chair of the Department of Psychiatry at NYU Langone Medical Center and director of the Steven and Alexandra Cohen Veterans Center and Military Family Clinic; and Daniela Schiller, assistant professor of psychiatry and neuroscience and head of the Schiller Laboratory of Affective Neuroscience at the Icahn School of Medicine at Mount Sinai. BBC journalist and author Kim Ghattas, who grew up on the front lines of Lebanon's civil war, will serve as moderator.

A new school program, geared toward students in grades 7–12, focused on the new exhibition as well: "Students explore the exhibition *On the Line:* Intrepid *and the Vietnam War*. Working in small groups, they examine and analyze Vietnam War–era objects and primary source documents from the Museum's collection and use these elements to 'curate' their own mini-exhibition narratives."[29] The education department also designed a professional development experience for middle school and high school teachers:

PROFESSIONAL DEVELOPMENT FOR EDUCATORS
ON THE LINE: INTREPID AND THE VIETNAM WAR
DATES: MONDAY, AUGUST 3–SATURDAY, AUGUST 8, 2015 (36 HOURS)
AUDIENCE: SOCIAL STUDIES AND HISTORY TEACHERS, GRADES 7–12
CREDIT: P CREDIT, AWARDED THROUGH NEW YORK CITY DEPARTMENT OF EDUCATION
This course provided middle and high school teachers with resources from the Intrepid Museum and expose them to the diversity of scholarship and debate on the Vietnam War. The course will deepen their understanding of the conflict and increase confidence in their ability to explore the subject thoroughly, critically and engagingly.

Teachers worked with expert scholars and Museum staff. The course will integrate primary sources such as letters, photographs, oral histories and other ephemera, along with the National Historic Landmark Intrepid, so that teachers gain skills, content knowledge and confidence using primary sources in planning, teaching and assessing standards-based instruction on the Vietnam War. This course is open only to New York City Department of Education teachers. There is a $75 fee, in addition to the DOE course fee, to take this 36-hour, three-credit course.

The success of *On the Line* has inspired the Intrepid Museum's staff to look ahead at other anniversaries to reimagine programming and exhibitions on other related topics. For example, the submarine *Growler* will be having a commissioning anniversary soon. "It is a very cool, immersive experience," said Williams, but it hasn't had the level of interpretation that it could have. So we're looking ahead to that." Anniversaries provide a focal point for museums to harness interest of a particular place in time. "Hopefully you can capture the visitors' interest in your particular story by taking advantage of publicity that you're not necessarily generating on your own," she said.

In fact, a previous anniversary inspired the approach the staff took when telling the story of Vietnam. "In 2013 we celebrated the 70th anniversary of *Intrepid's* commissioning," Williams said. "We had a homecoming weekend and reunion for former crew members. Nearly three hundred former crew members came, including sixteen from the first crew in 1943 who were in their eighties. Some of the World War II veterans had not been back on board the ship since they left. It was amazing, and at that moment we realized it was the last time we would be able to get a significant number of World War II veterans here." That anniversary kicked off the oral history project that ultimately led to the treasure trove of information on which *On the Line* is based. "One of the things we think about a lot is the ship doesn't do anything without the people," Williams said. "We needed to seize that anniversary to make that connection."

Chesapeake Bay Maritime Museum, St. Michaels, Maryland

To celebrate its 50th anniversary, the Chesapeake Bay Maritime Museum developed an exhibition called *A Broad Reach: 50 Years of Collecting*, featuring fifty outstanding artifacts from the museum's permanent collection. As Chesapeake Bay Maritime Museum president Kristen Greenaway told the *Star-Democrat*, the popular exhibition's run is limited. "The public's response to this exhibition has been outstanding. It's a rare opportunity to see fifty outstanding highlights from our collection, and this winter gives a great opportunity to visit us and take it all in, before we put our white gloves back on and meticulously store them all away."[30] Although the exhibition was designed as a temporary installation, it has been converted into a permanent digital exhibition that will live on long after the 50th anniversary festivities have ended.

The Chesapeake Bay Maritime Museum was founded in 1965 in response to the general feeling that times were changing and certain aspects of local culture were disappearing. What began as a repository of family heirlooms that helped document the region's past has become a compelling collection of artifacts, running the gamut from "humble to splendid," according to the exhibition's introduction.

In a press release, chief curatopr Pete Lesher described how selections were made for inclusion in the exhibition: "*A Broad Reach* reflects on the rich collections of the first half-century of this museum's history. In selecting these objects, we looked for those that not only have the richest stories to tell, but also those that are beautiful. Any list is a compromise, leaving out favorite items for some. The gaps in such a list further suggest that our work as a collecting institution is far from done; there are so many more stories out there to collect. And as the coming years unfold, new stories will emerge that we will need to preserve for the next generation who will come to appreciate the Chesapeake Bay and its vibrant heritage."[31] Highlights of the exhibition include the following:

- 16mm film clips documenting the last days of steamship service in the region in the late 1920s
- A fire ax from the steamboat City of Baltimore, which survived the fire that destroyed the boat in 1937
- A 450-pound figurehead from the schooner *Freedom*, which was used by the U.S. Naval Academy to train midshipmen in ship handling

- A late nineteenth-century pie safe featuring punched tin plate panels in a sailboat design
- An oil painting by Herman Herzog titled *Evening at Oxford*, depicting the height of the seafood industry, circa 1880
- An image of the buyboat *Winnie Estelle*, which served as a middleman between the fishing boats and city markets or large seafood packing houses (The *Winnie Estelle* itself is part of the museum's in water fleet and is available for rides.)
- A color lithograph poster advertising the Bon Ton Annapolis and West River Family Excursions, circa 1920
- A rare tin can from the Wild Duck Brand Raw Oysters, circa 1920
- A lithograph titled "Crab Pickers at St. Michaels" by Ruth Starr Rose, depicting the African American wives of the watermen who worked long hours processing crab
- A sail makers bench, sewing machine, and tools, circa 1946

A limited-edition, full-color hardcover commemorative exhibition catalog was also pro-duced. A few weeks before the exhibition closed, the museum hosted a free Members Night to catch a last look at *A Broad Reach*. Chief curator Pete Lesher led a tour, sharing the stories behind each artifact. The event quickly filled to capacity.

George Washington's Mt. Vernon, Mt. Vernon, Virginia

In 1999, Mount Vernon commemorated the bicentennial of George Washington's death, which was the biggest milestone the museum had seen in decades. One of the projects staff worked on was a large-scale traveling exhibition called *Treasures of Mount Vernon: George Washington Revealed*. "Our objective was not so much to focus on George Washington's death, but to celebrate his life and accomplishments, and to remind the public about them," said Mary V. Thompson, research specialist.[32] She came up with the idea for the traveling exhibit a few years before the bicentennial. "I recall saying I'll probably hate myself in the morning for saying this, but I think a traveling exhibition would be a great way to reach people who can't come to us." Launching a major traveling exhibition was a huge under-taking for the staff, so the museum hired the Washington, DC, firm Miles, Friedburg, and Molinaroli to design it. "None of us working on the exhibition had ever done a traveling show before and to start with something this big and important would not have been pos-sible without a lot of handholding on their part," said Thompson. The exhibition opened in late 1998 and traveled to five cities—New York, Los Angeles, Richmond, Atlanta, and Chicago—over the next eighteen months. Among the 190 items included were love letters to Martha, spurs Washington wore during the Revolution, and a dressing gown he may have worn during the brief illness that ultimately killed him.

An article in *Style Weekly*, published while the exhibition was on view at the Virginia Historical Society in Richmond, describes its appeal:

For good or ill, media-age presidents have been photographed routinely in relaxed mo-ments. What better captured FDR than shots of him grinning confidently with a cigarette clamped between his teeth? Or pictures of Jimmy Carter's toothy smile that betrayed a steely determination?

George Washington's life, of course, predated cameras: He died in 1799. And no portrait painter dared to depict the revered father of our country with lips apart. He is always shown stalwart and determined, even grim. Therefore, it is startling to wander through the elegant, softly lit galleries of the Virginia Historical Society and be confronted by the first president's false teeth—brownish stains and all, for heaven's sake, under carefully set lighting in a custom-made display case. Bizarre.

And if the exhibition's major aim is to de-mythicize the surveyor, soldier, gentleman-farmer and national founding political figure—to pull him off the dollar bill—this show succeeds. On the 200th anniversary of his death, the keepers of his beloved Mount Vernon, with support from Ford Motor Co., have mounted a handsome touring exhibition, rich with spectacular furniture, clothing, personal effects, maps, letters and period pictures.[33]

The exhibition's sections included the Man Behind the Myth, the Presence of Washington, Venturing Forth, the Pleasure of His Company, On His Own Farm, and Getting a Touch of Him. A one-inch scale, ten-foot by eight-foot "Mount Vernon in Miniature" also traveled with the exhibition. It took four years and $400,000 to build the model.

The publicity generated by the traveling exhibition and other bicentennial events that year translated to staggering admission numbers. "Visitation at Mount Vernon soared," said Thompson, "reaching 1,115,843 people, the highest level of visitation since the nation's bicentennial in 1976. In addition, 297,916 students came to Mount Vernon, the highest number ever. The 1999 bicentennial issue of Mount Vernon Handbook sold 61,000 copies in that year alone. The New York Historical Society saw a 368 percent increase in visitation during the time it was hosting *Treasures from Mount Vernon*. Mount Vernon's two websites recorded 1,900,000 hits in February 1999."

The bicentennial also produced several new books. "There were a number of publications, which Mount Vernon either published themselves or did in cooperation with other institutions," Thompson said. "We did a special edition of the *Mount Vernon Handbook*, as well as a book on the gardens, *George Washington's Gardens at Mount Vernon: Landscape of the Inner Man*, by Mac Griswold, and a coffee-table book on *George Washington's Mount Vernon*, which was edited by Wendell Garrett. We also republished Marcus Cunliffe's *George Washington: Man and Monument* and worked with the Society of the Cincinnati to publish a textbook entitled *Why America is Free*."

Morris-Jumel Mansion, Manhattan, New York

Historic house museums are often challenged to come up with ways to attract new audiences and to reimagine spaces that change very little over time. One way to shake things up is a modern art exhibition installation. In 2015, the Morris-Jumel Mansion celebrated its 250th anniversary with an exhibition titled *Colonial Arrangements*. It "showcased the work of British artist Yinka Shonibare," said Carol Ward, executive director. "It included recent

The exhibition Colonial Arrangements at the Morris-Jumel Mansion juxtaposed a 250 year-old historic house with the modern art of British artist Yinka Shonibare. Photo by Trish Mayo, courtesy of the Morris-Jumel Mansion.

Colonial Arrangements. Photo by Trish Mayo, courtesy of the Morris-Jumel Mansion.

works plus one work the museum specifically commissioned him to do about the longest resident of the mansion, Eliza Jumel. It was mounted throughout the museum in our various period rooms. Each piece was carefully selected to create a dialog between the historic topics of the museum and his contemporary works."[34]

Shonibare's work is rather startling against the backdrop of a 250 year-old house. But that was the point. According to an article at Art Fix Daily, "Set within the Mansion's well-appointed interiors, Shonibare's work elucidates, vivifies, and examines Morris-Jumel's multi-layered history, which spans the colonial period to the present. . . . Shonibare's art explores identity, race, gender and the cross-pollination of cultures through the use of life-sized mannequins adorned in period costumes rendered in Dutch wax fabric (the colorful, Indonesian textile introduced to Africa by British and Dutch merchant-colonizers)."[35] The headless figures, often mounted in odd positions, provided a layer of interpretation to the Mansion that was innovative and exciting.

Rutherford B. Hayes Presidential Library and Museums, Fremont, Ohio

One of the initiatives identified as a centennial project at the Rutherford B. Hayes Presidential Library and Museums was a complete redesign of the permanent exhibitions. Originally installed in 1968, the space had changed very little over the years. In fact, executive director Christie Weininger's modern color photographs of the exhibits were almost identical to the black and white images in the museum's archives.

"When they were installed, the exhibits were cutting edge," Weininger said. "Some people were attached to them, and there were parts that I hated to see go. Some of the backgrounds in the cases had been hand painted, which was very charming."[36] In response to some of the comments from people who were sad to see the exhibits go, the staff decided to throw a "going away party," where people could come and say goodbye to the old exhibits. As plans evolved, they decided to make it a 1968-themed party. Many of the 150 guests came in costume. "There was tie dye and peace signs and flowers in their hair," Weininger said. "We had fondue and Jell-O mold salads. People had a great time."

Renderings of the new exhibits were displayed at the party so guests could see what was planned for the space. Although they realized how much work had gone into the original exhibits, they were very much a product of their times. "In 1968, when you think of the type of history that was taught then, it was fact-based," Weininger said. "They didn't talk much about the servants or Lucy. It was all about Hayes." The old exhibits provided very little context about the times in which Hayes lived, how his decisions shaped the nation, and what the contemporary issues were.

"The story we're telling now is a lot more human," Weininger said. The facts that were in the previous exhibition have found their way into the new one, but visitors now see a much more in-depth presentation of those facts. Since Hayes kept a diary for most of his life, there is plenty of information regarding his anguish over a decision or what made him happy. While the previous exhibition about the First Lady featured her dresses and information about her children, the new exhibit talks about her volunteer work with wounded soldiers during the Civil War, for example, and how she would come home each night sobbing at the horrors she had seen during the day. "The new exhibits tell a more compelling story about Rutherford and Lucy Hayes, what they worried about, what they felt were solutions to society's problems and what they wanted to accomplish," Weininger said.

The new exhibition also places Hayes within the context of his world. "We never talked about the time period in the previous exhibit," Weininger said. "Now we talk about the Industrial Revolution, the growing gap between the rich and the poor, labor and the economy. We want people to come away with a sense of what it was like to be an American in that time period, as well as understanding Hayes and what motivated him." New gallery themes include the following:

- The White House Years
- Making of a President
- The Office of the President
- History of Fremont
- Former President: Private Citizen, Social Advocate
- Rutherford and Lucy's Early Years
- Life in the White House
- The Civil War Experience
- Administration and Issues
- The Hayes Family Gallery
- Evolution of a National Landmark
- 1876 Exposition
- Hayes 1876 Presidential Campaign
- Life and Times of the United States
- Hayes and Webb Ancestry
- Early Years in Politics

The exhibits officially opened at the museum's Centennial Celebration during Memorial Day Weekend 2016. Festivities included performances by the Ohio State Marching Band, since Hayes served as president of the Ohio State University's board of trustees, and "The President's Own" U.S. Marine Band, a nod to his U.S. presidency. Journalist Cokie Roberts served as the main speaker for the formal centennial ceremony, followed by a barbecue on the grounds. The weekend was also a "homecoming" for far-flung members of the Hayes family, some of whom had not been to the museum in several years. "If we were a university, they would be our alumni," Weininger said. "We want them to feel connected to this place."

Memorial Art Gallery of the University of Rochester, Rochester, New York

To celebrate its 100th anniversary in 2013, the Memorial Art Gallery installed three centennial exhibitions, created the Centennial Sculpture Park, and published a book commemorating the institution's history. The first exhibition, *It Came from the Vault: Rarely Seen*

Works from MAG's Collection, featured pieces that are not often on exhibit. The following description appeared in the March–April 2013 issue of the Gallery's newsletter *ARTiculate*:[37]

> A typical museum exhibits 10 percent (or less) of the objects entrusted to its care, and the Memorial Art Gallery is no exception. This exhibition is your opportunity to see works from MAG's permanent collection that are seldom on view to the public.
>
> The works, selected by staff and curators, include light-sensitive drawings that are infrequently shown because of their fragile nature, works that are awaiting conservation or repair or have recently undergone treatment, and odd but interesting objects that simply don't fit any of the Gallery's storylines.
>
> Scores of these works will come out of the shadows—some for the first time in decades—for this usual exhibition of hidden treasures.

A second exhibition, *Memory Theatre 2013*, explored the idea of how memory shapes your personal and cultural identities. The September–October 2013 issue of *ARTiculate* explained:[38]

> How do you define memory?
>
> According to the American Heritage Dictionary, it's the "mental faculty of retaining and recalling past experiences; the ability to remember." And that's just the first of 10 definitions, including some unknown before the computer age.
>
> Memory links us to our past and helps us imagine our future. It allows us to honor individuals like the gifted young architect to whom MAG is dedicated. It transports us across space and time, reminds us of what we hold dear, and sometimes (but not always) helps us avoid past mistakes. It's not always reliable, and when it disappears—whether through trauma, disease or aging—it alters our very being.
>
> One hundred years after Mrs. Watson founded the Gallery, this exhibition celebrates the role of museums as memory theaters that help us preserve our cultural identity. The objects on view, both historical and contemporary, include works in many media from MAG and other public and private collections.

Featuring pieces from three generations of the Watson family, *Connoisseurs around the Corner: Gifts of Art from MAG's Founding Family* rounded out the trio of centennial exhibitions. It included a wide variety of art, from ancient to modern works.

The Centennial Sculpture Park was dedicated on May 22, 2013, before a crowd of over three hundred people. In addition to the installation of several important sculptures, four artists were commissioned to create site-specific installations for the park, located on the grounds surrounding the gallery. The project began in 2010 when director Grant Holcomb announced plans for a reimagined outdoor space that he envisioned as "reminiscent of the old town square." Walkway beautification and a redesigned entryway set the plan in motion. Wrought iron fencing was removed, creating a more inviting environment for the appreciation of the sculptures. Interactive sidewalks along the park's border allow visitors to call a phone number and enter the first four letters of the key word engraved on the sidewalk to hear a poem or an excerpt of history.

The Memorial Art Gallery of the University of Rochester celebrated its 100th anniversary with the dedication of Centennial Sculpture Park. Family Day featured many activities, including dancers and other activities. Photo by Brandon Vick, courtesy of Memorial Art Gallery of the University of Rochester, Rochester, New York.

The ribbon-cutting ceremony featured the University of Rochester president, Rochester's mayor, the Monroe County executive, and the gallery's president of the board of managers. In a press release announcing its dedication, Holcomb said, "The new Centennial Sculpture Park, with its fusion of poetry (Poets Walk), Rochester history (Story Walk), and the visual arts, not only transforms the grounds of the Memorial Art Gallery but offers this community yet another beautiful and significant park to enjoy."

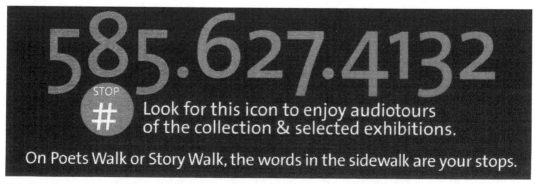

This bookmark explains how to interact with the Poets Walk or Story Walk, located in Centennial Sculpture Park. Memorial Art Gallery of the University of Rochester, Rochester, New York.

The gallery also published a lavishly illustrated book called *The Memorial Art Gallery: 100 Years*. Based on the web timelines created by librarian Lu Harper, the publication chronicles the history of the Memorial Art Gallery through its acquisitions and profiles of local artists, as well as regional and institutional history.

The Solomon R. Guggenheim Museum, New York, New York

For its 50th anniversary in 2009, the Solomon R. Guggenheim Museum published four books to commemorate the occasion. A press release announcing the museum's anniversary plans included the following descriptions of the publications:[39]

The Guggenheim: Frank Lloyd Wright and the Making of the Modern Museum
This first-ever book to explore the 16-year construction process behind one of the greatest modern buildings in America will examine the history, design, and construction of Wright's masterwork. Fully illustrated with preliminary drawings, models, and photographs, the book includes three major essays by Hillary Ballon, Neil Levine, and Joseph Siry. It is published on the occasion of museum's 50th Anniversary and in association with the Frank Lloyd Wright Foundation.

The Museum of Non-Objective Painting: Hilla Rebay and the Origins of the Solomon R. Guggenheim Museum
Considering the Guggenheim when it was initially known as the Museum of Non-Objective Painting, this volume reveals the museum's complex architectural history and the ambitious exhibition program organized by Hilla Rebay, founding director and curator from 1939 to 1952. The publication presents Rebay's unusual concepts for installation and framing practices in the museum's first location on East 54th Street in midtown Manhattan, and later in a temporary townhouse at 1071 Fifth Avenue. Illustrated with reproductions of architectural drawings, sketches, historical exhibition installation views, photographs, and color plates of artworks, the book includes extensive, previously unpublished archival materials.

I'd Like the Goo-gen-heim
First published in 1970, this timeless introduction to modern art for young readers is back in a new edition, with original text and illustrations by A. C. Hollingsworth. Hollingsworth was an artist and teacher with a special affinity for the iconic architecture of the Guggenheim Museum, and he produced a series of paintings illustrating its many building stages during its construction in the 1950s. Long out of print, his book was recently discovered at a library sale and reprinted with the approval of his widow.

Guggenheim Museum Collection A to Z
Revised and expanded, this new edition of the Guggenheim Museum's popular guide to its New York collection is a beautifully produced volume, not only a handy overview of the museum's holdings but a concise, engaging primer on 20th-century and early 21st-century

art. Organized alphabetically, the book consists of entries on more than 250 of the most important paintings, sculptures, and other artworks in the collection by artists from Marina Abramovic to Gilberto Zorio. Also included are definitions of key terms and concepts of Modern art, from "Action" to "Non-Objective" and beyond.

The anniversary also inspired a documentary film:

Art, Architecture, and Innovation: Celebrating the Guggenheim Museum
In honor of its 50th Anniversary, the Guggenheim has produced a documentary film on the history of its building, collections, exhibitions, and the development of its international network. The film combines archival materials—including talks given by Solomon Guggenheim and Frank Lloyd Wright—with contemporary footage featuring artists, art historians, architects, architectural historians, and curators. The 27-minute film will be screened regularly as a public program, offered free with museum admission, and will also be presented at the Guggenheim museums in Bilbao, Berlin, Venice, and as part of a 50th anniversary special exhibition program in Abu Dhabi.

A series of dynamic anniversary exhibitions "which honor its visionary history and founding collections as well as its dynamic present" explored the work of several artists, including *Frank Lloyd Wright: From Within Outward; Kandinsky; Intervals: Kitty Kraus;* and *Tino Sehgal*. Other exhibitions included *The Sweeney Decade: Acquisitions at the 1959 Inaugural*, featuring some of the works displayed when the museum first opened, and *Contemplating the Void: Interventions in the Guggenheim Museum Rotunda*, where 250 artists, designers, and architects were invited to reimagine the Frank Lloyd Wright rotunda via two-dimensional drawings. *Haunted: Contemporary Photography/Video/Performance* examined the ways in which photographic imagery has been incorporated into modern art to document "a widespread obsession with accessing the past." For the anniversary year the Deutsche Bank Series at the Guggenheim featured a major new commission and site specific installation called *Anish Kapoor: Memory*, which "challenged the museum's architecture through its improbable scale, measuring 47.6 × 29.4 × 14.7 feet and weighing 24 tons," according to the museum's website.

The Rockwell Museum, Corning, New York

In 2016 the Rockwell Museum celebrated its 40th anniversary with a complete transformation from top to bottom. "This is a pivotal moment in our institution's history," said Beth Manwaring, director of marketing and communication. "We've really leveraged the anniversary as a milestone year to be forward thinking and forward looking. We are setting the museum up for the next forty years, by developing a strategy for growth in collections, exhibitions, attendance, and audience. It was serendipitous because we were going through a reinvention of the museum anyway."[40] The museum had already dropped "Western Art" from its title, rebranding itself in a more broad context of American art. The anniversary year was perfect timing to make some major changes. The Rockwell Museum announced its anniversary plans in November 2015 when it was named the only Smithsonian Affiliate in upstate New York.

For the first time since 2000, the Rockwell went through a complete gallery by gallery reinstallation. As the galleries were completed, they opened throughout the anniversary year. New spaces included exhibits featuring everything from American illustrators to modern and contemporary art. A highlight of the anniversary year was an exhibition called *40 for 40*, curated by Steven and William Ladd, conceptual artist brothers who typically work in textiles, dabbling in fashion, beading, and even performance art. The Rockwell asked the cutting-edge artists to dive deep into its collection to mine it for "buried treasures" to be included in a spectacular anniversary exhibition. The concept centered around stories and memories, since the Ladds love to be storytellers. They worked closely with the curatorial team and chose pieces based on their own American experiences that were presented in a new context.

The Rockwell also capitalized on the centennial of the National Park Service (NPS) by mounting an exhibition of its collection of Hudson River School landscape paintings, many featuring scenes in national parks. They worked with NPS to create a map and guide with the centennial logo on it. Other anniversary initiatives included upgrades to the museum store and visitors' area, and a social media campaign featuring forty community members talking about their experiences at the museum. "The timing was just really right for us," said Manwaring. "It helps the public understand why we're doing what we're doing. An anniversary year is a good time for change."

Notes

1. Personal interview with author, July 1, 2015. All quotes in this chapter are from the same interview.
2. Personal interview with author, July 12, 2015. All quotes in this chapter are from the same interview.
3. "First World War Galleries," Imperial War Museums, accessed September 1, 2015, http://www.iwm.org.uk/exhibitions/iwm-london/first-world-war-galleries.
4. "From Street to Trench: IWM North explores impact of the First World War on North West England," Imperial War Museum, accessed September 1, 2015, http://www.centenarynews.com/article?id=1573.
5. Personal interview with author, July 8, 2015. All quotes in this chapter are from the same interview.
6. "30 Objects 30 Insights," Boise Art Museum, accessed July 15, 2015, http://www.gardinermuseum.on.ca/shop/30-objects-30-insights.
7. "30 Objects 30 Insights," Boise Art Museum, accessed July 15, 2015, http://www.gardinermuseum.on.ca/shop/30-objects-30-insights.
8. Personal interview with author, July 31. 2015. All quotes in this chapter are from the same interview.
9. Karen Von Hahn, "The Style Czar: Clare Twomey's Exhibit at Gardiner Breaks the Mould," Toronto *Daily Star*, October 8, 2014.
10. Eiteljorg Museum of American Indians and Western Art, 25th anniversary catalog, 2014.
11. Personal interview with author, August 30, 2015.
12. "About the Museum," Andy Warhol Museum, accessed November 1, 2015, http://www.warhol.org/museum/about/.

13. Personal interview with author, October 19, 2015. All quotes in this chapter are from the same interview.

14. "The Andy Warhol Museum Wall Text and Expanded Labels," Andy Warhol Museum, accessed November 1, 2015, http://www.warhol.org/uploadedFiles/Warhol_Site/Warhol_Responsive/Pages/visit/Warhol%20Museum%20Large%20Print%20Labels%202014.pdf.

15. Karen Lue, "My Mind Was Blown: Experiencing the Warhol's EPI Gallery," Andy Warhol Museum Blog, August 7, 2014, http://blog.warhol.org/museum/my-mind-was-blown-experiencing-the-warhols-epi-gallery/.

16. Matt DiClemente, "Andy Warhol's Silver Clouds: More Than Just Hot Air," Andy Warhol Museum Blog, April 3, 2014, http://blog.warhol.org/exhibitions/andy-warhols-silver-clouds-more-than-just-hot-air/.

17. "Inside the Auction," Paddle 8, accessed November 1, 2015, http://paddle8.com/auction/warholmuseum.

18. Personal interview with author, October 29 and 30, 2015. All quotes in this chapter are from the same interview.

19. Personal interview with author, October 30, 2015. All quotes in this chapter are from the same interview.

20. Personal interview with author, November 1, 2015. All quotes in this chapter are from the same interview.

21. Personal interview with author, December 8, 2015. All quotes in this chapter are from the same interview.

22. John D'Addario, "A Decade After Katrina: NOMA Looks at Memories, Loss, and Change in 'Ten Years Gone,'" The New Orleans Advocate, May 27, 2015, http://www.theneworleansadvocate.com/help/12433895-172/a-decade-after-katrina-noma.

23. "How Did River Lights Come About?," SB150, accessed March 1, 2015, https://downtownsouthbend.com/story.

24. Personal interview with author, November 18, 2015, and February 8, 2016. All quotes in this chapter are from the same interview.

25. Personal interview with author, December 15, 2015. All quotes in this chapter are from the same interview.

26. "On the Line: Intrepid and the Vietnam War," Intrepid Sea, Air and Space Museum, accessed January 10, 2016, http://www.intrepidmuseum.org/ontheline.aspx.

27. "Intrepid Museum Opens New Major Exhibition On the Line: Intrepid and the Vietnam War October 16," Intrepid Sea, Air and Space Museum, October 15, 2015, https://www.intrepidmuseum.org/About-Us/Press-Room/Press-Releases/INTREPID-MUSEUM-OPENS-MAJOR-EXHIBITION-ON-THE-LINE.

28. "Museum Tours and Talks," Intrepid Sea, Air and Space Museum, accessed January 10, 2016, http://www.intrepidmuseum.org/The-Intrepid-Experience/Current-Exhibitions/Intrepid-and-the-Vietnam-War/Museum-Tours-and-Talks.aspx.

29. "Education Programs," Intrepid Sea, Air and Space Museum, accessed January 10, 2016, http://www.intrepidmuseum.org/The-Intrepid-Experience/Current-Exhibitions/Intrepid-and-the-Vietnam-War/Education-Programs.aspx.

30. Sarah Drury, "A Broad Reach to Close for New Exhibition," The Star Democrat, October 15, 2015, http://www.stardem.com/news/local_news/article_a7f20f19-c4b1-552d-b3a4-4d622a986578.html.

31. "Museum Announces 'A Broad Reach' Online Exhibition and Catalog," Chesapeake Bay Maritime Museum, accessed January 10, 2016, http://cbmm.org/news/museum-announces-a-broad-reach-online-exhibition-catalogue/.

32. Personal interview with author, December 28, 2015. All quotes in this chapter are from the same interview.

33. Edwin Slipek, Jr. "A New Exhibition on George Washington Fills in Many Gaps about the Personal Life of Our First President," *Style Weekly*, accessed February 1, 2016, http://www.styleweekly.com/richmond/a-new-exhibition-on-george-washington-fills-in-many-gaps-about-the-personal-life-of-our-first-president/Content?oid=1388183.

34. Personal interview with author, December 7, 2015.

35. "Morris-Jumel Mansion Presents 'Yinka Shonibare MBE: Colonial Arrangements,'" Artfix-Daily, March 12, 2015, http://www.artfixdaily.com/artwire/release/4451-morris-jumel-mansion-presents-yinka-shonibare-mbe-colonial-arrang.

36. Personal interview with author, February 19, 2016. All quotes in this chapter are from the same interview.

37. *ARTiculate*, Memorial Art Gallery of the University of Rochester, March–April 2013.

38. *ARTiculate*, Memorial Art Gallery of the University of Rochester, September–October 2013.

39. 50th Anniversary Publications, Solomon R. Guggeheim Museum, accessed March 30, 2016, http://www.guggenheim.org/new-york/about-us/50th-anniversary/publications.

40. Personal interview with author, January 8, 2016. All quotes in this chapter are from the same interview.

CHAPTER 5

Audience Outreach and Community Involvement

ANNIVERSARIES AND MILESTONES provide an excellent opportunity to reach out to new audiences and get your community involved in your celebration. With social media, there are many free opportunities to spread the word about your plans, such as a simple hashtag campaign to promote what you're doing. Asking the community to participate in your exhibition or event in some way will not only make them feel invested in your anniversary, it will also boost your attendance. Don't miss your chance to get people excited about what you're doing!

McKinley Presidential Library and Museum, Canton, Ohio

While planning the 100th anniversary of the McKinley National Memorial in 2007, it was natural for the museum to plan an exhibition on its history. But the staff soon discovered there was very little material culture related to the memorial's history.

Director of education Christopher Kenney, author of *The McKinley Monument: A Tribute to a Fallen President*, served as guest curator for the exhibition Celebrating 100 Years: Building the McKinley National Memorial. "Our collection contains mostly small artifacts," said Kenney. "There are little souvenirs made from leftover pieces of granite, ribbons dignitaries wore to the dedication events, a bank used to collect donations. We needed something to fill up our cases."[1]

So Kenney came up with the idea of creating a series of contests for children and adults that would fill up the gallery space. He asked teachers to create drawings and 3D models of the McKinley National Memorial with their students, which provided a great visual element for the exhibition. The museum commissioned an artist to create a coloring contest page for younger students. And the non-artistic students had the option of writing an essay about what the memorial meant to them. A separate artistic photo contest was held for adults. Not

An exhibition celebrating the 100th anniversary of the McKinley National Memorial included a pulley interactive to show visitors how a piece of granite is easier to lift with more pulleys added to the rope. The interactive simulated the process used to build the Memorial between 1905 and 1907. McKinley Presidential Library & Museum, Canton, Ohio.

only did the students' work help the museum create a first-class exhibition, it also created a built-in audience to come see it. "There was a line at the door for the exhibition opening," Kenney said. "We almost never see that kind of a crowd for a temporary exhibition."

The McKinley National Memorial is rather unique among presidential grave sites. It is an icon in Canton, serving as a backdrop for all kinds of events from senior photo shoots to wedding pictures. "People don't always think of it as a mausoleum," Kenney said. "It is part of the community in ways that most presidential grave sites are not." To help commemorate this idea, people were encouraged to submit photos of the memorial that displayed this sense of community. Contributions included wedding parties, family reunions, Girl Scout troops, out-of-town guests, and events on the grounds—from all time periods. Not

To help fill the gap in artifacts for an exhibition on the 100th anniversary of the McKinley National Memorial, the staff held several contests for kids and adults, including drawing, coloring, and model making. McKinley Presidential Library & Museum, Canton, Ohio.

only were the photos included in the exhibition, but the staff was able to build the archival collection simultaneously.

Fort Wayne Children's Zoo, Fort Wayne, Indiana

One way to get your community to "buy in" to what you're doing is to ask for their help. When the Fort Wayne Children's Zoo started planning its 50th anniversary, the committee decided to crowdsource photographs of the zoo over the years. "We discovered some real gems," said Cheryl Piropato, education and communications director. "We found things we didn't have in our archives. Before we were a zoo, there was a small nature center here. But we didn't have a photo of it. Now we do. It really showed us how much the zoo means to families in Fort Wayne. People dug through photos from thirty or forty years ago. It was a great memory for them, and it was very meaningful to our staff."[2]

The zoo's marketing department used the photos in all of their advertising campaigns for the anniversary year. The possibility of seeing their photos on a billboard or television commercial was just the motivation people needed to participate. With today's technology, the staff was able to scan originals and return them to the owners on the spot. In total, the zoo received over one thousand photos.

The zoo also came up with a fantastic photo opportunity to help market the anniversary. After seeing kids posing to have their picture taken with a giant "2" when Yankee

The Fort Wayne Children's Zoo created an oversized "5" and "0" to promote its anniversary around town before it opened for the season. Throughout the summer, visitors took pictures of themselves with the numbers, which could be posted on social media. Fort Wayne Children's Zoo, Fort Wayne, Indiana.

legend Derek Jeter retired, Piropato asked a local sign shop to craft a "5" and a "0" for the zoo. Made of vinyl and PVC, the numbers stand about two-and-a-half-feet tall. Piropato took them around town and made promotional videos about the anniversary to post on the zoo's website and YouTube channel. "We took them everywhere," she said, "to the fire station, to the mayor's office. It's been a great visual." Youth volunteers set up a station at the zoo for visitors to take their own photos with the big numbers. People were encouraged to post them on the zoo's social media sites to help promote the year-long celebration.

Early in the planning process, the committee identified three goals for the anniversary celebration: attendance, awareness, and appreciation. All of the anniversary activities were planned with one of the three goals in mind. "We wanted to get people talking about the zoo and thinking about the zoo," Piropato said. But as a nonprofit zoo, which is funded entirely by earned income and donations, the top marketing goal is always to drive attendance at the gate.

The anniversary allowed the staff to come up with some fun ideas to promote the zoo around town and encourage visitation. For the first time, they got permission to paint orange tiger footprints on the roads leading to the zoo. Piropato said it was easy to get permission because it was part of the anniversary. She also got permission to hang banners on the light poles throughout town. The zoo also upgraded its mascot costume, since they expected additional appearance requests during the anniversary year.

The zoo set a new attendance record in its anniversary year, welcoming 618,498 guests in 2015. The previous record was 614,666 in 2009 when a new exhibit called African Journey opened. In addition to the visitation increase, the Fort Wayne Children's Zoo also celebrated its anniversary by welcoming several baby animals, such as a reticulated giraffe and an endangered Sumatran orangutan.

"We thank our entire community for your support during this record-breaking season," said zoo director Jim Anderson. "I'm proud of our staff for serving over 600,000 guests as we work to fulfill our mission of connecting people with animals."[3] The increase in attendance is directly connected to the zoo's anniversary activities. "Having a full-blown, season-long celebration can generate lots of publicity and keep your facility "top of mind" in the public eye," said Piropato. "For us, it resulted in huge attendance."

Imperial War Museums, London, Manchester, and Cambridgeshire, England

As part of its commemoration of the centennial of World War I, the Imperial War Museums (IWM) launched a digital legacy project called Lives of the First World War. "Personal discoveries of how the war changed lives and shaped our society are much aided by the digital age we now live in," said Gina Koutsika, head of national and international learning and engagement. "Digital technologies have given us exciting new possibilities for museum audiences to engage more widely and deeply with our content and collections."[4] Lives of the First World War brings materials together in one place from museums, libraries, archives, and family collections relating to World War I. IWM "appeals to users to explore the archive and existing archives, link them together, and add additional content and information," Koutsika said. "Through this crowd-sourcing project, we have started to bring together the personal stories of those who served, as well as those who worked on the home front. Our aim is for Lives of the First World War to grow into the definitive digital memorial to more than 8 million people from across Britain and Commonwealth. This will create a permanent digital memorial." Users can upload photographs, find records, add facts, and create communities. The project was created through a partnership with the genealogy website Findmypast.

The IWM also partnered with Ethe National Archives and Zooniverse, a collaborative project of the University of Oxford and the Adler Planetarium in Chicago that uses volunteers to identify and organize data for use by scientists and humanities researchers, to launch Operation War Diary in 2014. According to the project's website, "War diaries were kept for two reasons: to provide an accurate record of operations for preparing the official history of the war, and to collect information that would help make improvements in preparing the army for war. The war diaries contain a wealth of information of far greater interest than the army could ever have predicted. They provide unrivalled insight into daily events on the front line, and are full of fascinating detail about the decisions that were made and the activities that resulted from them."[5]

Through Operation War Diary, original documents from World War I were made available to the public online for the first time. The project created "citizen historians" who helped to review and tag key information in a series of digitized diaries from World War I. According to the project's website, the partners identified three goals:

- to enrich the National Archives' catalogue descriptions for the unit war diaries
- to provide evidence about the experience of named individuals in IWM's Lives of the First World War project
- to present academics with large amounts of accurate data to help them gain a better understanding of how the war was fought

The National Archives was responsible for the digitization of the materials, which are part of its collection. The data was made available free of charge via Zooniverse. Historians at the IWM helped to identify key questions to guide the exploration of the material in the following categories: military activity, people, weather, army life, and casualties. The project was designed to complement Lives of the First World War.

The Geffrye Museum of the Home, London, England

The Geffrye Museum of the Home explores the home and the way people have lived over the past four hundred years, with a focus on the urban middle class. The museum is located in the eighteenth-century almshouses of the Ironmongers' Company, where up to fifty elderly poor residents lived at a time between 1714 and 1912. One of the original almshouses has been restored and is open to the public for tours on a limited basis. The museum's collections include furniture, decorative arts, household goods, decorating manuals, cookbooks, and many other items related to the home. Period rooms showcase the evolution of the home, including simple seventeenth-century design, elaborate Victorian décor, and modern mid-twentieth-century style. The site also includes period gardens that complement the eras displayed inside the museum.

In 2014 the museum celebrated two significant anniversaries at once—the 100th anniversary of the museum's opening to the public and the 300th anniversary of the opening of the almshouse. The most successful program the Geffrye launched during the centennial celebration was designed for a younger audience. "The Centenary Celebrations project aimed to engage hard-to-reach young people, between the ages of 14–24, from the local East London community, many of whom had special educational needs, in learning about the history of the Geffrye and the local area, and re-interpreting the stories they heard about life behind the almshouse/museum walls," wrote Rachael Crofts, young people's programs manager, and Vanessa Weibel, Centenary Celebrations project coordinator, in their final report and summative evaluation of the project.[6] The project staff included the curator of exhibitions and interpretation and the web designer at the Geffrye, as well as a freelance artist, two freelance photographers, two freelance designers, and a freelance drama practioner.

The museum also partnered with Eastside Community Heritage (ECT) and Eastside Educational Trust (EET) on the project. ECT's mission is to document and preserve the experiences of different communities through social, cultural, educational, and historical activities. With a focus on oral histories, ECT was able to fill a knowledge gap in the museum's staff regarding digital recording and best practices for management and administration of oral history projects. EET's mission is to engage and educate school-age children, especially those with learning difficulties or disabilities, through direct participation in the arts. They seek to connect students with artists to co-produce projects that benefit the community.

Throughout the year, the museum used previously created youth-aimed Twitter and Facebook accounts to promote activities and events, encourage interaction through commenting, and post photos of events and projects in progress. Youth Advisory Panel members provided input for content on both social media sites. The Geffrye also created a project-specific blog called Heritage through the Keyhole to record and share information relating to the centennial youth projects. The keyhole theme was also used in the museum's annual appeal for the anniversary year. (See appendix F: Unlock the Future Special Appeal.)

The Centenary Celebrations encompassed several creative projects, including sculpture, oral history, and two photography and image-editing projects, all of which were displayed in the museum, on its website, on the project's blog Heritage through the Keyhole, social media sites, or in museum publications. The Young Volunteer Tour Guides also used these projects for inspiration for tours. A major component of the project was to train young people to properly handle archival materials and research stories through workshops and hands-on activities coordinated by museum professionals. "We wanted young people to co-produce a multi-layered and multi-sensory exhibition to be presented in the museum's front gardens, co-organize and facilitate the associated public programme of events, and produce interpretive digital resources on the museum's website that preserved their research and engagement with heritage," wrote Crofts and Weibel.

Access to primary documents, such as the 1881–1882 diary of Ernest Baker, the teenage son of an almshouse chaplain, captured their imaginations. "The young people found his perspective to be relatable and yet very different from their experiences today, and insisted on using material from his diary extensively in the programme," wrote Crofts and Weibel. "We wanted young people to examine the archive material and reveal the story of the museum, its historic almshouses, its inhabitants and its relationship with the local area." The goal of the project was for participants in the youth program to bring the museum to life for other young people. Organizers stressed that skills learned through the program were transferrable to other aspects of education, learning, and eventual employment.

The Geffrye began investing in youth participation initiatives in 2006 through funding from Renaissance London, Stories of the World (a program of the Cultural Olympiad), and Arts Council England. In 2009 staff began developing ways to ask young people themselves what they wanted from such a program through a Youth Advisory Panel. Members volunteer monthly, ensuring that the museum is more youth friendly. In 2012 the Geffrye established the Youth Consultants program, offering eight young people the chance to participate in decision making regarding development plans, strategic documents, and exhibitions through a yearlong paid appointment. Participants conduct research on a regular basis and present their findings to staff.

"Today we offer young people aged 14–24 a plethora of one-off or long-term voluntary, paid and informal engagement opportunities," wrote Crofts and Weibel. "These can emphasize creative or technical skills development, encourage CV enhancement and provide an opportunity to gain nationally recognized awards. Young people continue to inform future community, audience development and youth participation projects. The lessons learnt are seen as a model of good practice and inspired the conception of the Centenary Celebrations project."

According to Crofts and Weibel, the original aims of the project included the following goals:

Provide learning opportunities for:

- 75 young people aged 11–25 to explore the museum's archives, history and building and re-interpret this local heritage in a creative and engaging way.
- Young people to develop their research, documentation, photography, film, creative, technical and design skills, as well as lifelong learning/work skills such as: communication (speaking, listening, and writing), teamwork, planning, organizational leadership and project management, whilst improving their self-confidence and self-esteem.
- Local residents, museum staff and visitors to learn about the history of the almshouses.
- Museum staff to develop youth-participation skills, and benefit from new ideas and approaches to presenting the museum and its heritage through exhibitions and events.

Encourage youth-led participation by:

- Actively promoting a reciprocal relationship between staff and young people.
- Co-curating the overall Centenary Celebrations project with young people.
- Encouraging young people to take the lead on individual strands of the project: producing mobile and facilitated tours, creating sculptures and photographs, developing web resources, organizing workshops and events.

Celebrate their achievements by:

- Presenting them with a Certificate of Achievement outlining the skills they have developed.
- Investigating the use of accreditation through Arts Mark, Arts Award, vinspired V10/V50.
- Inviting all the young people to organize and attend a celebratory private view for friends, family, visitors and other stakeholders.
- Developing web resources which provide a long-term legacy for the project and enabling them to gain transferable skills applicable towards their CVs, portfolios, and future references.

Provide opportunities to gain heritage skills by:

- Delivering oral history training with Eastside Community Heritage.
- Organizing access to primary and secondary materials in the museum's and other archives (such as Hackney Archives or London Metropolitan Archives) for research.

- Delivering hands-on object-handling and collections-care training.
- Encouraging creative and technological skills development.
- Enabling young people to develop project management and interpretation skills by organizing public program events, exhibitions, web resources, and audio tours.

The projects ran from April 2013 through January 2015. Museum staff provided before and after questionnaires to gauge what participants expected to learn and what they gained from the experience. (See appendix G: Geffrye Museum Questionnaires). The Geffrye engaged disabled young people to explore the archives, take photographs, and create a "large-scale photo-cube to be displayed outside the museum." Another project called "Geffrye Ghosts" included a tour of the on-site cemetery, brainstorming about appropriate costumes, and a photo shoot throughout the museum's grounds. Students developed skills in technical digital photography, image editing, computer software, and communications. A five-day workshop helped young people develop individual garden sculptures inspired by the animals that have lived in the almshouses over the years.

Students produced fourteen podcasts and one film for an exhibition and digital timeline through the oral history project. Podcast themes included the Ironmongers' Almshouses, Life in Hackney, Visiting the Geffrye in the '30s and '40s, Childhood during the London Blitz, East London Air Raid Shelters, the Geffrye Air Raid Shelters, Summertime at the Geffrye, Childhood Geffrye Visits, School Trips to the Geffrye, the Geffrye Front Garden, the Geffrye Building, the Geffrye Playground, the Playground and the Branson Coates Building, and Exhibition Memories. As one participant observed, the project connected generations in a new way: "I think the project has gotten young people and older people involved with each other, it's closed the age gap and made it easier for older people to trust younger people." Youth gained skills in interview techniques, video camera skills, filming and editing, and scriptwriting. Footage from the oral history project also provided content for four additional short films as part of the Centenary Celebrations project that are available on the museum's YouTube channel on the following topics: Top Tips for Oral History Interviews, Exhibitions at the Geffrye, Ways the Geffrye Museum Has Changed, and Learning at the Geffrye.

In partnership with the Centenary Celebrations Project Steering Group, the Youth Advisory Panel planned a series of thirteen workshops for young people inspired by archival materials and local history research. Topics included the following:

- Object Handling and Photo Shoot: Participants met a professional photographer and members of the curatorial team, chose objects to research, and assisted with a photo shoot in the restored almshouses.
- Cool Cushions: Participants learned about the almshouse animals and made animal screen print cushions.
- Animal Frostings: Participants learned about the almshouse animals and the intricate art of icing cakes and created their own animal-themed cakes.
- Anim-8: Participants learned about everyday eighteenth- and nineteenth-century objects and created three short 2D animations in partnership with Chocolate Films.
- Stitch and Knit Gardens: Participants learned about the almshouse animals, gardens, and stitching techniques to create cushions and bags.

- Grand Garden Design: Participants learned about the almshouse animals, gardens, and ceramic and fabric printing techniques to create tiles and bags
- Futuristic Furniture: Participants learned about local furniture designers and created their own wire chair
- Picture Perfect Frames: Participants learned photography skills and Victorian paper-making and design to create their own frames
- Brilliant Bags: Participants used the "Useful and Beautiful" exhibition for inspiration to create their own bags
- Glorious Gardens: Participants used the museum's gardens as inspiration to create water color designs for their own gardens
- Perplexing Portraits: In partnership with Chocolate Films, participants were inspired by an artifact called a Monstrosity Scope, a toy almshouse resident Ernest Baker played with, to create portraits and distort them digitally
- Luminous Lanterns: Participants created decorative lanterns inspired by Ernest Baker's diary entries and patterns found on objects in the museum's collection
- Fragrant Candles: Participants created candles inspired by Ernest Baker's diary entries

Through the workshops, the young people who organized and conducted them gained important skills in budgeting, workshop facilitation, event management, evaluation, marketing, planning, peer leadership and mentoring, and teamwork.

A member of the Geffrye's youth team gives a centenary tour in the museum's gardens at The Geffrye Museum. The Geffrye Museum of the Home, London, England.

Thirteen young people worked with Geffrye curatorial and education staff to research, develop, and lead new tours for the public. A professional storyteller/drama practitioner helped students transform their research into a vibrant and engaging tour by developing public speaking skills and delivery techniques. The Youth Advisory Panel planned and assisted in a large-scale family event with activities for all ages inspired by archival materials and diary entries for more than one thousand visitors. The day included a craft workshop, historic garden games, storytelling, interactive musical programming, and youth-guided tours.

Throughout the centennial year members of the Youth Advisory Panel created tweets for the youth-directed Twitter feed, including the following:

- They viewed photos of the queen's visit to the museum in 1977 and wrote tweets about their own celebrity encounters.
- They toured the exhibition Almshouse Animals and wrote tweets about real and dream pets.
- At several meetings they read entries from Ernest Baker's diary and wrote tweets about Valentine's Day, home gadgets, leisure activities, and school.

In an article for *Museum Practice*, Weibel identified the challenges associated with a youth program such as this: "Challenges in delivering this aspect of the project have included: attendance, making more traditional archival material accessible and engaging, and sustainability. Staff developed approaches to mitigate these challenges, which included: planning in external sessions with partners, such as visits to archives to view and handle important materials, and tours of other key buildings; keeping members informed of other skills-building and training opportunities at the museum and elsewhere, and ensuring members had formal acknowledgement of their work and skills through project certificates and recognised awards such as vInspired and Arts Award."[7]

In total, 209 young people participated in some aspect of the project—278 percent more than staff expected—giving 3,055 hours of volunteer time to the museum. Through end of project evaluations, the Geffrye learned that 86 percent of the young people "felt that through their work/involvement they had made a positive contribution to the Geffrye Museum." One participant wrote, "I feel I've become more engaged with the museum's history. My highlight has been being trained and coached to become a better public speaker and I now have better research skills. I'll miss all the staff." In addition, 91.67 percent of participants "felt they had gained a better understanding of how a museum works."

Visitors also had a positive response after engaging with the young people. One said, "Good to see teenagers doing something positive, getting involved in the community, getting used to public speaking and talking about a subject they have researched." Another commented, "Listen carefully to a group of high intelligent, motivated and confident young guides. There is hope for humanity with such young people here!"

The museum staff also enjoyed the experience of engaging with students during the centennial year. Crofts and Weibel offered some advice to other museums seeking to replicate this program: "Working with young people often yields fresh, exciting perspectives that contribute to compelling and visitor-friendly interpretation, and this project was certainly proof of that. Thus, our strongest recommendation is to ignore stereotypes and clichés, and work with what are considered to be harder-to-reach audiences in order to broaden access to your organization, create rich learning experiences that benefit museum staff, participants and visitors, and to strengthen ties with your local community."

The Gardiner Museum of Ceramic Art, Toronto, Ontario, Canada

As part of its 30th anniversary celebration in 2014, the Gardiner Museum piloted a new program called "Clay on the Plaza." Throughout the summer, the Gardiner "welcomed a different group each week from the Albion Boys and Girls Club to participate in a full-day workshop at the museum," said Lauren Gould, development and programs manager.[8] For many of the participants, this marked the first time they had ever visited a museum. The workshops were held in a tent on the plaza in front of the museum to not only create a sense of animation in what can often appear to be a "boring" or "lifeless" building, but also "to reinforce our position as a community space," said Gould. A total of 198 students experienced claymaking during the pilot season of this program, which was made possible through a grant from the Pace Family Foundation.

Stan Hywet Hall & Gardens, Akron, Ohio

To celebrate the 100th anniversary of the completion of the mansion, Stan Hywet launched a seed packet initiative in partnership with the *Akron Beacon Journal*. The estate is well

This image accompanied the mailer Stan Hywet sent out in partnership with the *Akron Beacon-Journal*. Stan Hywet Hall & Gardens, Akron, Ohio.

known for its formal gardens, which made the seed packet idea a perfect tie-in. Thousands of Summit County residents received a large fold-out calendar detailing all of the year's events with a seed packet attached. Residents were encouraged to plant the seeds and enter a photo contest later in the season:

> Join the *BLOOM!*-ing Fun!
>
> Our zinnia packets are designed to help you create your own great garden during our milestone 100th anniversary season. Enter our garden zinnia contest and you might be a winner.
>
> Send us photos of your zinnia flowers in your garden space, flower pot or window box. We'll post images to our web site and our horticulture team will pick the best.
>
> • Plant your free zinnia seeds
> • Take a picture of your display
> • Upload your photos to stanhywet.org/blooming
> • You could win big prizes!

Contest winners were announced at a free Community Day on August 16, 2015.[9]

South Bend 150, South Bend, Indiana

As part of its yearlong sesquicentennial celebration, the city of South Bend launched a program called SB150 Challenge, a series of competitions encouraging citizens to get involved in their community and be a part of the festivities. The four themes were Serve South Bend, Show Up South Bend, Capture South Bend, and Envision South Bend. The following information appeared on the celebration's website and was created by Kylie Carter, SB150 program coordinator; Kara Kelly, director of communications, Office of the Mayor, City of South Bend; Aaron Perri, executive director for Downtown South Bend, Inc., and lead organizer for SB150:

Serve South Bend

To fund $10,000 in prize money for Serve South Bend, SB150 partnered with Teachers Credit Union. Categories for the challenge encouraged citizens to volunteer their time to improve their community:

• Volunteer for Back the Bend (Sponsored by Notre Dame, Back the Bend "Communiversity Day" encouraged students and community members to engage in a wide variety of projects, such as community clean ups, neighborhood home repair work, park landscaping, public art, playground improvement, and building projects.)
• Volunteer for SB150 Birthday Weekend
• Volunteer for South Bend Parks and Recreation
• Make Improvements to Your Yard or the Exterior of Your Property
• Host a Meal for Neighbors at Your House
• Spend a Day at a South Bend Park with Friends or Family

- Support Your Local Library
- Do-It-Yourself: Come Up with Your Own Act of Kindness to South Bend

Participants entered online and were required to provide a description of their project, as well as photographs of them doing it.

Show Up South Bend

This contest encouraged residents to attend Birthday Weekend with a chance to win a $5,000 prize. More than 300 photos taken at the SB150 Challenge Photo Booth on the Jefferson Bridge during the event were uploaded to SB150's Facebook page.

Capture South Bend

Sponsored by 1st Source Bank, the I Love South Bend Photo Contest asked residents to take pictures of what they love most about their city and upload them onto the bank's Facebook page. Visitors to the page voted for their favorite photo and the winner was awarded $1,500.

Envision South Bend

This challenge was aimed at K–12 students and focused on the future of the city.

SB150 also hosted a separate contest to design a new city flag. Described as "one final gift to the community" in honor of its 150th birthday, 168 people submitted over 200 different designs through an open competition for the flag contest. The following rules, published on the SB150 website, governed the contest:

ENTRY RULES

Flags should be designed in the standard US Flag 1:1.67 proportion. Submitted designs should be 1.5" × 2.5" in size. Acceptable file formats for image uploads are: jpg, gif, png or pdf, max 2MB in size.

Application form, including the narrative explanations, must be completed in its entirety to be considered.

Each entry may only contain one design. Individuals may submit up to three separate entries.

Application forms and designs must be submitted together, no later than 5:00 PM on Monday, November 23, 2015. Official entry form is at the bottom of this page.

All submitted flag designs should:

A. Include symbolic, visual or design representation of the four city-wide themes as conveyed by the SB150 Committee (see below).

B. Utilize the "South Bend color palette" (blue, red & yellow).

C. Adhere to the North American Vexillological Association's Five Basic Principles of Flag Design.

A. THEMATIC ELEMENTS to INCLUDE

The South Bend 150 Celebration Committee has come together to discuss major themes that collectively represent South Bend's identity. In some fashion, the following four items must be directly or indirectly represented in your flag design. The application form requires an explanation as to how each designer has symbolically represented these tenets:

1. The River

Not only is the St. Joseph River our city's namesake, it's ultimately why the city exists in the first place. What was an early travel route for the Potawatomi, the river became a major commercial route for European traders. The St. Joseph River provided power during the city's peak manufacturing era and has continued to be a source of recreation, natural beauty, and an engine for economic growth running through the heart of our community.

2. Connectivity

The St. Joseph River historically served as an important connection between the Great Lakes and the Mississippi River, and ultimately the Gulf of Mexico. In a similar way, South Bend became an important cross country road hub, with the intersection of the Lincoln Highway (New York to California) and the Dixie Highway (Canada to Florida). South Bend was, and still is, at the heart of several major highways and transcontinental railways. The South Bend International Airport connects the city to the rest of the world and adds value to the South Bend Foreign Trade Zone. In addition to being a hub for exploratory, commercial, logistical, and leisurely travel, South Bend's new economy is relying heavily on the fact it sits at the intersection of six national fiber routes—providing a form of digital connectivity that is unlike anywhere else in the country.

3. Ethnically Diverse Heritage

Our heritage is not only displayed on street names and in history books. It can be seen, felt and experienced in our deeply rooted neighborhoods, restaurants, churches, museums, performing arts centers, and special events. Miami, Potawatomi, French, Hispanic, Polish, Irish, Italian, African-American, Hungarian, Belgian, German . . . the list goes on. Our rich diversity is what made us who we are today and it's what will make us stronger tomorrow.

4. Innovation

South Bend is a city that has innovation built into its DNA. This has manifested itself through products like the Oliver Chilled Plow and Studebaker automobiles; companies such as Bendix and Honeywell; introductions such as hydroelectricity and the world's smartest sewer system; and through collaborations with world-class institutions such as Memorial Hospital and the University of Notre Dame. South Bend has proven itself as a place internationally renowned for advanced thinking and innovation. This spirit of innovation also includes reinvention, as South Bend has demonstrated a special tenacity to recreate itself and its economy.

While all four elements must be represented in some fashion, this does not necessarily mean there must be four symbols or graphics on every design proposal. A specific graphic design element may potentially represent two themes, a background color may represent a theme while a border may represent something different, etc. The narrative portion of your application is critical to explain these items.

B. COLORS:

The SB150 committee encourages the use of colors that are consistent with other imagery and logos frequently used in South Bend, which typically include blue, yellow, and/or red. For an example of these colors as they appear in South Bend and the surrounding region, please see the graphics below. Flag designs should be limited to using three colors at most (not all need to be used). Please note, white may be included as a fourth color if the design requires.

The committee was overwhelmed with the response to the flag contest. According to the SB150 website, entries came from "accomplished graphic designers, elementary aged artists, fifth-generation residents, someone in Spain, onetime University of Notre Dame or IU South Bend students who stayed on, Miss South Bend 2016, someone from Oregon who has never been closer than a flight layover in Detroit. The response of home folks and strangers alike is an inspiring sign of our city's energy and appeal. As one long-distance contestant wrote: 'I found this contest online and did research on South Bend. I found the city a great community worthy of a great flag to represent it.'"

Designs were evaluated by a committee of professional designers, marketers, vexillogists, academics and planners over a two-week period. Committee members reviewed not only the designs themselves, but the narrative submitted with the entry describing the meaning of each element. Two focus groups reviewed a narrow selection of entries that ultimately produced three finalists, and the public was invited to provide feedback on the designs online. The SB150 website saluted all contest participants, saying, "You are now part of the new wave of energy that our flag will represent."[10]

George Washington's Mount Vernon, Mount Vernon, Virginia

As part of the 200th anniversary of George Washington's death in 1999, Mount Vernon offered the opportunity for any community across the country to become an official "George Washington Bicentennial Community." In order to be included, the community had to plan at least four Washington-related events during the year, one of which was planned for the public. In total, 876 communities in all fifty states participated. According to Mount Vernon's 1999 Annual Report, "the range of local activities was nothing short of remarkable, including dozens of tree-plantings, Broadway-style musicals, essay contests, and history bees. This complex program was headquartered at Mount Vernon's new Volunteer Center. . . . The National Society of the Daughters of the American Revolution responded most enthusiastically to the plea for grassroots support, instigating almost 400 of the approved communities."[11] To identify these official communities, Mount Vernon issued a replica of the flag Washington used to mark his headquarters during the Revolutionary War. According to the 1999 Annual Report, "this commander-in-chief's flag, featuring white six-pointed stars on a rich blue field, literally traveled around the globe when former Senator John Glenn included Washington's colors during his historic return to space."

Rutherford B. Hayes Presidential Library and Museums, Fremont, Ohio

Two years before the Rutherford B. Hayes Presidential Library and Museums celebrated its centennial in 2016, the staff put together a brainstorming session, including community members, the mayor, elected officials, staff, volunteers, the Chamber of Commerce, the Convention and Visitors Bureau, the local community college's president, and others. One of the ideas that emerged was the idea of a "Flat Stanley." The staff created two life-sized cut-out figures of Rutherford and Lucy Hayes. "We thought it would be fun to send them to presidential sites throughout the United States on a goodwill tour," said Christine Weininger, executive director. "The tour created awareness for our organization and helped us develop relationships with other presidential libraries and sites. We wanted to have person-to-person contact with people at these sites, to explain the program."[12]

The figures folded up to fit inside a small box that was sent on to the next site on the itinerary by the last place they visited. Rutherford and Lucy traveled separately, which allowed them to stop at more places. Each site was asked to photograph the figures in significant spaces; the images were sent back to the Hayes staff. As the tour progressed, photos were posted on the social media sites. "Some of the pictures were absolutely hysterical!" Weininger said. "At the Adams site they have Sam Adams raising his mug of beer, and Lucy is standing next to him." (Sam Adams and President John Adams were second cousins.) The caption on the Facebook posts reads, "Lucy meets Sam Adams. Perhaps they discussed her views on temperance."

The last stop for the figures was the White House itself. Although the figures traveled alone through the mail from site to site, staff from the Hayes Presidential Library and Museums accompanied them to the White House.

A little closer to home, the staff planned another light-hearted event. Based on Rutherford B. Hayes's facial hair, the museum hosted a Centennial Beard Contest. The following text appeared on the official entry form:

> Like many men during the Civil War, Rutherford B. Hayes grew a full beard. He grew fond of the beard over the course of the war and kept it the rest of his life.
>
> To honor not only the spirit of President Hayes but also his impressive beard, the Hayes Presidential Library & Museums will have a beard contest on Saturday, May 28, during its Centennial Celebration. The contest is free to enter and is expected to begin at 2:15 p.m. The contest is sponsored by Mayle, Ray & Mayle, LLC.
>
> Prizes will be awarded to winners in three categories:
>
> - 100-day Beard Growing—This is a race to see who can grow the longest beard in 100 days. Registration is required for this contest by Feb. 18.

- Craziest & Most Unique Beard– Shape and style your beard into your most creative design! No pre-registration required.
- Most Hayes-Like–Who has a beard that most resembles the president's? No pre-registration required.

A representative from Beards of the Old Northwest will judge the contest. The contest is part of a weekend-long celebration of the Hayes Presidential Library & Museums' centennial. Events will include unveiling of the $1.3 million renovation to the museum/library building, performances by The Ohio State University Marching Band and "The President's Own" U.S. Marine Band, centennial ceremony followed by a public barbecue and festive celebration and more.[13]

The Repository, Canton, Ohio

To celebrate its bicentennial in 2015, Ohio's oldest continuously operating newspaper launched a series of initiatives to celebrate the occasion and thank the community. As a for-profit company, *The Repository*'s business model is different from a nonprofit, but many of the ideas they came up with would easily translate to any historical celebration. Bicentennial planning began seven years ahead of time as the newspaper was gearing up for its 195th anniversary in 2010. "Newspapers aren't often celebrated," said Maureen Ater, general manager of Gatehouse Ohio Media and chairperson of the Repository Bicentennial. "We are the narrator of the Stark County story in many ways . . . and we've done an excellent job of doing that."[14] This idea was echoed in the theme for the yearlong celebration: "The Story of Your Community."

Many organizations plan a black-tie gala as the grand finale of their anniversary celebration, but *The Repository* held its gala first to help defray costs of the community initiatives that followed. Many were free or low cost events but still required funding, and there was no budget planned for the bicentennial. "We wanted to kick things off big!" Ater said. Almost four hundred people attended the gala, which included live music, a documentary featuring community leaders and local historians, and a display of artifacts, such as the rare first edition of the newspaper dated March 30, 1815.

On the official date of the bicentennial—March 30, 2015—reporters set out to document "one day in the life of Stark County." Two days ahead of time, the newspaper published the following article:

The Repository wants to celebrate our 200th birthday by documenting a day in the life of Stark County.

Beginning at 12:01 a.m. Monday—200 years after Repository founder John Saxton began publishing the stories of Stark Countians in the newspaper—Repository reporters and photographers will begin visiting people and places across Stark County and sharing their stories over the next 24 hours.

We want to hear from you, too.

YOU'RE INVITED

The *Repository* planned its 200th anniversary gala as the first event of the celebration to help raise funds for other events planned throughout the year. *The Respository*, Canton, Ohio. Photo by Joe Albert.

Descendents of *Repository* founder John Saxton view the first edition of from March 30, 1815, which was on display for the gala. *The Respository*, Canton, Ohio. Photo by Scott Heckel.

You are invited to share your photos, videos and stories to help document a day in the life for residents of Stark County for an entire 24-hour period.

We want to see what Monday's sunrise (at 7:13 a.m.) looks like from your window. And the sunset, too.

We want to hear (and see) your tasty lunch—as well as hear the story about the feast you made for dinner that maybe was a little overdone.

We want to see photos and videos of your birthday party, your weekly card game, your best Monday nap ever, your happy hour, your new haircut or shoes, your treadmill workout.

If you're working Monday, snap a photo of your favorite co-worker or tell us if business is busy or slow. If you're babysitting, send us a photo of the kids or a video of your favorite activity together. Tell us about your favorite spot in the park or the best hole on the golf course.

We want it all—because it's all part of the portrait of our life in Stark County. #STARK24

To participate, post your photos, videos and updates on Twitter, Facebook, Instagram and other social media using the hashtag #Stark24. You also can email us at newsroom@cantonrep.com.

Then be sure to follow along with us Monday by visiting CantonRep.com. *Repository* reporters and photographers will be posting hourly updates—and incorporating your submissions—to reveal how even the most mundane of Mondays can become a day to remember and celebrate.[15]

Using social media any organization could replicate this idea.

In partnership with the United Way, *Repository* staff planned a series of "200 Acts of Kindness." These significant acts of charity or volunteerism were designed as way for the newspaper to "give back" to the community in honor of its bicentennial. Projects ranged from serving green eggs and ham at an inner city elementary school's family literacy event to participating in drives to collect dental hygiene projects and school supplies. The goal of the initiative was to create a sustainable program of volunteerism that would last beyond the bicentennial.

Throughout the year, the bicentennial committee organized a Brown Bag Lunch lecture series and several Reader Appreciation events, including a free picnic on the grounds of the McKinley Presidential Library and Museum. The newspaper provided more than four hundred free tickets to a Canton Charge game, the city's American NBA Development League minor league basketball team, owned by the Cleveland Cavaliers. "In August we held a community ice cream social on Market Square [in downtown Canton]," said Ater. "And, we had a free movie night at the Palace Theater in the fall. These events we loved and had such a good response that they will continue into the future." The newspaper also partnered with Canton Food Tours, owned by Barbara Abbott, to design a special tour that highlighted the *Repository's* bicentennial. "The tour included stops related to pertinent news topics," said Ater. "Many of the stops were stops that she makes on the regular food tours, but Barb

The *Repository's* free Brown Bag lunch series provided a forum for the community to meet some of the newspaper's staff. Programs often included a rare behind-the-scenes tour of the printing press and offices. *The Respository*, Canton, Ohio.

would incorporate news items or clippings related to that particular landmark or building." The *Repository* also "piggy-backed" onto an event that the Belden Village Mall was already hosting called "Art as Fashion." According to Ater, "The Rep team did research on fashion in the pages of the *Repository*, mostly from advertisements. The ads were categorized by decade and then provided to stylists who worked with mall stores to create a modern fashion show inspired by these vintage looks."

The *Repository* partnered with the theater department at Kent State University at Stark to produce an original play commemorating the bicentennial. Playwright Arwen Mitchell, who wrote material for the living history program at the Old State Capital in Lincoln's hometown of Springfield, Illinois, was selected to write the script. The theater department's website described the play: "Take an authentic walk into 200 years of life in Stark County as portrayed through the powerful lens of the media. In collaboration with *The Repository*, this tapestry play is the narrative of our community. Experience living excerpts of history that reveal where we came from, how we got here and where we are going."[16] The small cast included students and community members, who played multiple characters during the two-hour presentation.

The *Repository* was in a unique position to promote its own events in the pages of its newspaper, but creating a partnership with a local newspaper in your community could lead to such an arrangement. One of its most ambitious projects was to publish a reproduction of a historically significant front page inside the newspaper on page A3, every single day for a year. Although the newspaper itself researched material for its own bicentennial, a partnership between a museum and its local newspaper could yield the same results.

Sustaining a yearlong celebration can be a challenge for any organization, regardless of staff size. "From the very beginning, my concern was that we would lose steam trying to push a celebration throughout an entire year," said Ater. "In some ways, this did happen as the day-to-day duties we all have became more of a focus than the Bicentennial events. Despite a little lull after the first six months, we were able to create new events as the year went on. Also we found ways to lend the Bicentennial logo to other events to tie them into the celebration." The committee added a concert event featuring several local musical groups to end the celebration. "It was not planned at all, but seemed like a good way to cap off the year!" Ater said. "Newspapers are challenged each day with issues of relevancy. We work tirelessly to tell our story and share the evolution of local media. There was no better platform than the Bicentennial celebration to help share that story and garner enthusiasm and excitement around our organization."

The Rockwell Museum, Corning, New York

In order to draw a new younger audience to the Rockwell Museum, the staff used its 40th anniversary celebration in 2016 to launch a brand new series called Rockwell Roadhouse. "We have a team of young professionals on the Rockwell staff that worked together to establish a hand-selected group of community influencers who are strong in their peer group," said Beth Manwaring, director of marketing and communications. "We used them on a strategy team on how to engage a younger audience here at the Rockwell."[17] The Roadhouse idea came out of that group.

The concept is to have a high-energy live music series where participants can really cut loose and celebrate. The event includes a cash bar, hors d'oeuvres, and an opportunity to view the museum's art collection after hours. "We ditched all traditional marketing for Roadhouse," Manwaring said. They used only the newly established group to spread the word via word of mouth and social media. It worked very well for them, since the very first event was sold out.

Notes

1. Personal interview with author, July 15, 2015. All quotes in this chapter are from the same interview.
2. Personal interview with author, June 16, 2015. All quotes in this chapter are from the same interview.
3. "2015 Zoo Attendance Breaks All Records," Fort Wayne Children's Zoo, November 5, 2015, http://kidszoo.org/2015-zoo-attendance-breaks-all-records/.
4. Personal interview with author, June 18, 2015. All quotes in this chapter are from the same interview.
5. "Operation War Diary," Imperial War Museums, accessed August 1, 2015, https://www.opera tionwardiary.org/.
6. Rachel Crofts and Vanessa Weibel, "Final Report and Summative Evaluation," Geffrye Museum of the Home, 2015.
7. Vanessa Weibel, "Museum Practice," Museums Association, December 12, 2014, http://www .museumsassociation.org/museum-practice/teenagers/12122014-geffrye.
8. Personal interview with author, July 31, 2015.
9. In Bloom Brochure, Stan Hywet Hall and Gardens, 2015.
10. "SB150 Challenge," SB150, accessed February 1, 2016, http://sb150challenge.com/.
11. George Washington's Mount Vernon, *1999 Annual Report*.
12. Personal interview with author, February 19, 2016.
13. "Centennial Beard Contest," Rutherford B. Hayes Presidential Library and Museums, accessed February 20, 2016, http://www.rbhayes.org/hayes/newsroom/display.asp?id=1620.
14. Personal interview with author, July 16, 2015. All quotes in this chapter are from the same interview.
15. "Stark 24," *The Repository*, March 28, 2015, http://www.cantonrep.com/article/20150328/ NEWS/150329367.
16. "The Bicentennial Project," Kent State Stark, accessed February 15, 2016, https://www.kent .edu/stark/bicentennial-project.
17. Personal interview with author, January 8, 2016. All quotes in this chapter are from the same interview.

CHAPTER 6

Preservation Projects

A N ANNIVERSARY CELEBRATION may be just the leverage your institution needs to fund a preservation, restoration, or building project. Or maybe you have always wanted to launch a digitization project for a portion of your archival collection. An anniversary could provide the momentum you need to find funding from foundations or private sponsors to achieve long term preservation goals.

Shaker Heritage Society, Watervliet, New York

When the original 1851 Albany Shaker Church Family barn was destroyed by fire in 1914, the community immediately began planning for its replacement. The new design included the most efficient and technologically advanced features of the time, such as lightning rods, roof ventilators, and a track system for handling manure. The new barn was raised on May 20, 1915. Its foundation was made of early concrete, which was a new material at the time and not as strong as modern concrete. During upstate New York's frigid winters, the freeze/thaw cycle had caused the foundation to start pulling itself apart. With each passing year, the foundation became more and more unstable.

In 2015, the Shaker Heritage Society celebrated the centennial of the Church Family Barn Complex by completing a major stabilization project on the structure. Plans for its preservation had been in the works for over a decade, but the barn's approaching anniversary helped executive director Starlyn D'Angelo raise the funds needed to complete the project. She had hoped it would be finished several years earlier, but when that didn't happen, D'Angelo began looking ahead for ways the museum could leverage the centennial to secure funding. She and her staff identified two major initiatives for the centennial: to complete the barn's stabilization and to design a major exhibition at the New York State Museum. Both projects would increase the museum's visibility, which D'Angelo hoped would lead to more funding opportunities.

With grants from private foundations and the State of New York in place, the stabilization project's original budget was $310,000. But the attached manure shed turned out to be in much worse condition than expected. With the buzz surrounding the barn's centennial, D'Angelo was able to secure unanimous support for the barn project from the Albany County

Legislature, who voted to provide the $90,000 needed for additional expenses. "The reason that part of the Barn Complex is so important is because those types of structures tend to be lost over time," D'Angelo told the *Colonie Spotlight*. "They're becoming more and more rare."[1] The project was not quite done in time for the May 20, 2015, centennial, but the occasion was marked with an open house that also honored a state assemblyman who supported the project. The barn's stabilization was completed two months later. "We were lucky that we had the centennial," D'Angelo said. "Everyone was paying attention to what we were doing."[2]

Imperial War Museums, London, Manchester, and Cambridgeshire, England

The centennial of World War I provided an ideal opportunity for the Imperial War Museums to participate in the European Film Gateway (EFG) project to digitize films from the era in the museums' collection. EFG is an online portal providing access to the archival film collections of sixteen European museums. The original project was launched in 2008 and resulted in the digitization of thousands of films and film-related materials, such as posters, photos, censorship documents, and periodicals. As a follow-up project, the organization launched EFG1914 in 2012. The two-year project focused on digitizing materials related to World War I from twenty-one archives across Europe, including the IWM.

In the end more than seven hundred hours of film from or relating to World War I and approximately 6,100 documents were digitized. They are available to view through the project's website or Europeana.com, a "digital showcase" of artifacts from museums, libraries, and archives across Europe. EFG1914 also created a virtual exhibition called "European Film and the First World War," curated from these newly digitized archival materials. Sections include At the Front, Suffering In and After War, Beyond the Trenches, Neutral Countries, Film and Propaganda, Science and Technical Innovations, and Commemorating the War.

Mackinac State Historic Parks, Mackinaw City, Michigan, and Mackinac Island, Michigan

Mackinac State Historic Parks was able to reconstruct a new blockhouse and restore the earthworks at Fort Holmes as part of its commemoration of the War of 1812 from 2012 to 2015. The project was identified as part of the organization's strategic plan the Territory Ahead: 2012–2017. "We did not think we could raise the funds as quickly as we did," said deputy director Steven Brisson. "The idea was presented to [the friends group] Mackinac Associates in the summer of 2013. We broke ground the following summer and it was dedicated in 2015."[3]

The British originally built Fort Holmes on the southern end of the highest ridge on Mackinac Island to protect Fort Mackinac in 1814. It was originally called Fort George in honor of King George III of England. After the fort was transferred back to the United States at the conclusion of the war, it was renamed Fort Holmes in honor of American Major Andrew Hunter Holmes who was killed in the 1814 battle of Mackinac Island. The Americans abandoned it in 1817 and it fell into ruin. Through the Works Progress Administration, Mackinac State Historic Parks completed a reconstruction of the site based on original drawings in 1934. The centerpiece, a two-story blockhouse, was removed in 1969. According to its website, "the walls are made of mounded earth works and logs and the blockhouse is a two-story, hewn log structure with loop holes and port holes for musket and cannon fire."[4] The site includes interpretive signage inside the blockhouse and boasts spectacular views of the Straits of Mackinac.

The friends group secured the $500,000 needed to complete the project ahead of schedule. "The fundraising effort for Fort Holmes was a shock. They raised most of the $250,000 in a matter of days," Brisson said. "This funding leveraged the additional $250,000 appropriation through the State of Michigan. The reconstruction of Fort Holmes, which we technically had been 'planning' since 1969, only occurred because we were in the midst of the bicentennial. We seized the moment."

Schuyler Mansion State Historic Site, Albany, New York

Schuyler Mansion State Historic Site was the home of Revolutionary War Major General Philip J. Schuyler and Catharine van Rensselaer Schuyler. "Built between 1761 and 1765, the home was the first Georgian mansion in or around Albany, a city with a distinctly Dutch architectural streetscape," said Heidi Hill, historic site manager.[5] Schuyler was a member of the Continental Congress and became one of the first senators of New York State after the war. According to Friends of Schuyler Mansion, the home was "the site of military strategizing, political hobnobbing, elegant social affairs, and active family life. The wedding of daughter Elizabeth Schuyler to Alexander Hamilton took place in the house in 1780."[6] The house changed hands many times in its history. Its last private owner was St. Vincent's Orphan Asylum Society who sold the home to the State of New York in 1914. Over the next three years, the home was restored and opened as a museum on October 17, 1917, the 140th anniversary of the British defeat at Saratoga.

Looking ahead to the 100th anniversary of Schuyler Mansion being open to the public in 2017, Hill began planning several initiatives to improve the museum in 2010. "Anniversaries are always a good way to get projects done by rallying supporters around a reason to celebrate," she said. "We celebrate the saving of the house, the research and restoration work that has gone into it over the past one hundred years, the collections that have come back to the house, the period room restoration that has taken place thus far, the genealogical research and contacts we've made, as well as the interpretive projects and exhibits that have been presented over the years."

Plans included a new permanent exhibit in the Visitor Center to replace the one that has been in place since 1993. Hill and her team created a "Meet the Characters of Schuyler Mansion" interactive component, which provides multiple perspectives on Philip Schuyler, some of which are not positive. The new space also included a digital timeline, new exhibit script, and touch screen iPads that provide more in-depth information than exhibit text panels can provide.

The mansion itself was the main focus of the anniversary celebration. "We were tired of telling the public that we were a restoration in progress," said Hill. "Much of the restoration had been done years ago and we weren't so much in progress any longer. A big anniversary is the boost we needed in order to share some of our big transformational projects with others." Here are some of the projects that were included:

- Reupholstering the 1790s suite of Schuyler furniture for the Best Parlor
- Recreating the "Ruins of Rome" wallpaper using digital photography and printing, rather than handpainting
- Recreating the papier mache ceiling in the Best Parlor using 3D imaging
- Recreating the wallpaper and carpet in the Best Parlor
- Repairing and repainting the exterior of the mansion
- Installing UV glass in the mansion's windows to preserve and protect the furnishings
- Restoring the brownstone stoop at the front entry of the mansion
- Creating new landscaping through a five-year plan with the Albany County Cornell Cooperative Extension

One advantage of starting the anniversary initiatives seven years in advance is strategic fundraising opportunities. Several years ago the Friends of Schuyler Mansion was gifted a CD earmarked for restoration projects. Hill was able to pair that money with grant and corporate money to create a budget for the projects. "We need to roll with the project as funding becomes available," she said. "Many things need to be phased in or completed in chunks when money is in the budget. Some projects are split up over many different years." Being part of a state museum system can sometimes be a challenge. During the course of their project work was often postponed due to inadequate staffing or emergency repairs such as failing infrastructure at other state run historic sites.

As a state-owned museum, Schuyler Mansion does not have an endowment. The Friends of Schuyler Mansion is a nonprofit organization with a mission to support the "restoration, conservation, educational and cultural programs of Schuyler Mansion State Historic Site. The Friends also seek to increase public interest in this site, and develop an awareness and appreciation of 18th century history as it relates to the Schuyler family, the city of Albany, and the Upper Hudson River Valley region." The Friends group helped to raise funds for the anniversary restoration projects. One event was the History Happy Hour, featuring local beer, wine, and hors d'hoeuvres in the gardens of the mansion. The event included a self-guided tour of the home as well as eighteenth-century activities.

"This was actually the second History Happy Hour," said Hill. "It comes from a partnership with the city tourism bureau, the Hudson River National Heritage Area and the Albany museums to host a fun two- to three-hour Happy Hour for like-minded history people." The target audience for the event is twenty- and thirtysomethings, but Schuyler Mansion has also attracted museum professionals, reenactors, and preservationists. "I was asked to host it and I jumped on the opportunity," Hill said.

Because we are a state site, we are not able to technically host an event with alcohol and so I had to ask our Friends of Schuyler Mansion group to host it. The state provided tents, lights, tables, table cloths, decorations, the mansion and a fun scavenger hunt game. We also had to figure out how to do PayPal and Eventbrite in order to market and sell the event on line—that was a great learning opportunity for us and the Friends group. The partners provided the invite design, people who manned the alcohol (because the state staff couldn't and the Friends didn't want the liability), and someone to help with the PayPal square for people buying at the door.

The staff and Friends group hoped to sell fifty to eighty tickets. "We sold 120 tickets in the end and everyone had a blast," said Hill.

Mystic Seaport: The Museum of America and the Sea, Mystic, Connecticut

In 2008 Mystic Seaport began a major five-year restoration project on the 1841 Charles W. Morgan, America's last surviving wooden whaling ship. Mystic used the 70th anniversary of the Morgan's arrival at the museum to launch the public phase of its fundraising efforts to restore her. On October 11, 2011, the *Stonington-Mystic Patch* highlighted the significance of the commemoration:

> The anniversary is an opportunity to recognize the importance the Charles W. Morgan has had in the development of the Museum and the community since she was towed up the river on Nov. 8, 1941. The Morgan is the last wooden whaleship from the age of sail and is the oldest American commercial vessel still afloat. After an 80-year whaling career, the Morgan was at risk of being broken up when she was offered to the burgeoning Marine Historical Association (now Mystic Seaport). The acquisition of the ship raised the stature of the Museum significantly and helped put Mystic on the map of tourist destinations. The Museum estimates more than 20 million people have come to Mystic and walked her decks since 1941.[7]

In October 2011, Mystic launched a weeklong celebration to mark the occasion, including fireworks, concerts, performances, lectures, an antique car show, and a lantern lighting along the river. The week culminated with free admission on Saturday. "Celebrating the 70th anniversary of the Morgan's arrival presents us with an extraordinary opportunity to bring the community together in shared activities," said Melinda Carlisle, committee cochair, in the *Stonington-Mystic Patch*. A formal ceremony took place shipside, including a speech by historian Nathaniel Philbrick, author of *In the Heart of the Sea: The Tragedy of the Whaleship Essex*. The celebration also included the world premiere live performance of *Prince of Whalers*, starring Brian Dennehy, Joe Grifasi, and Linda Hart. The performance was described as "a dramatic telling of whales and whaling and the last wooden whaleship in the world, the Charles W. Morgan."

Following the anniversary celebration, Mystic Seaport president Steve White published an article in *The Day* on November 8, 2011, describing the purpose of the event:

> Mystic Seaport had an extraordinary day last Saturday as we celebrated the 70th anniversary of the arrival of the Charles W. Morgan in Mystic. No one who was standing on

the shore on Nov. 8, 1941 could have envisioned what the vessel would come to mean to the region. Mystic Seaport, then known as the Marine Historical Association, was a small collection of maritime artifacts, and Mystic was a quiet community with a proud maritime heritage. The Morgan would help change that.

Last weekend we kicked off the public phase of our fundraising campaign. This is the most crucial part, and will determine the success of this ambitious undertaking. With your help we can return the Morgan to sea stronger than she has been since she slid down the ways in 1841, so she can make history come alive for another generation of Americans. We invite you to join us on this new unprecedented voyage of exploration and discovery.[8]

The restoration project focused on the Morgan's condition beneath the waterline. Fresh water from rain had caused the top portions of the ship to deteriorate over time, so that section had been rebuilt four times in the past. The portion below the waterline was mostly original, and having been preserved by sailing in salt water, it did not need restoration previously.

The restoration project has been archived on Mystic's website, which includes the following description of the theory behind the project: "The restoration philosophy was to replace as little as possible. The guiding standard was whether the part in question could have a service life of 50 years. Those pieces needing replacement were carefully removed, thoroughly documented, and stored for future study. Mystic Seaport estimates 15–18 percent of the ship's fabric now dates to 1841, including her keel, the floor timbers on the bottom of the hull, and some of the lower planking."[9]

The restoration project was completed on time, and the Charles W. Morgan set sail on her 38th voyage on June 14, 2014. For eight weeks she toured historic ports in New England, including Provincetown, Newport, and Boston. Authors Andrew W. German and Daniel V. McFadden summarized the voyage in their book *The Charles W. Morgan, A Picture History of an American Icon*:

> There were many remarkable moments: beautiful sails to Newport, Vineyard Haven, and Provincetown; a joyous homecoming celebration in New Bedford; encounters with whales on Stellwagen Bank; America's two oldest ships berthed together for the first time. Along the way nearly 65,000 people toured the ship and the dockside exhibit, experiencing public history at its best.
>
> Undoubtedly though, the most significant aspect of the 38th Voyage was sailing the ship. No one alive had sailed an American whaleship. By sailing the Morgan, in the traditional way, the voyage helped rediscover and preserve the process and experience for a new generation. Now, returned to her berth at Chubb's Wharf at Mystic Seaport, she is back to her role as the flagship exhibit, but one with many new stories to tell.[10]

Notes

1. Emily Drew, "Celebrating the Barn," *Colonie Spotlight*, June 12, 2015, http://spotlightnews.com/news/2015/06/12/celebrating-barn/.
2. Personal interview with author, July 12, 2015.

3. Personal interview with author, August 30, 2015. All quotes in this chapter are from the same interview.

4. Fort Holmes, Mackinac State Historic Parks, accessed September 30, 2015, http://www.mackinacparks.com/fort-holmes-3/.

5. Personal interview, October 29 and 30, 2015. All quotes in this chapter are from the same interview.

6. Friends of Schuyler Mansion, accessed November 1, 2015, http://www.schuylerfriends.org/.

7. Bree Shirvell, "Mystic Seaport Celebrates 70 Years of the Charles W. Morgan," *Stonington Mystic Patch*, October 10, 2011, http://patch.com/connecticut/stonington/an--mystic-seaport-celebrate-70-years-of-the-charles-w-morgan.

8. Steve White, "The Charles W. Morgan, 70 Years Later," *The Day*, November 8, 2011, http://www.theday.com/article/20111108/OP05/311089941.

9. "Restoring the Morgan," Mystic Seaport, accessed February 15, 2016, http://www.mysticseaport.org/voyage/restoring-the-morgan/.

10. Andrew W. German and Daniel V. McFadden, *The Charles W. Morgan, A Picture History of an American Icon* (Mystic, CT: Mystic Seaport, 2014).

CHAPTER 7

Partnerships

ANNIVERSARIES PROVIDE a unique opportunity to build partnerships in your community and beyond. Some are obvious choices, but many are unique joint ventures that would likely not have been possible without the celebration bringing organizations together.

Fort Wayne Children's Zoo, Fort Wayne, Indiana

During the Fort Wayne Children's Zoo's 50th anniversary celebration in 2015, the local minor league baseball team the TinCaps approached them with an idea. Using Bill the Lion, one of the zoo's most famous residents, the team created commemorative jerseys with Bill's roaring face on the front and mane on the back. The team saluted the zoo's anniversary by wearing the jerseys at a home game on August 29, 2015.

After the game, the jerseys were auctioned off online through QTEGO.com as a fundraiser for the zoo. A total of thirty-five jerseys were available for bidding, including those worn by the players, batboys, coaches, and manager. QTEGO.com advertises itself as "America's #1 mobile bidding platform," with a client list that includes the Make-a-Wish Foundation and the American Cancer Society. According to its website, QTEGO invented mobile auction technology in 2009. The company is "passionate about equipping our clients to fund the causes and organizations that make our world a better place. We handle the technology so you can do what you do best—convey your message with your whole heart, rather than diverting your focus to the administrative headaches of paper-based silent auctions." Cheryl Piropato, education and communications director at the zoo, said the jersey auction was a successful fundraising event for them.

Imperial War Museums, London, Manchester, and Cambridgeshire, England

The Imperial War Museums (IWM) in the United Kingdom are quite unique; their history is inextricably linked to World War I itself. "We were founded in March 1917 and were collecting when the war was still going on," says Gina Koutsika, head of national and international learning and engagement. "Our intention then, as it is now, was to collect and display material as a record of everyone's experiences during the war—civilian and military—and to commemorate the sacrifices of all sections of society. With the First World War outside living memory, our collections are the voices of those veterans and eyewitnesses and of their stories."[1]

In 2010, the IWM led the global effort to commemorate World War I from 2014 to 2018 through the First World War Centenary Partnership. Over 3,400 local, regional, national, and international members represent museums, libraries, archives, universities, community groups, embassies, and other government entities in fifty-six countries. "Together we are stronger, more visible, and able to reach, inspire, and engage a much wider audience," said Koutsika. "With that in mind, we developed the First World War Centenary Partnership, adopting a model that is both inclusive and democratic." Any nonprofit that planned a commemoration for World War I could join free of charge. IWM created a special logo for the group so members could identify themselves as part of a larger community of institutions working toward the same goals.

The IWM curated a collection of digital resources for members to use, including photographs, images of artifacts, documents, and sound files. The IWM also designed several exhibitions on the war that could be downloaded by members and displayed either thematically or chronologically. In addition, the museum created a series of research guides to shape centennial planning on topics such as art, collections and research, learning, communications, and audience research. They were made available through the partnership's website at www.1914.org.

Before any planning began, the IWM used front-end evaluation to gauge the audience's knowledge of the war and interest in commemorating the centennial. "The First World War centenary really matters to a huge amount of people and that there is a tremendous appetite to engage with the centenary on a very personal level," Koutsika said. "This reflects not just a solemn responsibility to commemorate the enormous loss of life, but also an interest in learning more about the events which did so much to shape a century and the country we were to become. Many of us don't know what our families were doing in 1914—we believe that many will decide to find out."

Beaumier U.P. Heritage Center, Northern Michigan University, Marquette, Michigan

In 1957 Ishpeming, Michigan, native John Voelker (pen name Robert Traver) wrote the courtroom drama *Anatomy of a Murder*, a novel based on his real-life experience defending a husband who murdered a man who allegedly raped his wife. According to the University of Michigan, "In 1952 Voelker was asked to defend Army Lt. Coleman Peterson, who was accused of the murder of Mike Chenoweth, owner of the Lumberjack Tavern in Big Bay. After a six-day trial the jury returned a verdict of not guilty by reason of temporary insanity. Voelker turned over the events of the trial in his mind, and in 1953 he began tinkering with the idea of writing a novel based on the trial." The book was released in January 1958 and was an instant sensation, staying at the top of the *New York Times* best-seller list for almost six months. In 1959 film director Otto Preminger came to Marquette, Michigan, to make a film version of the book, starring James Stewart, Lee Remick, Ben Gazzara, Arthur O'Donnell, Eve Arden, and George C. Scott. Just like the novel, the movie was very well received and was nominated for several Oscars.

The 50th anniversary lasted for two years, celebrating both the publication of the novel and the making of the movie. "In 2008 the community came together to celebrate the initial publishing of the book," said Daniel Truckey, director/curator of the Beaumier U.P. Heritage Center, "but what meant the most to the community was the making of the film itself. So in 2009, several institutions joined forces to create a month-long celebration of events connected to the making of *Anatomy of a Murder*. It was the first Hollywood film entirely shot on location and for that reason, it involved the whole community. Many people who are alive remember the making of the film and/or were even used as extras. Many of the buildings, bars, restaurants, and hotels featured in the film are still in existence. It gave us an incredible ability to recreate the experience of the film for participants."[2] Having a Hollywood motion picture filmed in town was a major boost to the local economy, leaving a flood of good feelings in its wake.

The partnership included Beaumier U.P. Heritage Center, Marquette Regional Heritage Center, the Peter White Public Library, Central U.P. and Northern Michigan University Archives, Michigamme Historical Society, Ishpeming Historical Society, Carnegie Library of Ishpeming, Big Bay Historical Society, the *Mining Journal*, the John D. Voelker Foundation, and city governments in several local communities. The planning committee began meeting in 2007, a year before the 50th anniversary of the publication of the book. Plans for the second phase, commemorating the film's release, began in 2008. The celebration included an exhibition on the writer, the book, and the making of the film; bus and walking tours; special screenings of the film; a scholarly symposium; and events inside some of the buildings that were used in the film.

After its initial installation, the exhibition created by the Beaumier U.P. Heritage Center became a traveling exhibition that toured the Upper Peninsula and other parts of Michigan. *Hollywood Comes to Marquette: The Making of Anatomy of a Murder* consisted of twelve panels mounted on six collapsible banner stands, featuring rare images of the film-making process; timelines of Voelker's life, the book, and the movie; and links to oral histories with some of the participants. The exhibition was relatively inexpensive to produce, easy to transport and assemble, and booked for a period of four to eight weeks for a $50 fee per week. Museums can replicate this cost-effective process of creating a traveling exhibition through local vendors or online companies such as PopUp Stand. There is also an online version of the exhibition on the Central U.P. and NMU Archives website, which houses the John D. Voelker Papers. Through the website, users can access transcripts of the trial People v. Coleman Peterson (the trial on which Voelker based his novel), an interview with the last surviving juror, and photographs relating to the case.

For many, a highlight of the anniversary celebration was the opportunity to watch the movie in the very courtroom in which much of the film was shot. In addition, the walking tour of sites connected with the film ended at the old Roosevelt Bar, now Globe Printing, where there is a mural in the basement signed by all of the film's stars.

A strong community-wide partnership was essential for the anniversary's success. "This event could not have happened, or would not have been successful, without the partnership of several organizations," said Truckey. "Collaboration is key for events like this and made it all the more successful." With just one full-time and three part-time employees, the Beaumier U.P. Heritage Center has a very small staff. Yet they were able to accomplish great things by pooling resources with community partnerships. In retrospect, Truckey wished they would have made more connections with the local school districts to incorporate the book into the classroom. But overall, the celebration was a smashing success.

"I think other communities could easily create a similar type program dedicated to a local book or film," Truckey said. "We felt fortunate to have such a great connection to the book and film, and it made our jobs much easier." The community saw a small increase in tourism as a result of the celebration, and the local Convention and Visitors' Bureaus still uses the materials and information created to promote the region. "An anniversary creates public memory, develops a sense of place, and in the end is a great way to collect stories and artifacts," Truckey said. Plans are in the works to create another celebration to mark the 60th anniversary of the book and film.

McKinley Presidential Library and Museum, Canton, Ohio

In December 1933 an anonymous benefactor took out an ad in the local newspaper asking people to write to him describing their hardships, and he would send seventy-five of them $10 for Christmas. He promised not to reveal their identities or his, a promise he kept until his death. Several decades later his grandson, Ted Gup, discovered a suitcase filled with 150 letters from the same week in 1933, all addressed to a "B. Virdot." There were also thank you notes and canceled checks for $5, all signed by the mysterious "B. Virdot." He soon learned the name was a pseudonym his grandfather Sam Stone had created in order to anonymously distribute his Christmas gifts. He used parts of his daughter's names: Barbara, Virginia, and Dorothy, whom they called Dot. Evidently he had decided to help twice as many people as he originally intended, which caused him to cut each gift to $5 instead of $10. (In today's money, $5 is approximately $100.) Gup began to track down descendants of the letter writers to learn more about what happened to them. He wove the story of his grandfather's life, the general history of the Great Depression, and the individual stories of the Canton, Ohio, families who were recipients of these anonymous gifts into a book called *A Secret Gift*.

While researching his book, Gup contacted the McKinley Presidential Library and Museum (which is also the Stark County Historical Society) for information about Canton in the 1930s, his grandfather, and his business, Stone's Clothes. After the publication of *A Secret Gift*, he decided to donate the letters, thank you notes, and canceled checks to the museum's research library.

In 2013 the McKinley Presidential Library and Museum used those letters as the foundation for an exhibition and a series of programs to celebrate the 80th anniversary of Sam Stone's gifts to the community. At the same time the museum's activities were under development, Canton Symphony Orchestra president and CEO Michelle Mullaly was pursuing the idea of commissioning a musical piece based on the book. "When I first read the book, I instantly thought it needed to be set to music and put on the stage," Mullaly said.[3]

She contacted Gup, who informed her that the museum was planning an exhibition. Soon a community-wide partnership was born.

Each year Canton participates in the national program One Book, One Community. According to the Library of Congress,

> The "One Book" movement began in 1998 when Nancy Pearl, executive director of the Washington Center for the Book in the Seattle Public Library, initiated "If All Seattle Read the Same Book." With funding from the Lila Wallace Reader's Digest Fund and several local sponsors, she invited members of the public to read the novel *The Sweet Hereafter* by Russell Banks, and brought the author to Seattle for three days in December to discuss his book in a series of free public programs.
>
> In recent years, the "One Book" concept has been supported by a number of organizations. In 2003 the American Library Association (ALA), through its Public Programs Office, began providing librarians, library administrators and library partner organizations with guidance and information for the successful planning and execution of "One Book" initiatives. At the January 2004 ALA Midwinter meeting in San Diego, ALA hosted a "One Book, One Community" workshop, the first-ever national training opportunity for "One Book" programmers. The workshop was attended by librarians representing 54 communities in 23 states.[4]

When Canton's One Book, One Community committee met to discuss possibilities for their 2013 selection, Gail Martino made a strong case for *A Secret Gift*. "Many books were nominated by members of the Canton Mayor's Literacy Commission committee over the course of several months," Martino said.

> The committee discussed many aspects of each book, including mass appeal, suitability for high schools, access to the author (if living), length and difficulty of the book, how well the subject leant itself to community and school activities and access to the book itself. The list was narrowed to 5–6 titles and then all members read all of the books. A rating, using the aspects listed above, was used with discussion, and a book was selected. *A Secret Gift* fared well on all, especially the community and school appeal, and the fact that the author is alive and was willing to participate in our activities.[5]

As a member of several different organizations, Martino knew plans were in the works for a major community-wide celebration of this unique story. "Because I am a Canton Symphony Orchestra board member, working for the county educational service center, and on the One Book selection committee, I could see easily that there were many possibilities for collaboration," she said. "One of my favorite things to do was to help find a way to connect with the arts to draw the community in—either through a dramatization, which we did often, or a connection with the Canton Art Museum, the McKinley Museum, and/or the Canton Symphony."

After *A Secret Gift* was officially endorsed as the 2013 One Book, One Community selection, a meeting was scheduled for staff members of the museum and the orchestra, as well as a representative of One Book and a reporter who covers the "history" beat in the

Repository, Canton's local newspaper. The first meeting was extremely energizing as plans began to solidify for the celebration. "We had many collaborative discussions, lunches, and meetings to plot and plan the events and activities that year!" Martino said.

Naturally, all of the Stark County District Library branches would host free book discussions, which would also serve as a marketing opportunity for other book-related programming. The first event was an original theatrical performance by local playwright Frank Motz based on the book and performed in a small theater in downtown Canton. Some of the characters simply read the letters they had written to "B. Virdot." Others performed monologues or interacted with other characters to explain the circumstances surrounding their decision to answer the newspaper ad. The museum's director of education, Christopher Kenney, portrayed letter writer Frank Dick in the play. Dick's family had built a fortune through their business Dick Agricultural Works, but by 1933 the business was gone and the family was penniless. "It was powerful to almost become one of the people," said Kenney, "and to know what they had and what they lost, and how difficult it must have been for them to ask for help."[6] The play was so popular, the cast was asked to stay for a second performance immediately following the first one to accommodate the unexpectedly large crowd.

A free walking tour of downtown Canton pointed out locations mentioned in the book, with more information on the history of each. A roundtable discussion at one of the Stark County District Library branches featured people who lived during the Great Depression sharing their memories of what it was like to grow up in that era. Since a major component of author Ted Gup's research involved genealogy to track down descendants of the letter writers, the library's genealogy department led a workshop called The Making of a Secret Gift to explain how historical records were used in the search. Malone University in Canton hosted a Meet the Author event where Gup spoke about his project and then did a book signing of *A Secret Gift*.

The Canton Symphony Orchestra commissioned composer Eric Benjamin to write a musical piece based on the book that would also include spoken parts and a slide show of images relating to the people and places that made up the story. The McKinley Presidential Library and Museum already had a popular evening lecture series called Soup at Six, which included a signature soup for dinner, a program, and sometimes a tour of an exhibition. The museum asked Composer Eric Benjamin to discuss how he created his musical piece. It was a rare opportunity to talk to a composer about his creative process and how he chose which stories to include from the book. The Soup at Six event served as a preview of both the Canton Symphony Orchestra's performance and the exhibition *A Secret Gift* in the museum's Keller Gallery, which opened to the public the following day. Benjamin shared his inspiration for the piece, as well as digitally created recordings of special themes within the musical composition, since it had not yet been performed by anyone. After the lecture, guests were ushered into the gallery for their first glimpse of the exhibition based on the book.

While the exhibition was built around the letters, it needed more than just papers to create something compelling. As she read the book, the museum's curator saw the story in 3D, noting ideas for what artifacts could tell the story. She borrowed artifacts from the families that had belonged to the letter writers, including a lamp and table that came from Rachel DeHoff's home and several salesman's samples of agricultural equipment Frank Dick had used in his family business before it went bankrupt. The exhibition also featured items from the museum's collection that directly related to the stories in the book, such as the sign from

The centerpiece of the exhibition A Secret Gift was a recreation of the office where Sam Stone and his wife Minna wrote anonymous checks for those who contacted them in 1933. McKinley Presidential Library & Museum, Canton, Ohio.

Exhibition panels featured images of the letters and photographs of the letter writers. McKinley Presidential Library & Museum, Canton, Ohio.

the Fairmount Children's Home, the orphanage that figured prominently in the lives of two letter writers; a bottle from a dairy who continued to deliver milk to families who couldn't pay their bill; and a souvenir bell from Bender's restaurant, where Sam Stone regularly lunched. To round out the display, artifacts from the 1930s illustrated life during the period, including several handmade women's dresses, toys, household items, and an Ohio license plate from 1933. The centerpiece of the exhibition was a re-creation of Sam Stone's home office, which featured a set of furniture he actually used at the time he crafted the idea for his anonymous gifts. Ted Gup loaned Stone's desk, chair, and several bookcases and cabinets for the exhibition, which he later donated to the museum.

A panel for each family selected for the exhibition included pages from the letter itself, plus images that illustrated the family's story from the museum's archives. Each letter included the sender's address, so "B. Virdot" would know where to send a check. The museum used this information to create a map of where each letter writer lived in 1933. Contextual panels in the exhibition explained how and why the stock market crashed, as well as the cost of basic items such as milk, eggs, and shoes in 1933 so visitors would understand the impact of a $5 gift in that time period.

One case featured the suitcase where Gup had discovered the letters, with some of the original letters and canceled checks displayed inside. Other artifacts included a McKinley High School yearbook opened to Stone's wife Minna's photograph, a fragment of a shopping bag from Stone's Clothes, and several copies of *A Secret Gift* in foreign languages from around the world.

The museum also used the exhibition to create workshops for teachers and an immersion experience for students, both centered on using primary sources in the classroom. Archivist Mark Holland and director of education Christopher Kenney worked together to develop the immersion experience for high school students. "We used the exhibit itself to teach about the Depression, finances, and the reasons for the economic collapse," said Kenney. "We led some discussions about what it would have been like to live through the Depression and what they would have purchased with the money." After touring the exhibition, students met in the museum's archive where Holland used two of the letters to help students understand the human component of the Depression. "We used the Written Document Analysis Worksheet developed by the National Archives to examine two of the letters," Holland said. In addition to basic information such as the document's date, author, and physical characteristics, the worksheet asked students the following questions:

1. List three things the author said that you think are important.
2. Why do you think this document was written?
3. What evidence in the document helps you know why it was written? Quote from the document.
4. List two things the document tells you about life in the United States at the time it was written.
5. Write a question to the author that is left unanswered by the document.

Holland selected the letters for specific reasons. "I wanted to use a letter from a man and from a woman," he said. "The businessman's letter really showed the difference in his lifestyle before and after the Depression began, and how devastating it was." Holland chose the other letter because it told the story of children who were relocated to the Fairmount Children's Home, which was outside the city limits of Canton and made a better connection for students who lived in a rural area.

The final event of the series was the Canton Symphony Orchestra's concert "A Very Canton Christmas," which included the world premiere of Eric Benjamin's piece based on *A Secret Gift*. The performance included speaking parts by people who portrayed various letter writers, with author Ted Gup serving as narrator. A slide show on the stage behind the orchestra included photos from the museum's archival collection. Additional performances were held as part of the Orchestra's Young People's Concert series. The museum and orchestra offered a special discount on admission if teachers booked both the concert and a tour of the exhibition.

The partnerships created through *A Secret Gift* made each event more successful than it would have been on its own. Martino cited many benefits to working with community partners on this project: "Shared facilities, resources, different points of view and perspectives, and possibilities for bringing people into the One Book activities who perhaps never participated through their affiliation with one or more of the other organizations. This was the most rewarding and exciting One Book season of the seven in which I participated. It was moving, memorable, rich, and created an understanding of a critical time in Canton's history of which many of its current citizens were unaware. It was unforgettable!"

Representatives from the museum, the Canton Symphony Orchestra, and One Book, One Community came together one last time to present a panel discussion called Community Collaborations: How One Book United Canton's Cultural Organizations for Ohio Museums Association's annual meeting in April 2014. While this partnership was indeed exceptional, there are elements that can be adapted to any community. Working with the One Book, One Community committee in your town, or starting a group if you don't have one already, can provide a rich opportunity to create partnerships that might not always emerge in other ways.

Mullaly very much believes in the power of partnerships:

Stark County is fortunate that there are many arts organizations and other nonprofits, as well as a thriving arts district. Rather than working independently of one another, I think it's very important for us to work together. We have worked with the Stark Parks, the Professional Football Hall of Fame, the Canton Museum of Art, the Players Guild Theatre, the Canton Palace Theatre, the McKinley Presidential Library and Museum in Canton as well as the Cleveland International Piano Competition and the Dancing Wheels Company and School in Cleveland. Working together maximizes partnership funding as well as broadens our patron pool within the community and Northeast Ohio.

The best partnerships are those with common goals. "I think it's important to find a partner that has a similar mission or that wants similar things out of a partnership," Mullaly said. "For example, when we partnered with Stark Parks, their goal was to draw more people in to experience their parks. For us, we wanted to draw more people to hear our music in a setting other than the concert hall. It's also important to find a partner who is willing to meet you halfway. Our partners put as much into the relationship as we do and we both reap the benefits."

South Bend 150, South Bend, Indiana

Celebrated throughout 2015, South Bend's sesquicentennial (known as SB150) began as an initiative through Downtown South Bend, Inc., the city's downtown organization, in cooperation with the city. "But soon leaders brought in our local museums, and also encouraged methods through which any number of organizations—local businesses, nonprofits, etc.—could identify events as part of SB150," said George Garner, curator at Indiana University South Bend Civil Rights Heritage Center. Like many anniversary celebrations, SB150 looked to the past and the future at the same time. "South Bend, like many industrial centers in the twentieth century, is looking to reidentify itself in the twenty-first century," said Garner. "SB150 was a way to celebrate 150 years of innovation in the city, while serving as a launching point for the innovation that will occur in the next 150 years. SB150 became a focal point for a city in the midst of transition from an industrial past to an uncertain future. It put our city's history in front of tens of thousands of people throughout the entire year."[7]

Downtown South Bend executive director, Aaron Perri, led the anniversary efforts, creating a team that included over eighty local leaders to plan the yearlong series of events and programs. Committees included Executive, Marketing and Promotions, Fundraising and Finance, Grants, Community Partners, Programming and Events, and Volunteers. The Executive Committee began meeting a year in advance to outline goals and broad ideas, including a big birthday celebration. Perri held a series of meetings around the city seeking community partners. "Organizations were told about the themes behind SB150 and encouraged to come up with their own ways to incorporate the SB150 themes into what they do," said Garner. "No idea was a bad one, so long as it had some connection to the city, its history, and/or [the number] 150. A local church, for example, published a recipe book with meals that were 150 calories each, and restaurants offered drink specials for $1.50." The SB150 website highlighted the goals of the celebration and provided ideas for community partners to get involved (website content was created by Kylie Carter, SB150's program coordinator; Kara Kelly, director of communications, Office of the Mayor, City of South Bend; Aaron Perri, executive director for Downtown South Bend, Inc., and lead organizer for SB150):

SB150 will

- emphasize and celebrate the role South Bend has played in our nation's history.
- show off our best in arts, culture, and heritage.
- motivate people to take part in the yearlong celebrations and increase citizen engagement.
- leave a positive legacy for South Bend residents to continue to build on our proud history.

Residents and organizations are encouraged to help celebrate South Bend's milestone by hosting their own events throughout the year, from small neighborhood gatherings to sponsored community-wide festivals. Events can be simple or complex, and could include the following:

- Attaching the SB150 logo to your advertising and promoting it through the SB150 marketing channels

- Hosting an event or offering product specials that cost $1.50
- Adapting the theme of an event to be "South Bend's Past, Present, Future"
- Working 150 into your event/activity/exhibit performance—for example, 150 great artists, 150 days of art, 150 different techniques, and so on
- Dedicating a play, performance, or piece of art to South Bend
- Adding a float to an existing parade, themed to reflect South Bend's past, present, future
- Organizing a group project designed to make the city a better place

With the goal to "leverage every corner of the city," SB150 made it easy and exciting to become a partner in this anniversary celebration. Businesses or organizations who wanted to be recognized as an "official" partner were invited to submit their ideas via an online form. The "SB150 Celebration Partner Manual" explained the criteria for submissions.

Approved events should

- describe in clear language how your activity or event contributes to the SB150 Celebration. Please be specific as to how you plan on incorporating the SB150 theme into your event.
- be open for the community to participate.
- be consistent with SB150's mission, vision, and values.
- make efforts to be a zero-waste event to save resources, reduce waste, promote "green living," and to uphold sustainability initiatives in South Bend. See Zero-Waste Events Guide on SB150.com for suggestions and best practices.
- receive approval from the SB150 Marketing and Promotions Committee via online registration form.
- take place in South Bend, during the year 2015.

Another section of the guide highlighted some of the benefits of partnership:

GRANT SUPPORT
Recognized Celebration Partners will be eligible to apply for limited grant funding to be made available in early 2015. Grant funding is NOT guaranteed to Celebration Partners. All approved Celebration Partners will be notified of grant opportunities as they become available.

SB150 MARKETING RESOURCES
SB150 Logo
Hi-resolution and vector versions of the SB150 Logo are available for use to approved Celebration Partners by emailing kcarter@sb150.com. Please follow the Logo Usage Guidelines, which can be found on SB150.com.
Website
SB150.com is a valuable tool to display SB150 updates, events, sponsorship recognition, etc.

SB150 will be using the following social media platforms to engage the community:
- Friend us on Facebook: SB150
- Follow us on Twitter: @southbend150
- Follow us on Instagram: sb150

Media Partners

The SB150 Marketing and Promotions Committee is developing strategic media partners to effectively highlight events and stories throughout the year. Celebration Partners will be notified of opportunities to leverage this broad media coverage.

Marquee Celebration Activities

Celebration Partners will have opportunities to highlight their events at select marquee celebration activities such as the Birthday weekend and Discover . . . South Bend Series.[8]

Communication between the partners became a slight issue during the planning phase. Many of the partners were younger, ranging in age from twenty to forty, and preferred to communicate digitally. "Some older residents found themselves left out of the planning," said Garner, "not out of malice, of course, but by those younger digital natives favoring their method of communication." If your partners represent several generations, it is important to keep in mind the ways in which the older members prefer to or are able to communicate.

SB150 was a resounding success, due in large part to the dynamic partnerships that were created for the celebration. It was possible to carry out big ideas because so many organizations were working toward a common goal. "Big, bold celebrations of a city's past can and should happen everywhere," said Garner. "What are you proud about in your city's past? What mistakes has your city made? Each weaves into your city's story, and it's that story that informs its present and its future. Use it, embrace it, and celebrate it! History can unite the people in your city. It can also reignite old divisions. But all in all, it gets the conversation going, and it can focus your community around your city's successes and its opportunities. It's great history, it's great for your institution, and it's great for modern businesses. I would challenge other museums to share the agency for 'doing history' with many different types of organizations—you may be surprised and incredibly pleased with what comes from it!"

National Baseball Hall of Fame, Cooperstown, New York

When planning its 75th anniversary celebration in 2014, the National Baseball Hall of Fame partnered with the I Love New York tourism program to launch an eighteen to twenty-four month media blitz. Working with an organization that had access to more funds than the museum allowed them to reach out further than they could have on their own. "We built a campaign featuring Joe Torre across the state of New York and neighboring states," said Brad Horn, vice president of communications and education. "That was a major influence in driving attendance that year."[9] Admission numbers climbed to just under 300,000 from 250,000 the year before, which was a primary goal of the anniversary observance. "We wanted to raise our national profile," Horn said, "which would in turn fuel attendance to the museum, aid funding goals, and position us for a three to five year window of riding the coattails of the celebration."

The increased publicity generated by the 75th anniversary provided several major marketing opportunities for the Hall of Fame. "President Obama gave a speech from the plaque gallery, which was the first time a sitting president had come to visit," said Horn. The *Today Show* broadcast live from Cooperstown on the Thursday before Hall of Fame Weekend. "The anniversary brought to light what we do every day," said Horn. "People's interest is spurred by having a shiny anniversary. And you get attention from a nice round number."

Notes

1. Personal interview with author, June 18, 2015. All quotes in this chapter are from the same interview.
2. Personal interview with author, August 19, 2015. All quotes in this chapter are from the same interview.
3. Personal interview with author, October 30, 2015. All quotes in this chapter are from the same interview.
4. John Y. Cole, "One Book Projects Grow in Popularity," Library of Congress, accessed November 15, 2015, http://www.loc.gov/loc/lcib/0601/cfb.html.
5. Personal interview with author, October 12, 2015. All quotes in this chapter are from the same interview.
6. Personal interview with author, July 15, 2015. All quotes in this chapter are from the same interview.
7. Personal interview with author, November 18, 2015, and February 8, 2016. All quotes in this chapter are from the same interviews.
8. "South Bend Celebrates 150 Years," SB150, accessed February 15, 2016, http://www.sb150.com/.
9. Personal interview with author, December 21, 2015. All quotes in this chapter are from the same interview.

CHAPTER 8

Commemorative Products and Souvenirs

MANY ORGANIZATIONS choose to create commemorative products and souvenirs to sell or give away as a tangible reminder of an anniversary celebration. You know your budget and audience best. What already sells well in your shop? Will a priccy, high-end product sit on a shelf, collecting dust? Or can you produce a "limited edition" of something that you can market as an exclusive anniversary product? Do you have the budget for a range of options? Or do you want to pick one thing that you know you can sell, like a Christmas ornament, t-shirt, or travel mug? It is possible to offset the cost of a giveaway or even increase the profit margin of merchandise by finding a sponsor. This chapter is full of ideas that have worked well at other institutions.

Cincinnati Preservation Society, Cincinnati, Ohio

As part of its 50th anniversary in 2014, the Cincinnati Preservation Society launched a public voting project online for the top fifty buildings that defined Cincinnati. Executive director Paul Muller set up an account on Offerpop.com, a consumer engagement marketing company, and modified a photo voting contest template. Although there is a fee to use Offerpop, no additional software was required. The public nominated, voted, and commented on the buildings. "We sat back in wonder," Muller said.[1]

In the end, CPS took the top 104 buildings and created two decks of playing cards. Each set was $15 wholesale for a very high-quality coated card. They sold some for $25, but most of them were used as giveaways at their anniversary gala. A deck was given to one person at each table whose birthday was closest to May 2, the day the Preservation Society was founded.

Fort Wayne Children's Zoo, Fort Wayne, Indiana

Cheryl Piropato, education and communications director at the Fort Wayne Children's Zoo, had ten thousand buttons and five thousand car window stickers made to celebrate the zoo's

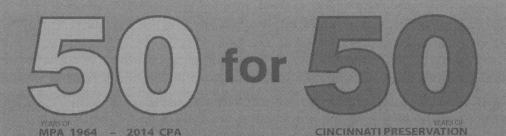

YEARS OF
MPA 1964 — 2014 CPA

YEARS OF
CINCINNATI PRESERVATION

We asked the public to help make the list.

Over 12,000 people spoke up and created the 50 historic buildings and sites list.

"Why should Union Terminal be considered one of Cincinnati's gems? Because when I walk into that rotunda, I still go weak in the knees."

— Karli Kathleen

To celebrate our 50th anniversary, CPA invited the public to select the 50 buildings that express the unique character of Cincinnati. People were able to nominate and vote for historic buildings and sites on our Facebook page. The result is a wonderful mosaic that shows the passion of the people of Cincinnati for the City's historic resources.

D-005
50-for-50

Cincinnati Observatory:

"Simply beautiful. You've got to visit this gorgeous campus or you haven't seen all of our city."

— Lael Anderson Truss

Take a minute to write a suggest a building or site that needs preservation action.

Tell us what to do next!

The Cincinnati Preservation Society asked the community to nominate and vote for 50 significant historic properties thoughout the city. Cincinnati Preservation Society, Cincinnati, Ohio

50th anniversary in 2015. Thousands of the buttons and stickers were given away for free at the zoo's official birthday party, but they were also distributed before and after the event. "It's fun to walk around the zoo with stuff in your pocket to give away!" Piropato said.[2] She also set aside some for the staff, board, and volunteers so they could help promote the zoo's anniversary.

Imperial War Museums, London, Manchester, and Cambridgeshire, England

The Imperial War Museums (IWM) created several commercial projects to commemorate the centennial of World War I. IWM commissioned "Bob and Roberta Smith" (Patrick Brill's pseudonym) to create original works of art specific to the commemoration that would "explore how art can help us all understand the complexity, terrible loss and personal tragedy of 1914–1918," according to the museum shop's website. The museum provided the artist with access to the collections for inspiration. He also consulted with historians on staff, and drew from his own grandfather's recollections of the war.

Bob and Roberta Smith's painting, titled *Lost Artists*, featuring just a few names of the artists, poets, and composers who died in the war, was available as a limited edition print. According to the museum shop's website, the piece "asks you to think about what European culture would have been like if a whole generation's creativity had not been distorted and destroyed by war." The image was also available on a silk scarf or on the cover of an artist sketchbook. The artist also created a gold tone button, featuring the question "How do we understand 1914–1918?" written in a spiral. Other commemorative products included a presentation pack for a UK £2 coin designed by military artist David Rowlands honoring the Royal Navy, and a bag, pin, magnet, and keychain featuring the First World War Centenary logo.[3]

National Baseball Hall of Fame, Cooperstown, New York

As part of its 75th anniversary celebration in 2014, the Baseball Hall of Fame participated in the U.S. Mint's Commemorative Coin program. According to the U.S. Mint's website, Congress has authorized the U.S. Mint to issue two commemorative coins per year since 1982, honoring "American people, places, events, and institutions. As well as commemorating important aspects of American history and culture, these coins help raise money for important causes. Part of the price of these coins is a surcharge that goes to organizations and projects that benefit the community. For example, surcharges on the U.S. Capitol Visitor Center commemorative coins helped build a new visitor center under the U.S. Capitol's East Plaza."[4] By 2016 the program had raised over $506 million "to help build new museums, maintain national monuments like the Vietnam War Memorial, preserve historical sites like George Washington's home, support various Olympic programs, and much more." The U.S. Mint also produces a series of lesson plans and classroom activities related to the coins they issue, which are available for free at usmint.gov.

Commemorative coins since the modern program began in 1982 have included these:

- 2016   Mark Twain Commemorative Coin Program
- 2016   National Park Service 100th Anniversary Commemorative Coin Program
- 2015   U.S. Marshals Service 225th Anniversary Commemorative Coin Act
- 2015   March of Dimes Silver Dollar
- 2014   Civil Rights Act of 1964 Silver Dollar
- 2014   National Baseball Hall of Fame Commemorative Coin Program
- 2013   5-Star Generals Commemorative Coin Program
- 2013   Girl Scouts of the USA Centennial Silver Dollar
- 2012   Star-Spangled Banner Commemorative Coin Program
- 2012   Infantry Soldier Silver Dollar
- 2011   Medal of Honor Commemorative Coin Program
- 2011   United States Army Commemorative Coin Program
- 2010   Boy Scouts of America Centennial Silver Dollar
- 2010   American Veterans Disabled for Life Silver Dollar
- 2009   Abraham Lincoln Commemorative Silver Dollar Program
- 2009   Louis Braille Bicentennial Silver Dollar Program
- 2008   Bald Eagle Commemorative Coin Program
- 2007   Little Rock Central High School Desegregation Silver Dollar Program
- 2007   Jamestown 400th Anniversary Commemorative Coin Program
- 2006   San Francisco Old Mint Commemorative Coin Program
- 2006   Benjamin Franklin Commemorative Coin Program
- 2005   Chief Justice John Marshall Silver Dollar
- 2005   Marine Corps 230th Anniversary Silver Dollar
- 2004   Lewis and Clark Bicentennial Silver Dollar
- 2004   Thomas Alva Edison Commemorative Coin
- 2003   First Flight Centennial Commemorative Coins
- 2002   West Point Bicentennial Commemorative Coin
- 2002   Olympic Winter Games Commemorative Coins
- 2001   American Buffalo Commemorative Coins
- 2001   U.S. Capitol Visitor Center Commemorative Coins
- 2000   Library of Congress Bicentennial
- 2000   Leif Erikson Millenium
- 1999   Dolley Madison
- 1999   George Washington
- 1999   Yellowstone National Park
- 1998   Robert F. Kennedy Memorial
- 1998   Black Revolutionary War Patriots
- 1997   United States Botanic Garden
- 1997   Franklin Delano Roosevelt
- 1997   Jackie Robinson
- 1997   National Law Enforcement Officers Memorial

- 1996   Smithsonian Institution Sesquicentennial
- 1996   National Community Service
- 1995   1996 Atlanta Centennial Olympics Games
- 1995   Civil War Battlefield
- 1995   Special Olympics World Games
- 1994   World Cup USA
- 1994   Thomas Jefferson
- 1994   U.S. Veterans
- 1994   U.S. Capitol
- 1993   James Madison—Bill of Rights
- 1993   World War II 50th Anniversary
- 1992   1992 Olympics
- 1992   White House
- 1992   Christopher Columbus Quincentenary Coins
- 1991   Mount Rushmore
- 1991   Korean War Veterans Memorial Thirty-Eighth Anniversary
- 1991   United Services Organization's 50th Anniversary
- 1990   Dwight David Eisenhower
- 1989   Bicentennial of the United States Congress
- 1988   1988 Olympics
- 1987   Bicentennial of the United States Constitution
- 1982   George Washington
- 1986   Statue of Liberty—Ellis Island
- 1985   None Listed
- 1984   1984 Olympics

The coins are produced with a limited run and are only available for a limited time. The Baseball Hall of Fame's coin was the best-selling coin in the history of the program, according to Brad Horn, vice president of communications and education. The process begins several years before the coin issued. The National Baseball Hall of Fame Commemorative Coin Act (Public Law 112-152) was signed into law on August 3, 2012, allowing for the creation of up to fifty thousand $5 gold coins; four hundred thousand $1 silver coins; and seven hundred fifty thousand half-dollar clad coins. According to the U.S. Mint, "Prices for the coins will include surcharges of $35 for each gold coin, $10 for each silver coin, and $5 for each half-dollar, which are authorized to be paid to the National Baseball Hall of Fame, an independent not-for-profit educational institution, to help fund its operations."[5]

A nationwide competition took place for thirty days in 2013 for the obverse design of the coin. According to the U.S. Mint, the following process was followed to select a winner:

Three United States Mint sculptor-engravers and a Bureau of Engraving and Printing banknote designer reviewed all 178 designs and scored them based on 1) artistic merit and 2) how well they would translate into a coin format. Based on these scores, the semi-finalists were selected.

The semi-finalist designs were then shown to five members of the National Baseball Hall of Fame. These esteemed members of the baseball community completed their evaluations of the semi-finalist designs and submitted their scores to determine the finalists. These designs became available for public viewing on July 18, 2013, and were presented to the U.S. Commission of Fine Arts (CFA), the Citizens Coinage Advisory Committee (CCAC), and the National Baseball Hall of Fame and Museum for review and comment.

The Acting Director of the United States Mint made a final recommendation to the Secretary of the Treasury after considering all relevant factors, including the comments and recommendations of the National Baseball Hall of Fame, the CFA, and the CCAC. The Secretary of the Treasury made the final design selection in early September 2013.

The U.S. Mint's website describes the coin in detail:

> The common obverse (heads) design depicts a glove that, combined with the baseball design featured on the reverse, exemplifies the most basic elements of our national pastime or a simple game of catch in the backyard or at the local sandlot. The glove design also highlights the unique concavity of the coin.
>
> The winning design, submitted by Cassie McFarland, was selected from the finalists by the Department of the Treasury on September 4, 2013, after consultation with the National Baseball Hall of Fame and U.S. Commission of Fine Arts and review by the Citizens Coinage Advisory Committee.
>
> The common inscriptions on each coin's obverse are *LIBERTY, IN GOD WE TRUST*, and 2014. The obverse design was sculpted by United States Mint Sculptor-Engraver Don Everhart.
>
> The common reverse (tails) design of each coin depicts a baseball similar to those used in Major League Baseball®. The final design, also designed and sculpted by Everhart, was approved by the Department of the Treasury on May 20, 2013, after consultation with the National Baseball Hall of Fame and U.S. Commission of Fine Arts and review by the Citizens Coinage Advisory Committee.

The coin was the first-ever curved design, which heightened interest among coin collectors. Although the coin itself did not make reference to the 75th anniversary, it was marketed as an anniversary commemorative piece. In 2016 the Baseball Hall of Fame coin was awarded Coin of the Year (COTY), an annual global coin competition. It also won the Most Innovative Coin Award for the U.S. Mint's first "cupped clad coin." The $5 gold coin won in the Best Gold Coin category.

An organization who is interested in being selected for the U.S. Mint Commemorative Coin program should begin by contacting their elected officials several years in advance. The U.S. Mint has established the following selection guidelines:

CRITERIA FOR COMMEMORATIVE COIN SUBJECT SELECTION
Our nation's coinage should be a permanent reflection of its values and culture. The Citizens Commemorative Coin Advisory Committee is committed to the selection of themes and designs for commemorative coins that represent the noblest values and achievements

of the nation, recognizing the widest variety of contributions to our history and culture. A primary goal of the committee is to ensure that all commemorative themes and designs meet the highest standards for artistic excellence.

In furtherance of these goals, the Citizens Commemorative Coin Advisory Committee has established the following criteria for the selection of commemorative themes for coins of the United States:

- Historical persons, places, events and themes to be commemorated should have an enduring effect on the nation's history or culture. Their significance should be national or international in scope.
- Events to be commemorated should have national or international significance and draw participation from across America or around the world.
- No living person should be honored by commemoration on U.S. coins.
- United States commemorative coins should be issued in the appropriate year of commemoration.
- Historical events should generally be considered for commemoration on important or significant anniversaries.
- Commemorative themes and designs should not be considered if one treating the same subject has been issued in the past 10 years.
- Commemorative coinage designs should reflect traditional American coin iconography as well as contemporary developments in the arts.
- Designs should be determined in consultation with sponsoring organizations but should not be determined by legislation.
- Commemorative coinage should not be required to contain logos and emblems of non-governmental organizations as part of the design.
- Coins should be dated in the year of their issuance.
- Legislation authorizing the production of coins should be enacted no less than nine months prior to the date on which the coins may first be available to the public.

The Solomon R. Guggenheim Museum, New York, New York

In commemoration of its 50th anniversary in 2009, the Solomon R. Guggenheim Museum launched a new line of products featuring the iconic images of the museum, including a steel-cased watch by Bulova, which sold for $150. Lower price point items included a mini wall calendar, umbrella, tie, scarf, totebag, notecard set, and a Megara lamp. The museum also debuted a brand-new line of children's items for the first time, based on the picture book *I'd Like the Goo-gen-heim*. Products included a backpack, t-shirt, and games.

Notes

1. Personal interview with author, July 1, 2015.
2. Personal interview with author, June 16, 2015.

3. IWM Shop, accessed September 1, 2015, http://www.iwmshop.org.uk/category/1429/Bob_and_Roberta_Smith.

4. "Commemorative Coin Programs," U.S. Mint, accessed January 15, 2016, https://www.usmint.gov/mint_programs/?action=commemoratives.

5. "First Curved Coin from the U.S. Mint," U.S. Mint, accessed January 15, 2016, https://www.usmint.gov/batterup/?action=curvedcoin&pf.

Conclusion

The pages of this book have highlighted a wide variety of ideas for your anniversary that can be scaled up or down depending on the size of your organization, your resources, and your budget. But before setting out to make the most of this special time in your institution's history, it is important to be practical about what you can reasonably accomplish. It's great to have big ideas, but be sure you have a strategy to follow through on them. Take some advice from those who have already been through what you're about to discover.

Many museums that have already planned and executed major commemorations cited the extra time and energy required as a possible area of concern. "Anniversary celebrations are exciting and can energize the staff and board," said Melanie Fales, executive director/CEO of the Boise Art Museum, "and they can also provide a challenge of the potential for burnout, particularly when they are yearlong initiatives. It is important to consider the work that may have to be set aside to achieve the anniversary year goals and to decide where the priorities lie."[1]

Mary Thompson, research specialist at George Washington's Mount Vernon, cautions institutions to be realistic about staffing needs for any major project. When planning events for the bicentennial of George Washington's death in 1999, "three staff members, including myself, ended up in emergency rooms with chest pains. The diagnosis was stress."[2]

As coordinator of the Ohio Civil War 150 initiative, Amy Rohmiller, program coordinator, local history and AmeriCorps at the Ohio History Connection in Columbus, learned it's important to select the right kind of people to help. "Make sure your planning committee has a mix of thinkers and doers because you need both," she said. "You can do a lot with a little. Whatever you're already doing can be tweaked to fit whatever you're commemorating."[3]

Planning an anniversary celebration is often a lot of work, but the benefits always outweigh the costs. "It was fun and brought us to a new level of prominence in the community," said Cheryl Piropato, education and communications director at the Fort Wayne Children's Zoo. "For a smaller organization, we feel this even more because I think people take for granted the things in their [own] community. You can really elevate your profile and make people realize how significant you are because you've been there for fifty years. It makes people appreciate you a little bit more. In that sense, it's definitely worth making the effort."[4]

Fales agrees: "Anniversaries are good opportunities to instill a sense of pride in those who have helped create an enduring resource in the community," she said, "to raise awareness of the organization and its longevity, to assess the organization's current position and determine direction, and to galvanize an organization around a specific set of short-term and long-term goals."

These events can also help to motivate staff to complete projects that have been simmering on the back burner for a while. "Anniversaries present opportunities for increased public engagement, increased funding from public and private sources, and the incentive to complete or tackle projects that may otherwise seem too daunting," said Lauren Gould, development and programs manager at the Gardiner Museum of Ceramic Art in Toronto.[5] The Gardiner had planned a major transformation of its porcelain galleries in 2016, but the momentum of the 30th anniversary celebration in 2014 allowed them to reach the goal much faster. According to the museum's website, the project's goals included the following:

- Make one of the world's finest porcelain collections accessible and engaging for a broader public
- Animate and reinterpret the porcelain collections with new state-of-the-art lighting, interactive displays, labels, and signage
- Better tell the story of clay with a narrative describing their place and significance within human history and relevance to our daily lives
- Show more of our collection; 55 percent of our objects are in reserve storage but a new display will allow us to put these on public exhibition
- Create interactive displays that will provide a multimedia introduction to ceramic techniques and their history[6]

By seizing on the financial opportunities associated with the excitement of an anniversary, the Gardiner was able to open the new galleries one year ahead of schedule.

Historic New England has also enjoyed an extraordinary period of growth since celebrating its centennial in 2010. "Historic New England's centennial strategy was very successful," said Diane Viera, executive vice president and chief operating officer. "We now stand at the brink of some remarkable milestones. This year we will exceed fifty thousand children served through our education programs, which have grown every year since their inception in 1985. We will serve a record two hundred thousand visitors at our historic sites, and we are in our sixth consecutive year of increased membership. In summary, Historic New England maximized its centennial opportunity in the following ways:

- Looking forward and launching the next century, not focusing on the past
- Making it all about the public and not being self-absorbed
- Strategizing how we could "centennialize" what we're already doing, and planning new activities to complement or fill in gaps to make the centennial special
- Looking beyond twelve months; investing wisely in things that will have longer impact
- Using the excitement of the centennial as an opportunity to get visibility and funding for initiatives that we already wanted to do
- Involving the entire organization; a committee or team can take the lead in ensuring things happen but the centennial initiatives should be an institution-wide priority and integrated into the work of everyone[7]

Historic New England's remarkable series of centennial events included a gala, birthday bash, two exhibitions, a symposium, an expansion of its magazine, and a new program called 100 Years, 100 Communities, an ambitious initiative documenting twentieth-century history in underserved communities in all six New England states. Today the program is known as Everyone's History.

Without exception, everyone I interviewed for this book was proud of what their institutions were able to accomplish during their anniversary years. Many saw a ripple effect from their efforts continue years later. People are drawn to celebrate anniversaries and commemorate tragic events in our past. These milestones provide just the right catalyst to achieve long-time institutional goals, engage new audiences, reenergize your base, and generate media attention. The museum field is notoriously creative and resourceful. I hope these ideas from your colleagues will inspire you to reach even higher than you thought possible, and that your anniversaries bring you all the benefits included in this book—and more.

Notes

1. Personal interview with author, July 8, 2015. All quotes in this chapter are from the same interview.
2. Personal interview with author, December 28, 2015.
3. Personal interview with author, December 3, 2015.
4. Personal interview with author, June 16, 2015.
5. Personal interview with author, July 31, 2015.
6. "Transformation of the European Porcelain Galleries," Gardiner Museum of Ceramic Art, accessed January 25, 2016, http://www.gardinermuseum.on.ca/support-us/transformation-of-the-european-porcelain-galleries.
7. Personal interview with author, October 30, 2015. All quotes in this chapter are from the same interview.

Appendix A

Ohio Civil War 150: Interpretive Framework

Introduction

An interpretive framework organizes diverse information and perspectives on a topic in history, culture, or nature. It organizes these materials into an integrated, meaningful, and useful instrument for the development of engaging and relevant public programs that are firmly rooted in high quality, contemporary scholarship.

This Interpretive Framework for Ohio Civil War 150 consists of an Overarching Statement and three Primary Themes. Embedded within the Overarching Statement and the Primary Themes are several exemplary storylines. The specific stories identified within the Interpretive Framework are included to provide readers with sample stories that can bring to life the broader, more abstract ideas presented here. In other words, these illustrative storylines are included in part to fuel the imagination and suggest a range of possibilities. If this approach succeeds, individuals and groups interested in the Civil War will be inspired to use this framework for programs, research, writing, and more, and they will add their own layers of meaning and analysis to it.

While this document draws on the contributions of some of Ohio's finest historians, all of us are committed to telling well-constructed stories that speak to a modern-day audience. We are not engaged in the pursuit of history for history's sake alone. Rather we are firm in our resolve to discover a past that will shed light on the present, that will place contemporary issues and concerns in a larger, historical context. At root we are asking some fundamental questions: What does the experience of the Civil War generation have to tell us today? What can we learn from the quest, struggles, and achievements of that time? How did this formative event in American history impact who we are as a culture? How can new perspectives on this historic event help us to gain new perspective on ourselves today? In attempting to answer these questions, we believe that the past—in this instance, the Civil War—can serve as a distant mirror, reflecting and illuminating contemporary aspirations and enterprises.

Like the Civil War generation, we too live during a time of immense change and substantial turmoil, a time when democracy, the role of government, the rights of the individual, racial and gender relations, and memory itself are being debated and reworked. We hope that this Interpretive Framework and the public programs that spring from it will serve to raise questions, inspire exploration, prompt discussion, and enrich our understanding of the past and present in Ohio and our nation.

Overarching Statement

The American Civil War was the most important *collective public event* in the history of Ohio, if not in the nation. Virtually everyone alive in the state between April 1861 and April 1865 partook in a common experience, no matter which side they supported. The fact that there was little fighting within the borders of Ohio did not alleviate the constant worry about invasion. Most knew someone killed or wounded on battlefields in distant, previously unknown places, such as Shiloh, Tennessee; Kenesaw Mountain, Georgia; and Gettysburg, Pennsylvania.

Close to 320,000 Ohioans—roughly sixty percent of males between 18 and 45—served in the Union Army; more than 35,000 died in battle or as a result of wounds, infection, or illness. Thousands of Ohioans also fought and died for the Confederacy. These divisions reflected serious political conflicts about slavery and the role of the federal government.

By the time Ohio natives Ulysses S. Grant and William Tecumseh Sherman led the Grand Review of the triumphant Union Armies through the streets of Washington, D.C., in May 1865, few remembered exactly how and why the war had begun. But they knew that so personal and so profound a sacrifice of blood, sweat, and treasure demanded explanation. Those Ohioans who survived the Civil War spent much of their lives trying to give it meaning. They decorated graves, erected statues, debated the rights—or lack thereof—of African Americans and women, wrote histories, planned public ceremonies, and sought reconciliation with southern comrades. And they continued to disagree with each other about the war's causes and consequences. As the citizens of Ohio became prominent Americans in the century after the Civil War, they often claimed that their subsequent achievements were a direct consequence of their continued devotion to the values and institutions that they believed had led the North to victory in 1865.

Today, the Civil War seems remote to most Ohioans, familiar only through clouds of romance and sentiment. We aim to change this. Between 2011 and 2015, we will remind ourselves of the war's importance in our history and reflect upon its enduring legacy in our lives. We will celebrate the abolition of chattel slavery and the promise of equality before the law for all citizens of the United States. To talk about the Civil War is to talk about Ohio's future as well as its past, to address its failures as well as its successes. That is the spirit with which we begin the commemoration of the sesquicentennial anniversary.

Primary Theme #1

Democracy: Visions, Challenges, Breakdown and Expansion

The American experiment in democracy has long been a challenging and unpredictable endeavor, and the tumultuous events of the Civil War era provide a case in point. Though the Founders sought to restrict suffrage, the Revolution unleashed social and political forces that transformed the United States into an increasingly democratic country by the late 1820s. During the time of the early republic, however, the vast majority of Americans understood democracy to mean universal white male suffrage only. Women and African Americans did not have the right to vote and this was as true for Ohio and Massachusetts as it was for South Carolina and Virginia.

Similarly, though the Founders believed that a spirit of "faction" was disruptive and destructive, robust political parties with strongly contrasting views on government surfaced early on, and they successfully mobilized large voter turnouts. It was common for elections to attract 80 percent of the electorate. These parties flattered the common (white) man and argued, in effect, that the common (white) man possessed the civic virtue necessary for a successful democratic polity precisely because he *was* common.

For the enfranchised, this system seemed to work initially. The two major parties—the Whigs and Democrats—were equally matched and enjoyed support in all parts of the country. Keenly aware that the issue of slavery could split the country along sectional lines, Whigs and Democrats managed to exclude it from national political discourse for two decades.

The War with Mexico (1846–1848) changed the political dynamics of the era and raised an immensely divisive issue: whether to permit slavery in the territories that the United States had acquired as a result of its victory over Mexico. From then on, the issue of slavery was at the heart of the national political dialogue, and by 1854 a major new party—the Republicans—emerged, largely on the basis of its opposition to slavery in the western territories. At stake was a fundamental question about the nature of the United States. Was it a *free* republic with pockets of slavery or a *slaveholding* republic with pockets of freedom?

After the passage of the Fugitive Slave Act of 1850, African Americans and their political allies waged a prolonged struggle that included militant self-defense in the face of slave catchers who tried to capture and re-enslave them, even though they thought they had found safety in free states like Ohio. Indeed, Ohio's historical record is replete with memorials, petitions, and other evidence that African Americans tried to expand their political rights and protections during this tumultuous period.

In Ohio, African Americans fought for political rights and guarantees through a movement for a state black convention and through the Ohio Equal Rights League at a time when the North as a whole was deeply divided on the issues of slavery and black equality. African Americans in Northern states faced a precarious situation prior to the Civil War: Abraham Lincoln denied any intent to abolish slavery, candidly regarded African Americans as inferior to whites, and thought the racial problem could best be solved by sending the African American population to colonies in Africa or the Caribbean.

Notwithstanding these publicly espoused convictions in the years prior to Lincoln's inauguration, the Deep South regarded his election as a mortal threat. During the winter of 1860–1861 seven states seceded from the Union rather than accept the verdict of a fairly conducted election whose winner was never in dispute. Last minute efforts at a compromise solution went nowhere, and when Lincoln, early in his administration, attempted to "hold, occupy, and possess" federal installations in the seceded states, the newly created Confederacy fired upon the U.S. garrison at Fort Sumter in Charleston Harbor rather than accept lawful authority. Lincoln's call for 75,000 militia troops to suppress the rebellion led four states of the Upper South to join the Confederacy.

With the outbreak of war, African Americans seized the opportunity to prove their citizenship, defend their integrity, and advance their rights. In Ohio and other northern states, substantial numbers of African Americans volunteered for military service, only to be met with rebuffs, denials, and claims that they were not citizens. Despite this widespread insistence that African Americans were not citizens, in Cincinnati during the early years of the war free black men were hunted down, rounded up, and pressed into military service.

Although these black recruits served with honor and were later formally organized as the Black Brigade, Ohio's Black Brigade was not a combat unit. Rather, African American men in the military were only allowed to perform menial duties like building fortifications and digging ditches. Those who wanted to fight in battle had to leave the state and volunteer their services elsewhere, for example the Massachusetts 54th. Eventually, Ohio formed its own African American regiment.

As a consequence of the Civil War, the nation redefined itself anew in regard to democracy and racial relations. On the battlefield and at the ballot box, Americans of that generation reworked and amended the political arrangements that the Founders had embedded in the Constitution. It took four years, ten thousand military engagements, and 620,000 dead to resolve through violence an issue that the democratic process had utterly failed to resolve peacefully. It was a great triumph that came at the cost of terrible carnage. It marked a breakdown in the American democratic process as well as its expansion and renewal.

Primary Theme #2

The Transformation of Ohio and America

Well before the outbreak of war in 1861, the United States and Ohio were in the midst of enormous social, political, and economic changes. The events and the demands of the Civil War let loose, accelerated, and compounded a whole host of transformations that restructured everyday life in America. Although there were elements of deep-seated continuity during this era, pronounced changes during a time of already existing rapid change recast both the state and the nation.

During the war, thousands of ordinary Ohio residents—people who tended farms, worked in factories, fought in the trenches, cared for the wounded and transported supplies—contributed to this multitude of related changes in concrete and specific ways. A microcosm of the nation at that time, Ohio was a complicated blend of rural and urban, eastern and western, northern and southern, and its population consisted of transplants from all sections of the country. In addition, immigrants from many other lands settled in the state. As a result, successful leaders, inventions, products, procedures, and ideas that first emerged and then flourished in Ohio proved subsequently to be popular and effective in other parts of the nation as well. Changes in Ohio were part of the larger transformation of American life during that era.

While the arenas and consequences of change were diverse and innumerable, certain aspects of the transformation were more prevalent and apparent than others. The following dimensions are rich with possibilities for exploration and public programming.

Racial Views

The Civil War was a watershed moment in race relations not only in the nation at large but also within Ohio itself. The 13th, 14th, and 15th amendments to the Constitution are among the most striking manifestations of the dramatic changes in racial relations, but there were also many others, some subtle and some palpable. For example, military families from Ohio had a large stake in this issue because of their sacrifices during the war years. There are documented cases of white Union soldiers from Ohio who entered the war believing that African Americans should never have political rights or equality but who, as a consequence of firsthand experience, were transformed by what they learned about African American men on the battlefield. By war's end, they supported the extension of citizenship rights to African Americans.

Women's Roles

As a consequence of wartime disruptions in daily life, women seized previously unavailable opportunities and assumed new responsibilities. Their efforts precipitated substantial changes in gender roles, expectations, and possibilities. Many women not only served as nurses but—like Mary Ann Bickerdyke—also advocated, organized, and directed substantial health care efforts on behalf of soldiers. Similarly, during the war years women performed new duties (in homes, on farms, and at businesses) that previously were reserved almost exclusively for men. In the public sphere, women raised funds to support the war effort, collected supplies for the armies, and, in certain instances, vocally promoted the cause of freedom. Other women—weary and resentful of the war and its effects on their families—spoke publicly on behalf of the Peace Democrats' agenda. Some women simply wrote powerful and defiant letters expressing their disenchantment with the carnage and human cost of war. In these ways and others, women actively worked in spheres formerly considered the province of men only.

Ohio in the Nation

The status of Ohio in the nation changed markedly as a consequence of the Civil War. Ohio-born army generals like Ulysses Grant, William Sherman, and Philip Sheridan were prominent in major military campaigns that made the Union victory possible. Similarly, Ohio provided the nation with key members in the wartime cabinet and high profile representatives and senators in the halls of Congress. Ohio's industrialists and financiers generated both the materials and the funds for a successful war effort. After the war, Ohio continued to play a leading role in the nation's public life. Prior to the Civil War, no native-born Ohioan had been president; over the next two generations, seven Ohio-born men were elected to this office. Five of these presidents were former officers in the Union army.

Other related manifestations of change are similarly cogent, significant, and worthy of pursuit. Examples include changes in the make-up of the state's population, the foundations of its burgeoning economy, the relationship between the state and national governments, and also the relationship between contemporary citizens and their government. These are all areas in which Ohioans initiated and experienced substantial change—both intended and unexpected—during this time of war, upheaval, innovation, and reorganization.

Primary Theme #3

Memory and Commemoration

Searing experiences and deeply ingrained memories from the war were enduring and life altering for a large number of Americans of the Civil War generation and in subtler ways for succeeding generations of Americans as well. To this very day, the aftereffects of the Civil War in combination with collective memories of that era—handed down from one generation to another and, in the process, modified and reworked—reverberate throughout American culture and society, simultaneously shaping and reflecting contemporary attitudes and perspectives in diverse ways.

The Civil War was a series of interrelated cataclysmic events that profoundly affected the everyday lives of a vast number of Americans. During the years of fighting, over 320,000 soldiers from Ohio participated in the Civil War and approximately 35,000 never returned home. In the country as a whole—North and South—approximately 3 million Americans served in the military from 1861 to 1865, and over 600,000 died. For those who came home as well as for those who remained in the state while loved ones fought in military campaigns, life was forever changed by the conflict. Although the war ended after four years, its repercussions continued to generate a wide array of challenges, and powerful memories—private and public, individual and shared, prized and horrific—played a substantial role in the new realities confronting ordinary Americans in the succeeding decades.

In the years following the war, towns, cities, and counties throughout the country dedicated memorials and performed communal rituals of commemoration. In Ohio today, Civil War memorials can be found in 85 of the 88 counties, with the overwhelming majority constructed between 1865 and 1930. The Civil War memorials reflect the values, priorities, experiences, and compromises of the generation and the era in which they were constructed. Most of those memorials honor soldiers who died during the conflict, while only a very few make reference to the anti-slavery dimensions of the struggle, to the killed and wounded African American troops who fought for freedom and the integrity of the Union, or to the large number of ordinary women who supported the war effort and assumed unusual duties on the home front. They are testimony to some of the ways in which memory itself fluctuates over time, for as new memorials to war are crafted today, they include a more diverse viewpoint.

Another means by which memories from the Civil War era emerged publicly in the aftermath of the conflict can be found in the organized gatherings of veterans in subsequent years. In 1866, shortly after the war's end, a small band of veterans formed the Grand Army of the Republic in Decatur, Illinois. By 1890, the organization claimed over 400,000 members nationally with 7,000 local chapters or posts; in Ohio alone there were approximately 700 posts.

In the late 1800s and early 1900s, G.A.R. members marched in annual Memorial Day parades, created soldiers' homes, lobbied for veterans' benefits, and endorsed candidates for public office. The organization also convened a yearly national encampment where veterans assembled to renew old bonds, recall wartime experiences, and provide support for one another. In 1888, one of the largest of these encampments was held in Columbus, Ohio, where tens of thousands gathered. By 1949, however, the G.A.R. consisted of only sixteen members, and in February 1951, the last remaining Civil War veteran died at age 104.

Still, communal memories of the Civil War lived on in a variety of ways, and new organizations were born to replace veterans' groups: the Sons of Union Veterans of the Civil War and the Daughters of the Confederacy are still active today, among others. Other initiatives, such as national observances, public school education, history textbooks, and scholarship, letters and memoirs, popular novels, Hollywood films, and public television documentaries have reflected each succeeding generation's modification and reinvention of Civil War memory in light of its own experiences, struggles, concerns, attitudes and perspectives.

In a related vein, each generation also forgot aspects of the Civil War, sometimes because certain parts were too horrible and uncomfortable to remember and sometimes because memory, both individual and collective, is subject to subtle as well as blatant negotiations, lapses, and distortions. In this sense, both memory and forgetfulness are purposeful social constructions, and, consequently, what we forget is as illuminating and revealing as what we remember. As a nation we have again and again reframed and reformulated the narrative of the Civil War. These interpretations of the war, its causes and its consequences are very much a reflection of the era in which each is cast and fashioned.

The Civil War 150 offers Ohioans an opportunity to investigate the individual and collective memory of the Civil War era through its legacies today, to explore the variety of ways in which the meaning of those memories changed over time. For local communities, the commemoration can also serve as an occasion to consider together what the war meant to the people who inhabited Ohio towns, cities, and counties in earlier eras, to think about the values and ideals of those who struggled to understand the conflict in generations past, and to reflect on the experiences, circumstances and beliefs that both connect and separate modern-day residents from previous ones. By focusing on the theme of memory and commemoration over 150 years, Ohioans can reinvigorate not only the war's legacies and our shared heritage but also the richly textured quality of contemporary community life in the state and the nation.

Credits

This work was made possible by a grant from the Ohio Humanities Council. Facilitated by Shomer Zwelling & Associates.

Academic Advisors

- Andrew Cayton, Miami University
- Tom Culbertson, Hayes Presidential Center
- Scott Gampfer, Cincinnati Museum Center

- John Grabowski, Western Reserve Historical Society & Case Western Reserve University
- Mark Grimsley, The Ohio State University
- John Haas, Ohio Historical Society
- Carol Lasser, Oberlin University
- Kelly Selby, Walsh University
- Nikki Taylor, University of Cincinnati

Appendix B
MacArthur Planning Timeline

Planning Timeline — 50th Anniversary

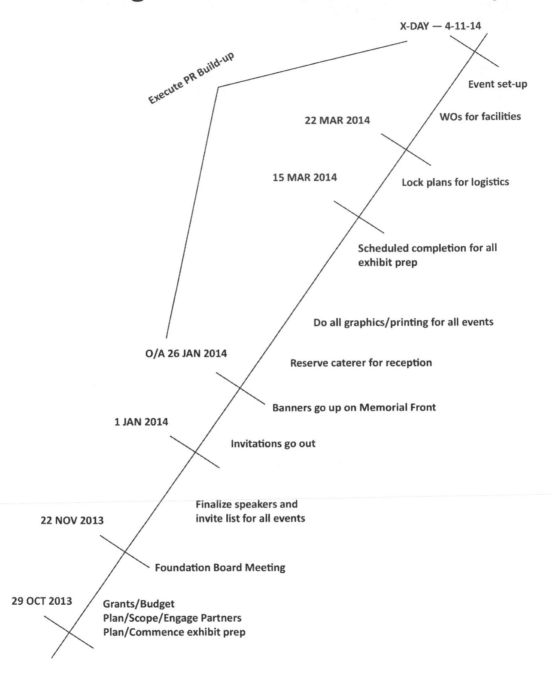

X-DAY — 4-11-14

Execute PR Build-up

Event set-up

22 MAR 2014

WOs for facilities

15 MAR 2014

Lock plans for logistics

Scheduled completion for all exhibit prep

Do all graphics/printing for all events

O/A 26 JAN 2014

Reserve caterer for reception

Banners go up on Memorial Front

1 JAN 2014

Invitations go out

Finalize speakers and invite list for all events

22 NOV 2013

Foundation Board Meeting

29 OCT 2013

Grants/Budget
Plan/Scope/Engage Partners
Plan/Commence exhibit prep

Appendix C

The Gardiner Museum Year at a Glance

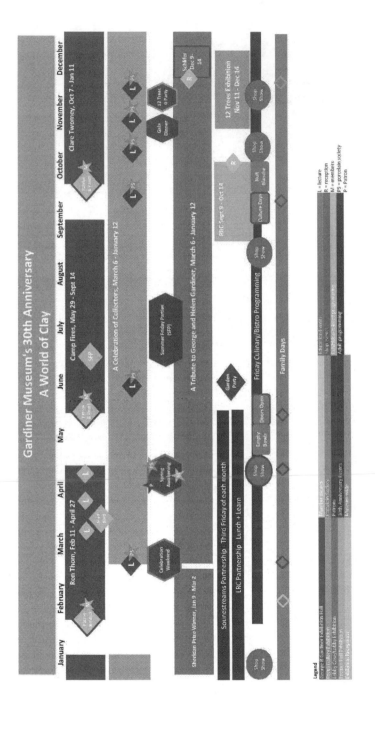

Appendix D
SB150 Brief Book

Section I: Early History: « 1864		
South Bend is on land once called *Zen Bi Nak*, or "Ribbon Town," by people of the Potawatomi nation. Soon, waves of people from European and African descent come to settle. They built the city we know today, but forever changed the lives of the Potawatomi who called this land home. [Words: 51] [Flesh-Kincaid: 68.5] [Avg. grade level: 8.1]		
Text	**Artifact/Image**	**Caption / Credit Line**
A. Potawatomi Potawatomi peoples live in a vast area along the Great Lakes. Here they build bark houses, farm, and trade. They create art and play beautiful music. They tell stories of the Seven Grandfathers, who each shared a gift with the people–wisdom, love, respect, bravery, honesty, humility, and truth. [Words: 49] [Flesh-Kincaid: 66.6] [Avg. grade level: 8.4]		Leopold Pokagon, leader of the Potawatomi living along the St. Joseph River. Courtesy of The History Museum.
B. European and African American settlers Waves of people from European and African descent come down the St. Joseph River. They cut trees, build mills and homes, and forge a new city. [Words: 26] [Flesh-Kincaid: 83.0] [Avg. grade level: 6.2]		The cabin Pierre Navarre built along the St. Joseph River in what is now Leeper Park. Courtesy of The History Museum.
1. Pierre Navarre A trader for the American Fur Company, he builds a cabin along what is now Leeper Park. Navarre marries a woman from Potawatomi descent and starts a large family. When the Potawatomi are forcefully removed in 1838, he goes with them. They return a few years later to continue building the young village. [Words: 53] [Flesh-Kincaid: 59.3] [Avg. grade level: 8.3]		Courtesy of The History Museum.

2. *Farrow Powell* The first settlers of African descent come soon after the first European Americans. Farrow and Rebecca Powell are not the first to arrive, but they are the first to establish a lasting family line. They also help found Olivet AME Church, the first majority African American church. The Powells have descendants living here today, with many generations of leaders in between. [Words: 62] [Flesh-Kincaid: 47.8] [Avg. grade level: 10.8]		Image shared through the courtesy of Mr. John Charles Bryant.
3. *Father Edward Sorin* During a snowy winter in 1842, eight Holy Cross priests arrive. French native Father Édouard Sorin is one of them. Together they build *L'Université de Notre Dame du Lac* a short walk from the new cabins on the river. Less than two years later, the state of Indiana officially charters it the University of Notre Dame. [Words: 57] [Flesh-Kincaid: 63.2] [Avg. grade level: 7.7]		Image shared through the courtesy of the University of Notre Dame Archives.
4. *Mother Angela of St. Mary's* Eliza Maria Gillespie is asked to run Michigan's St. Mary's Academy in 1850. Five years later, she moves it near her fellow Catholic college, the University of Notre Dame. When the Civil War breaks, Mother Angela builds hospitals across the nation to care for hurt soldiers. [Words: 48] [Flesh-Kincaid: 53.1] [Avg. grade level: 9.1]		Image shared through the courtesy of the St. Mary's College Archives.

Section II: Incorporation: 1865–1914

South Bend begins an amazing transformation. From lone shops come booming factories. A once tranquil river teems with human activity. New ideas and new technologies change the city faster than any point before or since.

[Words: 35] [Flesh-Kincaid: 57.8] [Avg. grade level: 9.1]

Text	Artifact/Image	Caption / Credit Line
A. An Incorporated City, An Industrial Core Before electricity, water powers industrial machines. The bend in the St Joseph River powers dozens of new businesses that invent new technologies. Some become international icons known for generations. [Words: 29] [Flesh-Kincaid: 22.0] [Avg. grade: 12.5]		The original office and wagon shop on the corner of what is now Michigan and Jefferson Streets in downtown South Bend. Image shared through the courtesy of the Studebaker National Museum.
1. The Studebaker Brothers Manufacturing Company The Studebaker brothers grow a modest blacksmith shop into the world's largest wagon company. Their father's advice, "Always give more than you promise," helps. As horse drawn vehicles give way to gas powered vehicles, Studebaker is the only wagon company to survive and thrive in the auto age. Their innovative and beautiful designs draw fans around the world. [Words: 60] [Flesh-Kincaid: 56.3] [Avg. grade level: 9.9]		Image shared through the courtesy of the Studebaker National Museum.
2. The Oliver Chilled Plow Works Sixteen year-old Joseph Doty Oliver works in the foundry of his father's Oliver Chilled Plow Works. Four years later, he runs the factory and turns it into a major farm supplier. Upon his father's death, J.D. leads it to international success at a time when farming is becoming less individual and more industrial. He funds many buildings in South Bend, including his family's home, the beautiful Oliver Mansion. [Words: 68] [Flesh-Kincaid: 68.6] [Avg. grade level: 7.5]		The sprawling Oliver Chilled Plow Works factory. Courtesy of The History Museum. *(continued)*

Text	Artifact/Image	Caption / Credit Line
3. J.C. Birdsell and Sons Clover seeds are a great animal feed and fertilizer. John C. Birdsell's huller let farmers extract seeds faster and easier than ever. At the company's height, 95% of the clover hullers in the world are made by Birdsell right here along the St. Joseph River. [Words: 47] [Flesh-Kincaid: 76.1] [Avg. grade level: 6.8]		The Birdsell Clover Huller factory was, for a time, the largest factory in the entire city. Courtesy of The History Museum.

Section III: Peak Industry: 1915–1964
South Bend's factories are booming. Tens of thousands of workers clock in every day making quality Studebaker automobiles, Oliver plows, Birdsell Clover Hullers, and more. The city is teeming with art and culture. Downtown streets are filled with life. [Words: 40] [Flesh-Kincaid: 59.2] [Avg. grade level: 9.0]

Text	Artifact/Image	Caption / Credit Line
A. Downtown Thrives Downtown is a hub for shopping and socializing. Hundreds, sometimes thousands a day walk to restaurants, theaters, and stores brightened by big electric lights. The places listed here are among the many that remain in the hearts and memories of generations of residents. [Words: 43] [Flesh-Kincaid: 56.5] [Avg. grade: 10.9]		Courtesy of The History Museum.
1. Blackstone/The State Theatre First opened as the Blackstone Theatre Vaudeville House in 1921, it reopened as the State Theatre in 1933. Major movies flickered on its single screen for more than forty years. [Words: 70.4] [Flesh-Kincaid: 70.4] [Avg. grade level: 7.3]		The State Theatre with its original marquee. Courtesy of The History Museum.

Text	Artifact/Image	Caption / Credit Line
2. Morris Performing Arts Center When it opened as the Palace Theatre in 1922, the luxurious space made attendees feel like royalty. Acting troops from New York and Chicago brought culture, while Vaudeville acts and silent films brought laughs. *Knute Rockne: All American*, a 1940 film about the legendary University of Notre Dame football coach, made its world premier here to a crowd of thousands. [Words: 60] [Flesh-Kincaid: 55.4] [Avg. grade level: 10.9]		The Morris Performing Arts Center as it was originally named, The Palace. Courtesy of The History Museum.
3. Robertson's Department Store Robertson's, a local department store, delighted customers for generations. In an age before malls and Walmart, families went here to eat, explore, and buy just about anything—all under one roof. Trips to Robertson's often made for happy memories. [Words: 41] [Flesh-Kincaid: 52.7] [Avg. grade level: 10.6]		Robertson's was the largest department store in downtown South Bend. Courtesy of The History Museum.
B. Separate, Not Equal Factory jobs at places like Studebaker lure thousands of African Americans to leave the segregated South. Yet, these new residents are not warmly welcomed. Almost every downtown business has segregated spaces for people of color. The Engman Public Natatorium, which opens in 1922 as the largest indoor swimming pool in the state, completely bans African Americans. Segregation remains until the 1950s, when public facilities choose to, or in cases like the Natatorium, are forced to allow access to all of South Bend's citizens. [Words: 84] [Flesh-Kincaid: 41.7] [Avg. grade: 11.7]		Today, the Engman Public Natatorium has reopened as a center for civil rights history through Indiana University South Bend. Image credit of the Civil Rights Heritage Center Collection of the Indiana University South Bend Archives. Photograph taken by Matt Cashore. *(continued)*

Text	Artifact/Image	Caption / Credit Line
C. *Dom. Otthon. Huis.* Home. Polish. Hungarians. Belgians. With ample jobs, people from Eastern Europe fill South Bend's factories by day and its neighborhoods by night. They bring with them their language and their culture. Packis and Dyngus Day celebrations are just some of the lasting impacts made by these generations of new Americans. [Words: 50] [Flesh-Kincaid: 66.4] [Avg. grade: 8.2]		Members of South Bend's Polish community outside the Polish National Hall. Courtesy of The History Museum.

Section IV: Rediscovery: 1965–2014
Industry changes across the United States. Industrial cities like South Bend are affected the most. Studebaker closes. Oliver closes. Dozens more move or shrink. South Bend tries new ideas to figure out its future. Sometimes, in the process, it forgets about its past. [Words: 43] [Flesh-Kincaid: 66.8] [Avg. grade level: 7.6]

Text	Artifact/Image	Caption / Credit Line
A. Urban Renewal City and business leaders use millions of dollars adapting to a new economy. Huge one-way roads are meant to bring cars quickly to and from the new suburbs. An outdoor, downtown mall tries to lure shoppers back. Historic buildings are replaced by modern skyscrapers. While many of these attempts are criticized today, city leaders were desperately trying to stop the loss of industry, talent, and people. [Words: 67] [Flesh-Kincaid: 61.9] [Avg. grade: 9.4]		The former Colfax Theatre in downtown South Bend is nearly removed. Courtesy of The History Museum.
		New buildings take the place of older ones, like this one at the corner of Washington and Main in downtown South Bend. Courtesy of The History Museum.

Text	Artifact/Image	Caption / Credit Line
B. Old Industries, New Ideas From old industries come new, 21st century ideas. Rail lines that once moved Studebakers are conduits for high-speed data. A public high school becomes apartments for hip downtown living. In every South Bend neighborhood, eager people bring life back into the city. [Words: 43] [Flesh-Kincaid: 64.1] [Avg. grade: 8.9]	**VSBM/Contemporary local photographer**	Credit.
C. *Nuevas Poblaciones* / New Populations *Spanish translation first.* South Bend has always been a city of immigrants. Beginning in the 1950s, Latino residents add to South Bend's culture and history. Organizations like La Casa de Amistad, the YWCA, and others work to integrate our newest peoples. [Words: 39] [Flesh-Kincaid: 52.6] [Avg. grade: 9.6]	**Contemporary local photographer**	Credit

Section V: New Era: 2015 ››
Today, we embrace our city's past to help inform its future. We remember what made South Bend great and adapt it to the 21st century. Our next 150 years are about the opportunities in front of us, and the decisions that we make to build them. [Words: 47] [Flesh-Kincaid: 77.5] [Avg. grade level: 7.1]

Text	Artifact/Image	Caption / Credit Line
N/A	**VSBM/Contemporary Local Photographer**	Credit.

Credit Panel	
Project Leader:	**George Garner** *Studebaker National Museum*
Lead Designer:	**Ali Letchlitner** *Visit South Bend/Mishawaka*
Review Board:	**Brandon Anderson** *The History Museum* **Dave Bainbridge** *Retired Senior Curator, The History Museum* **Andrew Beckman** *Studebaker National Museum* **Elicia Feasel** *Historic Preservation Commission of South Bend and St. Joseph County* **Muhammad Shabazz II** ***Community Activist*** **Marcus Winchester** *Pokagon Band of Potawatomi*
Operational support:	**Cara Grabowski** **Carolyne Wallace** *St. Joseph County Chamber of Commerce*
Special thanks to:	Kylie Carter, Sam Centellas, Travis Childs, Hannah Jensen and Dave Matthews from Matthews LLC, Carol Nichols, Jennifer Parker and her team from Hesburgh Libraries of Notre Dame's Architecture Library, and Marilyn Thompson from The History Museum. Extra special thanks to the members of the Pokagon Band of Potawatomi for demonstrating their life and culture, to our costumed interpreters for their time and energy, and to those who loaned items from South Bend's industrial history.

Appendix E
SB150 Logo Guidelines

SOUTH BEND 150 LOGO GUIDELINES

SOUTH BEND 150 IS A YEARLONG, COMMUNITY-WIDE CELEBRATION OF OUR RICH HISTORY AS WE FORGE OUR PROMISING FUTURE.

The South Bend 150 logo is a distinguishable graphic intentionally created to build awareness of the occasion while celebrating the 150th anniversary of the incorporation of the City of South Bend. When working with the official logo, please follow these standard logo guidelines. Event planners and organizers are encouraged to use the logo on any publicity materials and event collateral to signify official affiliation with the yearlong SB150 celebration. Please see the "community partners" information on the SB150 website for information on how to designate your event as an official part of the SB150 calendar. Vendors are welcome to reproduce the logo on items for sale, provided they follow the guidelines listed below. The logo, in various formats, can be downloaded here: **SB150.com**. For more information or clarification, please email logo@sb150.com

SIZING & WHITESPACE

Minimum size for print is 1" in width; please use that as a general guideline when showing it on screen. Leave a buffer of space around the logo no less than the width of the "D" in BEND.

COLOR

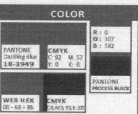

PANTONE Dazzling Blue 18-3949	CMYK C: 92 M: 57 Y: 0 K: 0
WEB HEX 00 - 6B - B6	CMYK C:0, M:0, Y:0, K:100

R : 0
G : 107
B : 182

PANTONE PROCESS BLACK

The two colors for the logo are PMS 18-3949 & Flat Black (100%). If the color logo doesn't work with your design, use the black & white versions.

COLOR/SHAPE INTEGRITY

When using the color logo maintain the integrity of the white interior shapes that spell: SOUTH BEND 150 & SB150.com.

BLACK & WHITE VERSION

This version is ideal for collaborative projects with light backgrounds, one color printing and projects that have an existing color palette that conflicts with the PMS Blue. Please maintain the integrity of the white interior shapes.

REVERSED WHITE VERSION

This version is ideal for collaborative projects with dark backgrounds and for projects that have an existing color palette that conflicts with the PMS Blue. When used on dark photographs, the opacity can be reduced by 10%.

DO NOT ALTER ELEMENTS

DO NOT ALTER/CHANGE COLOR
If the color logo doesn't work, use the black & white versions. Never edit the color.

DO NOT ADD EFFECTS

DO NOT ADD FILTERS OR EFFECTS
Never use: drop shadows, glows, bevels, embossing, feathering or any other effect.

DO NOT ROTATE OR TILT

DO NOT CHANGE THE ANGLE
Never rotate the logo clockwise or counter clockwise to alter the logo-type baseline.

DO NOT STRETCH OR SKEW

DO NOT SCALE VERTICALLY, HORIZONTALLY, SHEAR OR CROP
The logo should always be a true circle.

Appendix F

Geffrye Museum of the Home Special Appeal

The Geffrye is a place of memories
To unlock them, we need to unlock our future

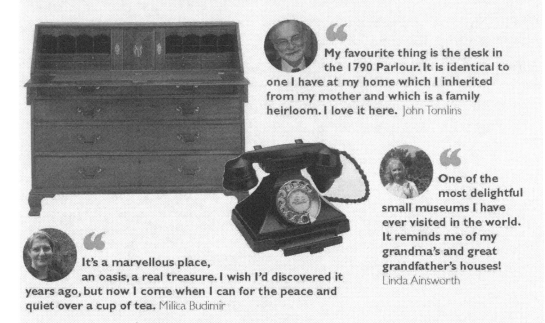

My favourite thing is the desk in the 1790 Parlour. It is identical to one I have at my home which I inherited from my mother and which is a family heirloom. I love it here. John Tomlins

One of the most delightful small museums I have ever visited in the world. It reminds me of my grandma's and great grandfather's houses! Linda Ainsworth

It's a marvellous place, an oasis, a real treasure. I wish I'd discovered it years ago, but now I come when I can for the peace and quiet over a cup of tea. Milica Budimir

Unlocking the future

Whilst taking care to preserve what we all love about the Geffrye, we will make improvements to the museum so more people can enjoy our buildings and collections.

- A new gallery and library will allow more of our treasures to be displayed and enjoyed
- Creating better spaces for our award-winning learning programmes and activities will allow more people of all ages and abilities to participate.
- Preserving the buildings, creating more garden spaces and protecting our collections will safeguard the Geffrye for generations to come.

We need your support to

Revealing the past

Home decorating has been a craze longer than we think. This catalogue of printed furnishing fabrics is from the 1890s, and is one of many decorating catalogues that reveal how our home-making tastes have changed. **We need a purpose built library and archive to make these wonderful items available for study and display.**

Staying in these days probably involves the sofa and the telly! But what did people do for comfort and fun in the past? We have a much-loved armchair from the 1720s with its original upholstery, a very rare survival, and a collection of games, radios and TVs you might remember from your childhood. **With a new gallery we could put them on display.**

Housekeeping chores haven't changed much, but how we do them has. This illustrated pamphlet from 1787 is *A Complete Guide for a Servant-maid; or the Sure Means of gaining Love and Esteem.* These days, we have endless gadgets to make life easier. **Our collection of weird and wonderful contraptions is largely in overcrowded storage and rarely seen. They deserve better conditions where they can be seen to be believed!**

make all this happen!

Your Geffrye
Unlock the future
Reveal the past

The Geffrye Museum of the Home is a special place, and no wonder: home is where the heart is! It is a place of memories, brought back through the displays of not-so-distant home life, set in wonderful historical surroundings and tranquil gardens.

The Geffrye is housed in former almshouses built 300 years ago, and the museum itself opened 100 years ago this year. It is a trove of treasured furniture and belongings, the things that make a home, well, home. But it is also a bit cramped. There is not enough room to display everything we would like to share. And on busy days it is overcrowded and congested.

The **Unlock the Future** Special Appeal will allow us to reveal more of the museum's treasures so more people can enjoy them, with better facilities and better access, while retaining the special nature of the museum. It will allow us to look after and create more memories.

The Geffrye and its memories are yours.
Please support the Unlock the Future Appeal!

www.justgiving.com/geffrye-museum

Development Office
The Geffrye Museum
136 Kingsland Road
London E2 8EA

Registered charity number 803052

THE GEFFRYE
MUSEUM OF THE HOME

www.geffrye-museum.org.uk

Appendix G

Geffrye Museum of the Home Questionnaire for Teens

YOUR THOUGHTS ON THE PROJECT & MUSEUM

As part of the evaluation for this project we would like to find out what your views of the museum and project are at the start.

1. How did you find out about this project/event?

> [blank box]

2. Before coming to the Geffrye Museum for this project, when was the last time you visited the Geffrye Museum?

○ Within the last 1 year
○ More than 1 year ago
○ Had heard of the Geffrye Museum but not visited
○ Did not know about the Geffrye Museum

We want to find out what your thoughts are on the project. Please rate the following on how strongly you agree or disagree with them:

3. DEVELOPING SKILLS

I WANT TO…

	Strongly Agree	Agree a little	Neither agree nor disagree	Disagree a little	Strongly disagree
Learn or improve my IT/ technology skills	○	○	○	○	○
Improve my teamwork skills	○	○	○	○	○
Improve my communication skills	○	○	○	○	○
Improve my organization and management skills	○	○	○	○	○
Develop my creative skills	○	○	○	○	○
Improve other skills	○	○	○	○	○

Improve other skills? Please tell us more:

> [blank box]

4. THE COMMUNITY

I WANT TO...

	Strongly agree	Agree a little	Neither agree nor disagree	Disagree a little	Strongly disagree
Feel more a part of my community	○	○	○	○	○
Change the way Geffrye visitors feel about young people	○	○	○	○	○
Get the opportunity to make a contribution to the Geffrye Museum	○	○	○	○	○
Understand more about the Geffrye and history/ heritage of the local area	○	○	○	○	○

5. THE MUSEUM/GALLERY

I WANT TO...

	Strongly agree	Agree a little	Neither agree nor disagree	Disagree a little	Strongly disagree
Better understand how a museum/gallery works	○	○	○	○	○
Make decisions that will influence the Geffrye	○	○	○	○	○
Help improve the way the Geffrye works with young people	○	○	○	○	○

6. GENERAL THOUGHTS

I WANT TO...

	Strongly agree	Agree a little	Neither agree nor disagree	Disagree a little	Strongly disagree
Increase my self confidence	○	○	○	○	○
Have fun	○	○	○	○	○
Gain experience for my CV	○	○	○	○	○
Get the opportunity to do something different	○	○	○	○	○
Meet other people	○	○	○	○	○

YOUR THOUGHTS ON THE PROJECT AND MUSEUM

Now you have come to the end of this project we would like to find out what your views are of it. The surveys are sent to a central office and your answers will help us with future projects so please answer honestly.

1. DEVELOPING SKILLS

THROUGH THIS PROJECT, I...

	Strongly Agree	Agree a little	Neither agree nor disagree	Disagree a little	Strongly disagree	Not Applicable
Learned or improve my IT/ technology skills	○	○	○	○	○	○
Improved my teamwork skills	○	○	○	○	○	○
Improved my communication skills	○	○	○	○	○	○
Improved my organization and management skills	○	○	○	○	○	○
Developed my creative skills	○	○	○	○	○	○
Improved other skills	○	○	○	○	○	○

Improved other skills? Please tell us more

2. THE COMMUNITY

BECAUSE OF THE PROJECT, I ...

	Strongly agree	Agree a little	Neither agree nor disagree	Disagree a little	Strongly disagree
Feel more a part of my community	○	○	○	○	○
Changed the way Geffrye visitors feel about young people	○	○	○	○	○
Got the opportunity to make a contribution to the Geffrye Museum	○	○	○	○	○
Understand more about the Geffrye and history/ heritage of the local area	○	○	○	○	○

3. THE MUSEUM/GALLERY

DURING THIS PROJECT, I...

	Strongly agree	Agree a little	Neither agree nor disagree	Disagree a little	Strongly disagree
Better understand how a museum/gallery works	○	○	○	○	○
Made decisions that will influence the Geffrye	○	○	○	○	○
Helped improve the way the Geffrye works with young people	○	○	○	○	○

4. GENERAL THOUGHTS

THROUGH THIS PROJECT I...

	Strongly agree	Agree a little	Neither agree nor disagree	Disagree a little	Strongly disagree
Increased my self confidence	○	○	○	○	○
Had fun	○	○	○	○	○
Gained experience for my CV	○	○	○	○	○
Got the opportunity to do something different	○	○	○	○	○
Met new people	○	○	○	○	○

5. Is there anything else you want to tell us?

[blank text box]

6. After this project I intend to...

	I have done this	I want to do this	I may do this	I have not thought about this	I do not think I will do this
Do more of the activity I enjoyed	○	○	○	○	○
Keep in touch with the museum	○	○	○	○	○
Visit museums/galleries	○	○	○	○	○
Find out more about museums/galleries	○	○	○	○	○
Keep in touch with the people I have met on this project	○	○	○	○	○
Put this experience on my CV	○	○	○	○	○
Do some more Volunteering	○	○	○	○	○

Further improve the skills I gained on this project	○	○	○	○	○
Take part in other museum/gallery projects	○	○	○	○	○
Take part in other creative/community projects	○	○	○	○	○
Find out more about London	○	○	○	○	○

7. Has this project influenced you to do anything else?

8. How happy were you with this project?

○ Very happy

○ Fairly happy

○ Neither happy or unhappy

○ Fairly unhappy

○ Very unhappy

9. I found the project...

○ Much better than I expected

○ A little better that I expected

○ About the same as I expected

○ Worse than I expected

○ I did not have any expectations before the project

10. How likely are you to recommend a visit or taking part in a project at a museum/gallery to others?

○ Very likely

○ Fairly likely

○ Haven't really thought about it

○ Fairly unlikely

○ Very unlikely

Index

About the Author

Kimberly A. Kenney graduated summa cum laude from Wells College in Aurora, New York, with a major in American history and minor in creative writing, where she became a member of Phi Beta Kappa. She earned her master of arts degree in history museum studies at the Cooperstown Graduate Program. She became curator of the McKinley Presidential Library & Museum in October 2001. This is her sixth book. Other publications include: *Canton: A Journey Through Time, Canton's West Lawn Cemetery, Canton's Pioneers in Flight, Canton Entertainment,* and *Through the Lens: The Photography of Frank Dick.* Her work has appeared in *The Public Historian,* the journal of the National Council for Public History; *White House History,* the journal of the White House Historical Association; *The Repository; The Boston Globe; Aviation History;* and the literary magazine *Mused.* She serves as editor of the Museums website at BellaOnline.com, where she has authored several ebooks, and is a member of the MuseLab Advisory Council at Kent State University. She has appeared on *The Daily Show, First Ladies: Influence & Images,* and *Mysteries at the Museum.* Her program "The 1918 Influenza Pandemic" was featured on C-SPAN's series *American History TV.* Kim has served as the Region 5 representative for the National Digital Newspaper Project in Ohio, a field reviewer for the Museums for America grant program through the Institute for Museum and Library Services, and a grant reviewer for The History Fund. She is an adjunct faculty member at the University of Mount Union and teaches online museum studies courses through the Northern States Conservation Center. She was awarded the Oakley Certificate of Merit from The Association of Gravestone Studies for her interpretive projects at West Lawn Cemetery and the Jane Weston Chapman Award from the University of Mount Union for her dedication to women's history programming. She lives in Canton, Ohio, with her husband Chris and her cats Snickers ("Doodle") and KitKat.

62729887R00138

Made in the USA
Lexington, KY
16 April 2017